➤ I-WRITING

I-WRITING

The Politics and Practice of
Teaching First-Person Writing

➤ KAREN SURMAN PALEY

Southern Illinois University Press
Carbondale and Edwardsville

Library of Congress Cataloging-in-Publication Data
Paley, Karen Surman, 1947–
I-writing : the politics and practice of teaching first-person writing / Karen Surman Paley.
  p. cm.
Includes bibliographical references (p.) and index.
1. English language—Rhetoric—Study and teaching. 2. English language—Rhetoric—Study and teaching—Political aspects. 3. English language—Rhetoric—Study and teaching—Social aspects. 4. First person narrative—Study and teaching (Higher). 5. Bias-free language—Study and teaching (Higher). 6. Creative writing—Study and teaching (Higher). 7. Report writing—Study and teaching (Higher). I. Title.

PE1404 .P34 2001
808'.042'0711—dc21   00-039505
ISBN 0-8093-2350-8 (alk. paper)
ISBN 0-8093-2351-6 (pbk. : alk. paper)

The paper used in this publication meets the minimum requirements of American National Standard for Information Sciences—Permanence of Paper for Printed Library Materials, ANSI Z39.48-1992. ♾

To my sons, Derek and Sean Paley,
and my friend Susan Ellard

✦ CONTENTS

✦ PREFACE

Robert Emerson and his coauthors write, "Ethnographic research involves the study of groups and people as they go about their everyday lives" (1). My book is grounded in a semester-long ethnographic study of two female writing faculty at Boston College, a young African American doctoral student and a Jewish, middle-aged, white lecturer. Transcripts of their classes, one-to-one student conferences, as well as interviews with participants, based on twenty-eight sixty-minute audiotapes, allow me to triangulate the empirical data.

Emerson and his colleagues tell us that field notebook entries of subjective reactions deepen the "'analysis-in-description'" (106). They argue that "the ethnographer's task is to write description that leads to an empathetic understanding of the social worlds of others" (72). The purpose is not to judge or to display "a better-than-thou attitude" (72). Yet the reader will find in my work that there are judgments and that at times I am critical of the teachers. One of the strategies I was taught in working as a family therapist was to make the covert overt. Apparently not having fully let go of my former career, I occasionally intrude into the sites of my inquiry. As Clifford Geertz tells us in his book *Works and Lives: The Anthropologist as Author*, "It may be that in other realms of discourse the author . . . is in the process of dying; but [he] . . . is very much alive among anthropologists" (6–7). Furthermore, in writing up my observations, I found that there was no way to mask my opinions. There is neither a neutral posture nor neutral language. The task of the ethnographer, as Geertz puts it, is "how to get an I-witnessing author into a they-picturing story" (84). My attempt at solving this problem takes the form of incorporating into my text the informants' objections to my observations and conclusions. The subjects talk back. When I am incorporating their glosses on the text itself, I put their remarks in quotation marks within brackets. At other times, I reprint e-mail commentaries or report their oral disagreements as part of a dialogue between us. Some of their responses came during the active phase of research while I was conducting the on-site observations, and others came in subsequent discussions.

In the first chapter, "The Social Construction of 'Expressivist' Pedagogy," I discuss what I see as some commonalities in the pedagogy of classrooms that have been identified as "expressivist": allowing students the authority of their own experiences; close working relationships between students and teachers in one-to-one conferences, which can create space for some self-disclosure; and a belief that most students can become strong writers. My observations of two teachers at Boston College, supervised by two tenured faculty trained at the University of New Hampshire, demonstrate the kinds of writing and approaches to writing that deconstruct the social construction of "expressivism" as a naive pedagogy. The students in their classrooms produced a range of essays that situated the narrator within families and communities where issues of race and class and gender were well attended. At the same time, the use of first-person experience in their prose motivated the students and engaged the readers in a way that recalled Aristotle's injunction to excite the emotions of the audience.

I then respond to the social constructionist representation of "expressivism" in the work of Lester Faigley and that of James Berlin. For example, underlying Faigley's summary of a student essay about the alcoholism in her family is contempt for the female protagonist that is not present in the student's version. Drawing on Aristotle, I argue that the much-maligned notion of "authentic voice" is the basis of ethos and that this ethos is essentially the logos of personal narrative. It is the very mechanism of persuasion.

In chapter 2, "In Situ: The Political Elbow," I discuss Kathleen

Cassity's ethnographic study of the man who in contemporary circles is perhaps most frequently associated with the pedagogy of "expressivism," Peter Elbow. Cassity belies the way Elbow has been represented by the social constructionists as someone who is apolitical and totally absorbed with "the private vision" of the solitary writer; we see Elbow directly challenge his students' sexism, racism, and heterosexism.

In "Ethnography: A Postmodern Way of Seeing the World," the third chapter, I explain my ethnographic methods and my relationship to the research site and to the people who are the subject of my study. Two research questions guided me: How do faculty teach personal narrative without crossing over a boundary and acting as if they are psychotherapists? Furthermore, are the skills taught in this mode of discourse transferable to expository or persuasive writing? Chapter 3 concludes with an introduction of "Helena," my first informant, an African American doctoral student and teaching fellow, at the time she received a teaching award during a period of antiracist struggle at Boston College.

The focus of chapter 4, "Confronting Bias in Student Texts," is Helena's work with "Janet," a white middle-class student who consistently produced essays grounded in her volunteer work with the homeless. Janet was locked into locating the causes of homelessness within individual or family defects, resisting course material that emphasized social causes. Toward the end of the semester, Helena's tolerance for Janet's biases ebbed and, in class, she challenged Janet's declaration that a particular panhandler was an "idiot." I felt frustrated that Helena had not been more directive with this student earlier in the semester. Helena argues back, in the text, that she dealt with Janet as "a budding consciousness." Helena wanted to plant new ideas rather than strong-arm Janet to gain ideological compliance for the sake of a grade.

In the fifth chapter, "'I'm Just Really Struggling in This Class': Facing Student Self-Doubt," I represent Helena's work with "Catherine," a young woman who was as insecure as Janet was overconfident. Catherine's first essay was a trenchant narrative about her alcoholic family. Helena masterfully responded to this troubling text with purposeful compassion; she had to balance her concerns about rhetorical issues with an acute awareness that there was much at stake for the student in this essay. A key moment in their relationship occurred when Catherine insisted on using the word *malice,* claiming that she wanted to bring harm to her father. As Catherine learned to step beyond single observations and incorporate research within her opinions and personal experiences, her confidence increased and her writing ability improved. I see Helena's work as testimony that one can address current traditional concerns about sentence-level error and still be humane.

In chapters 6 and 7, "Developing Voice, Developing Agency," and "'African Americans Have This Slang': Grammar, Dialect, and Racism," I introduce "Debby," a white woman in her mid fifties who had been teaching at Boston College for seventeen years. I highlight Debby's work with "Tanya," an African American senior from an inner city who finds herself on a majority white campus and the only student of color in Debby's advanced writing seminar. Tanya developed sufficient trust in her instructor to impart the story of her teaching internship in a wealthy white suburb. Because she used some Black English in oral discourse, her supervisor told her that she had "problems with grammar," and she was pressed into repeating her practicum. In addition to producing a hybrid essay that mixed elements of personal narrative and a critique of a racist institution, Tanya became less anxious about subsequent assignments and developed into an active participant in the seminar. As I struggled with transcripts of taped interviews, I became painfully aware of my own racism, manifesting itself in biases against Black English. I explore the issue of grammar instruction in the process-writing classroom.

In chapter 8—"The Personal in Social Constructionist Pedagogy: A Visit to the Classroom of Patricia Bizzell"—I examine different types of critical pedagogy, confrontational versus dialogic, and in the process discover my own assumption that social constructionism is necessarily confrontational. I draw on bell hooks's "engaged pedagogy" as a model for good teaching practice. As a counterbalance to the earlier discussion of Elbow's classroom, I offer a description of my visit to the classroom of social constructionist Patricia Bizzell. The class was divided into a cultural studies discussion and a more personal part dealing with her students' feelings of inadequacy as peer tutors. While I find Bizzell's practice more dialogic than confrontational, to achieve consensus at times differences were not explored. However, I was struck by how warm and personal the class became as her students discussed their anxieties related to peer tutoring. I include a teaching memory of my own that was evoked by the classroom observation. In an effort to heal the Merrillean "broken home," the split in the field of composition, Bizzell's responses to my remarks are interspersed through the text. I call for more collegial interactions of people from different theoretical backgrounds and suggest we do ethnographic work to share pedagogies.

In the conclusion of the book, I examine the ethics of having students write personal narratives, listing specific objections made by various theorists. While I acknowledge the potential for abuse of power when representatives of institutions assign autobiographical writing, I also lament the way postmodern theory separates discourse and experience and suggest that it may be detrimental to a writer who very much wants to communicate an experience. I then outline what I consider to be a responsible response to these texts. Sometimes the reader is directed to ascertain if the essay is meant to describe an event that happened. If this is the case, a clear support statement from the teacher should precede the discussion of the paper. At other times, I suggest that the teacher obey certain rhetorical signals, such as the use of the third person, and avoid asking personal questions. Either way, once the essay becomes the subject of critique, I suggest that the instructor always refer to the narrational *I* of the essay as *the narrator* to limit blurring rhetorical critique with psychological assessment. Personal narrative has a significant place in the composition classes of those instructors willing to learn how to teach it.

The purpose of *I-Writing* is to demonstrate that "expressivist" programs are much more complicated than they have been made out to be and that first-person writing can be simultaneously highly personal and highly politicized. At a time when the world fibrillates daily with ethnic conflict, we need to be mindful of our own essentializing of academic others.

✎ ACKNOWLEDGMENTS

Many individuals have put a considerable amount of time into reviewing versions of this manuscript, making it more informed and readable. Among these people I include the reviewers from Southern Illinois University Press, Wendy Bishop and Lucille Schultz, and my acquisitions editor, Karl Kageff. David Bleich and Bonnie TuSmith were especially helpful with the manuscript in its earliest stages.

As *I-Writing* grew, several people gave me moral support, a boost when the ego was failing. They include Lad Tobin, Thomas Newkirk, and Patricia Sullivan. My sons, Sean and Derek, rooted for me much as I had once cheered them on. The comments and support of Susan Ellard were indispensable.

Kathleen Cassity's unpublished ethnography of Peter Elbow provided immediate empirical evidence of the theoretical points I wanted to make. Without Bonnie Stone Sunstein's assistance with a pilot study at the University of New Hampshire, this project would have had many more fits and starts. Pat McLure and her students were very helpful during my observation of their class. Patricia Bizzell's generosity in allowing me to visit her class is appreciated, as is the time she spent rereading my representations of the visit.

Finally, I want to acknowledge the courage and integrity of two teachers from Boston College, "Helena" and "Debby," for inviting me into the intimate spaces of their classrooms. "Janet," "Catherine," "Tanya," and others taught me much about what it is like to be an undergraduate composition student these days.

➤ I-WRITING

➤ INTRODUCTION
The Birth of Critical Consciousness

There is a scene in Art Spiegelman's *Maus II* that I find particularly distressing. Françoise, Artie's wife, stops the car to pick up a black hitchhiker. Vladek, a Holocaust survivor and Artie's father, reacts. Using Yiddish syntax, he yells, "A HITCH-HIKER? AND—OY—IT'S A COLORED GUY, A SHVARTSER! PUSH QUICK ON THE GAS!" (98). Françoise ignores him and picks up the hitchhiker. After they drop him off, Vladek says, "WHAT HAPPENED ON YOU, FRANÇOISE? YOU WENT CRAZY, OR WHAT?! I HAD THE WHOLE TIME TO WATCH OUT THAT THIS SHVARTSER DOESN'T STEAL US THE GROCERIES FROM THE BACK SEAT!" Françoise is furious. "THAT'S OUTRAGEOUS! HOW CAN YOU, OF ALL PEOPLE, BE SUCH A RACIST! YOU TALK ABOUT BLACKS THE WAY THE NAZIS TALKED ABOUT THE JEWS" (99).

The word *shvartser* was used seven times in this scene. Every time I read it, I flinched. It brought back to me a childhood memory that remains powerful. Somewhere between the ages of six and eight, I can recall paying attention to a feeling of distress that I had experienced many times before when overhearing my mother talk with her mother on the telephone. Her discourse was punctuated with words like *shvartser* and *goyim*. On this particular day, I stopped and thought about these words. Perhaps it was the birth of a critical consciousness. Some ethical sensibility told me that it was not right to use those words because it was not good to dislike other people for not being white or for not being Jewish. I never expressed this awareness to my mother because I was afraid of her, a fear that grew over the years as her drinking problem progressed.

I have a related memory about my maternal grandmother. I wrote about it in an essay called "I Remember, Nana."

> Your arteries packed full of other people's despair so that in March of 1975, at the age of 77, you needed open heart surgery again. . . . I find you in an open ward with women of many ethnic groups. Your joy was kinetic and you were like a young girl, Nana. I was so happy for you because the "goyim" days had ended. (25)

In that visit, I experienced my grandmother as a changed woman, someone who had revised her attitude toward other Others in the world.

I still feel emotional pain when I hear disparaging remarks about various cultural groups, and the pain is even harsher when I hear the remarks inside my own head, when I realize that I have internalized ethnic and religious contempt. There is a racist ideologue who resides within me. Lisa Delpit tells us that "we do not really see through our eyes or hear through our ears, but through our beliefs." She asks us to "put our beliefs on hold." "It is painful . . . because it means turning yourself inside out, giving up your own sense of who you are, and being willing to see yourself in the unflattering light of another's angry gaze" (297). The way Delpit connects sense of self and political beliefs resonates for me. My cultural consciousness does not exist in some detached theoretical realm but in what has been a very private memory of what it was like to grow up in my particular white, lower-middle-class Jewish family. In other words, my politics are grounded in personal experience.

For me, the personal has always been invested with political tension and the political, in turn, imbued with pathos and with family memories. As Ira Shor writes in his foreword to *Sharing Pedagogies* by Gail Tayko and John Paul Tassoni, "Critical pedagogies evolving from Freirean roots (as well as from feminist and multicultural roots) situate the personal in the social and the social in the personal for an historical reading of experience" (xi). This intermingling of the social and the personal seems to underlie the purpose of the book that follows. Tayko and Tassoni tell us that the essays

in the volume are not meant to be "blueprints for course designs."
In fact, because

> they represent complex interactions between students and teachers,
> they do not *sound* or *feel* like typical academic articles. . . . It is, how-
> ever, through these portrayals of the particular and the individual,
> the personal and the emotional, that articles in *Sharing Pedagogies*
> enter the lore of teaching practices and accrue considerable theoreti-
> cal value. (10)

This rhetorical strategy of drawing on the "personal and the
emotional" to develop theory calls to me because it duplicates my
own sense of the blended tensions that are woven into my life. I am
reminded of the inseparability of these tensions when I read poet
James Merrill's description of his writing process.

> Presently minimal bits of information, like the tesserae of a mosaic,
> flicker and reassemble before my eyes. . . . Line after line wavers in
> and out of sense, transpositive, loose-ended, flimsy as gossamer, until
> a length of text is at last woven tightly enough to resist unmaking. Then
> only do I see what I had to say. (*Different Person* 202)

The tiles of my consciousness are grouted into a mosaic. The pattern resists unmaking. So it is that I have an adverse reaction to
impersonal theory, politics, or exposition; and personal writing that
lacks some suggestion of social or political implications does not feel
quite right to me. I think Sherrie Gradin, author of *Romancing
Rhetorics,* might call me a "social-expressivist."

Blended Tensions

I received a master's degree in education in 1972 at what was then
Boston State College (now the University of Massachusetts–Boston),
and I became certified to teach secondary-level English. Instead I
spent the next twenty years engaged in other kinds of activities, such
as raising two sons (the desire to brag here feels as strong as the urge
to push during childbirth), working as a therapist for families with
substance-abuse problems, and publishing essays in regional and
national magazines.

When I resumed my graduate training at the University of New
Hampshire (UNH), I did not know that I had landed in what some
scholars have called a hotbed of "expressivism." I took doctoral

seminars with Patricia Sullivan and Thomas Newkirk; students raised many objections as we read works like Susan Miller's *Textual Carnivals.* The composition graduate students and faculty at UNH did not recognize their pedagogy in her representation of it. One of Miller's points is that the topics raised in composition classes are inconsequential outside the classroom. If this were true, we wondered why the father of one student was threatening to sue a composition teacher for assigning a book by Maya Angelou.

When I completed my master's work at UNH, I began a doctoral program at Northeastern University. As soon as it was feasible, I gravitated toward the composition courses. There I was reading Susan Miller and Lester Faigley as if their representations of "expressivists" were as ideologically indisputable as common sense. The conflation of the two disparate readings felt like what meteorologists call *wind shear,* the sudden penetration of cooler air that is powerful enough to cause a plane to crash. Not long into my doctoral work, I knew that I would write a dissertation that would examine these very different air masses in composition in an attempt to ameliorate the wind shear, to land if we must, but not with a crash.

When I enrolled at Northeastern, I was also invited to teach part-time at Boston College (BC) by Lad Tobin, who had received his Ph.D. at UNH. After combining my perceptions of the goals of the writing faculty at UNH with my observations of BC writing faculty, including myself, I knew that the way "expressivist" practice was being depicted in some journals and books was reductive. It was apparent to me that the theorists were basing their critiques solely on texts their scholarly counterparts were publishing, on simulacra as it were. Thus, the methodology for my research emerged out of a desire to display some semblance of what was transpiring in these classrooms.

I had read Shirley Brice Heath's long-term ethnography, *Ways with Words,* as a student in Thomas Newkirk's class. Then I read his essay "The Politics of Composition Research: The Conspiracy Against Experience." Newkirk responds to the positivistic objection that "descriptive or observational studies" lack generalizability. He writes,

> There is no *internal* mechanism for generalization, no assurance that the student [that Nancy] Atwell describes is typical of other special-needs students. But as readers, we perform this act of generalization—

we determine if Atwell's Laura or Emig's Lynn resembles students we've seen. . . . Paradoxically, the case study gains generalizability through particularity—through the density of detail, the selection of incidents, and the narrative skill of the researcher. (130)

What Newkirk was saying here made sense to me: particularity can prompt the reader to generalize. I wanted to observe and describe classroom situations in an "expressivist" program. Were these classroom situations really as apolitical as certain theorists were saying? Like researchers Barbara Walvoord and Lucille Parkinson McCarthy, who conducted a long-term ethnographic study of writing in the disciplines, I chose "naturalistic inquiry to answer my research questions" because I too know that "realities are multiple and are constructed by people as they interact within particular social settings" (19). I hoped I could follow their lead in another way. To "ensure trustworthy findings," I would not try to mask "negative cases, that is, cases that lie outside [my] tentative categories and findings" (48). The representation of negative cases would be a challenge for me as I felt a deep sense of injustice over the way "expressivist" pedagogy was being represented.

In the summer of 1996, I returned to UNH to take a course in ethnography with Bonnie Stone Sunstein. I felt like I was back home. One of the many high points of that summer was when my adviser from Northeastern went with me to class and met Sunstein. Social constructionist and ethnographic "expressivist" were consorting. Again I turn to James Merrill. His poem "The Broken Home" is written from the perspective of a child of divorced parents.

> Crossing the street,
> I saw the parents and the child
> At their window, gleaming like fruit
> With evening's mild gold leaf.
>
> (*Selected Poems* 109)

I too had a fleeting moment of unity.

For my project, I observed Pat McLure's writing class in the New Hampshire Summer Writing Program. During my first week, I found a birthday card for my twenty-four-year-old son Sean in the campus bookstore. It represented my trepidation as I began the work, my projection of how the informants would regard me. Two adult bears are talking in front of a tree from which an anthropologist, sporting field glasses, is hanging by his shirt collar. One bear says to the other,

> His name's Bradshaw. He says I come from a single parent den with inadequate role models. He senses that my dysfunctional behaviors are shame based and codependent and he urges me to let my inner cub heal . . . I say we eat him. (See Paley, "Next Week")

I anticipated that McLure's class would resent my intrusion into their space and that they would just as soon get rid of me. They did demand of me an accountability I would not have predicted, and they started me on the way to write this book. Although it feels as if a few individuals have gnawed at my extremities along the way, to my knowledge no one has eaten me.

1 ❯❯ THE SOCIAL CONSTRUCTION OF "EXPRESSIVIST" PEDAGOGY

A Psychosocial Take on Personal-Experience Essays

In his introduction to *The Art of the Personal Essay,* a nearly eight hundred page anthology from the classical to the contemporary era, Phillip Lopate writes,

> The personal essay is the reverse of that Chinese set of boxes that you keep opening, only to find a smaller one within. Here you start with the small . . . and suddenly find a slightly larger container, insinuated by the essay's successful articulation and the writer's self-knowledge. (xxviii)

This capacity of the personal essay to open itself up, the way it relies on an implied induction to be realized in the mind of the reader, makes it a versatile genre that can communicate a social significance that extends deeper than the folds and crevices of one human navel.

One purpose I have in writing this book is to affirm the value of teaching, or rather allowing, our students to write narrative (as well as expository, descriptive, and persuasive) essays in the first person. I realize that taking such a position may not be thought of as intellectually smart in a climate in which the personal narrative has been critiqued, even ridiculed, by some composition theorists.

For example, categorizing the personal essay as "sentimental realism," David Bartholomae called the genre "corrupt" in 1995 ("Writing" 71). Apparently attempting to repair it, in the fifth edition of *Ways of Reading* (1999), an anthology that appears to be far more popular with instructors than with their students, Bartholomae and coeditor Anthony Petrosky continue to include autobiographical assignment sequences.[1] The assignments included in "Autobiographical Explorations" are not spontaneously written narratives that might be guided by the false purposes of "display or self-promotion, or to further (rather than question) an argument" (802). Unless student writers follow the editors' assignment guidelines, they are at risk of "produc[ing] each week only more of the same, the same story written in the same style" (803). Instead, in their introduction, Bartholomae and Petrosky direct the student "to imagine [his] own familiar settings through the images, metaphors, and ideas of others" (4), and this directive is later mystified as free topic choice. The clause "you can write about anything you want" (804) is qualified by the parenthetical statement "but you would be *wise* to stay away from childhood experiences and to stick with more adult experiences" (804, emphasis mine). The ruling out of childhood experiences as topics is not explained; the student whose mind did drift there might feel ashamed, as he has been judged as not wise. Neither do Bartholomae and Petrosky see any need to explain the ban. Using a pedagogy that is at once classical in its imitative purpose and controlling in its injunction to avoid childhood occurrences, the editors seek to shape the representation of experience with models they feel are appropriate. "[Y]our job in this assignment is to look at your experience in [Richard] Rodriguez's terms, which means thinking the way he does, noticing what he would notice . . . seeing through his point of view" (805). Why can't students frame whatever experiences they select in the way they choose and then do a revision framing it from Rodriguez's perspective?

Coeditors Bartholomae and Petrosky are indicative of the widespread knee-jerk dismissal of classrooms and pedagogy in which individual students write essays that situate them inside their families (without prescribed scaffolding). Yet, as Hephzibah Roskelly and Kate Ronald point out in *Reason to Believe*, "[P]ostprocess theorizing rarely speaks to classroom contexts and actual students" (2). While I address some of the postmodern criticism on a theoretical level, the bulk of the following chapters contain the results of an ethnographic study that I conducted at Boston College (BC), a program that would be identified as "expressivist." To my knowledge, the only substantive ethnographic study of an actual "expressivist" classroom is the chapter on Donna Qualley in *Academic Literacies* by Elizabeth Chiseri-Strater.

I take you into the classrooms of two writing faculty. Through transcripts of one-to-one conferences, interviews, and classroom discussions, you can "see and hear" how Helena, an African American doctoral student in her late twenties, worked with two very different white female students. One student did most of her writing on homelessness, and the other targeted the impact of alcoholism on families and on college students. You also meet Debby, a middle-aged woman, white and Jewish, who had been teaching at BC for nearly twenty years. I highlight her work with Tanya, the only student of color in an advanced writing class, as she wrote and workshopped a paper on a racist, humiliating experience as a student intern. Despite the accusation that the autobiographical nature of the writing in "expressivist" programs is solipsistic and apolitical, that the topics are insignificant outside the immediate classroom, I introduce students who eagerly wrote about topics that mattered not only to them but to the gender, economic class, family, and ethnic group from which they emerged.

The readings, the class discussions, and the student papers in these classes brought together the individuals' experiences and those of larger communities. For example, Helena's student, Janet, initially produced an essay about a rift in her family that led to her being cut off from her grandmother. She then went on to write about the problem of homelessness. The psychological problem in her family (an emotional homelessness) became the material problem in the lives of poor people. Similarly, Catherine first wrote about the devastating effect of her father's drinking on the family and on her individual development; she began her next essay with a description of a hungover roommate and ended it with a discussion of binge drinking in college. These students' portfolios illustrate Lopate's reversed Chinese boxes. They began with the small package and grew larger. However, the perceptions, feelings, and experiences of the individual writer, or rather the narrator that the writer constructed to represent her in public, remained very much a part of the essays even as they expanded. The teacher did not attempt to squelch the "personal" aspect of the essay or to hide the seams of the individual's perceptions behind a declaration that it was merely a "reproduc-[tion] of the master narrative of family life" (Bartholomae, "Writing" 67).

Is There "Expressivist" Pedagogy?

The word *"expressivism"* is problematic. As Peter Elbow put it in an e-mail to me,

> I hate the term expressivism. It tends to be used only by people who think it's a bad thing. And [it] tends to connote that I (or expressivists) are more interested in writing about the self or expressing the self than writing that is trying to be accurate or valid about things outside the self.

Given that the word is both widely used and loaded with insinuation, I put it in quotation marks.

While the word *"expressivist"* has been chosen for me, I might have easily chosen any number of other words. In a review of three teacher texts, Mariolina Salvatori writes,

> [T]he practices of the personal go by many different names, often used as if they were interchangeable: personal criticism, autobiographical criticism, narrative criticism, personal narrative, self-writing, life-writing, auto-graphy ([Jeanne] Perrault), confessional criticism ([Aram] Veeser), rhapsodic criticism ([Frank] Lentricchia). Although such a varied nomenclature may be taken to indicate the richness of the genre as a "category in process" (Perrault), or its need and right to self-definition, I suggest it might also be taken as a sign of a certain anxiety about its functions and possibilities. (567)

I concur with Salvatori: the sheer circulation of so many synonyms or near synonyms may be indicative of anxiety about the personal in the academy, a point I return to shortly. On the other hand, the multiple names may reflect the versatility of the form itself.

Let me develop a working description of *"expressivist" pedagogy.* A key feature seems to be an elevation of the importance of ordinary human experience, beginning in the mid-nineteenth century according to Lucille Schultz. In her history of composition, Schultz argues that the influence of the educational reformer Johann Heinrich Pestalozzi can be seen in John Frost's 1839 textbook, *Easy Exercises in Composition.* As Pestalozzi believed children should learn through objects rather than abstractions and rules, Frost's work opened with "pictures of objects for description," not with grammar rules; it was illustrated with scenes from children's lives at home and school; it invited children to write about their own lives; and it advised the young composers to write "freely and boldly." (Schultz 6–7)

Schultz locates Frost as the source of experience-based assignments in American grammar schools, and it was decades before similar assignments appeared in textbooks for college students (84). She concludes that experience-based writing "made space for students whose lives were situated in the world of manual labor and the world of work" (162). It was a progressive, democratizing pedagogy.

In his essay "Personal Writing Assignments," Robert Connors tells a different story. He tells us that Aristotelian topics and the process of invention relied more heavily on logos, "the nature of the subject," than on ethos, "the nature of the speaker." The orator's personal experiences and opinions were not relevant to his or her speech (167). Connors cites the introduction of vernacular literature in the seventeenth century and the concomitant "rise of the middle classes and the increasing threats they presented to the traditional hierarchies" (169) as the death knell of the classical tradition and the movement toward more personal topics. The shift away from public topics was enhanced by "the disappearance of classical study from the vernacular grammar schools" (171); thus it would seem that students knew of nothing else to write about than their immediate experiences. Since these students had not received a classical education, composition teachers "began to reject abstract, impersonal topics" (172). Connors does not mention Frost's 1839 work for grammar school children but instead cites John Hart's 1870 *Manual of Composition and Rhetoric* as the key text in "really open[ing up] the floodgates to personal writing in composition courses" (173).

A historical look at the pedagogy of personal writing must also include John Dewey and his book *Experience and Nature*. To determine the validity of any philosophy, Dewey argues that we must refer its conclusions back "to ordinary life-experiences and their predicaments" and determine whether the conclusions render these experiences "more opaque than they were before" or whether they "increase the power of ordinary things" (7). Dewey is opposed to philosophies that "disparage and condemn primary experience" (8).

James Britton is another educator who has influenced "expressivist" pedagogy along similar lines. Britton identifies three types of discourse (expressive, transactional, and poetic) without placing them in a hierarchy of significance. Expressive writing, which is "primarily written down speech," shows that the writer "stays in the writing and doesn't disappear" (97). Like Dewey, he valorizes everyday experience. In school, children "should write about what matters to them to someone who matters to them" (110). Instead of initially trying to teach the students academic discourse, Britton wants to bridge the language and culture of home and school. The teacher ought to "nourish the speech of the home and the neighborhood and [help] it find the kind of expression, in story, poem, or play, which can communicate the spirit of the subculture to a multicultural audience" (203). This kind of bridge is especially important when those of us who are teaching today realize how much our students' desire to fit in may be a function of an ethnic shame fostered by schools where what Bonnie TuSmith calls "the Englishes of ethnic folk" are not welcome.

More recent representations of "expressivist" pedagogy include the notion that respect for the experiential and cultural knowledge that students bring to their essays enables their writing abilities to develop fairly quickly. Here I turn to Thomas Newkirk who has been influenced by the teaching practices of Donald Murray and Robert Graves at the University of New Hampshire, as well as the work of Peter Elbow and Ken Macrorie. In "Locating Freshman English," his introduction to *Nuts and Bolts: A Practical Guide to Teaching College Composition,* Newkirk refers to "the archetypal writing-process story [of the] student who comes into our class with a history of past failure" (9).

> With the encouragement of the teacher, the student begins to write on a topic of deep personal interest and importance and suddenly there is an eloquence and power that the writer's early work did not even suggest. . . . The teacher did not teach this fluency but created conditions, particularly a relationship of trust, that enabled the writer to dip into this rich territory. . . . Proponents of academic literacy may dismiss [this assumption] as irrelevant to the task of mastering the discourse of the academy. I have found it happen too often to dismiss it. *And I feel that it is pedagogically healthy to assume that all students can produce writing that is genuinely effective* and not simply a fair approximation of someone else's language. (9, emphasis mine)

Thus, rather than have the student struggle clumsily to "invent the university," the teacher in an "expressivist" classroom might be more interested in creating a space for what the student has to offer within the university. As Elbow shapes the difference in his debate with Bartholomae, "[T]he basic subtext in a piece of student writing is likely to be, 'Is this okay?' In contrast to students, the basic subtext in a [professional] writer's text is likely to be, 'Listen to me, I have something to tell you'" (*Being* 81).

With these examples in mind, I define "expressivism" as a pedagogy that includes (but is by no means limited to) an openness to the use of personal narrative, a particular type of the narrative mode of discourse. Personal narrative takes the writer's own experience as its focus. It involves the use of a narrational *I* that seems to be the actual voice of the person who writes. Sometimes the narrator may appear to isolate individual consciousness, and sometimes he or she may represent the self in one or more social contexts, such as the family or college community. The narrator may or may not explicitly link the particular situation with those experienced by others.

When I first drafted the previous paragraph, I wrote, "'Expressivism' frequently concerns itself with personal narrative." I changed the clause to "includes an openness to the use of personal narrative" after an interview with Lad Tobin, director of first-year writing at BC. In the field of composition, he is regarded as an "expressivist." By the winter of 1997, he had studied about six hundred fifty syllabi for courses in which nearly ten thousand students have been enrolled. Tobin reports that only 25 percent of the assigned writing in his program falls into the genre of personal narrative. The rest of the assignments would be considered cultural criticism, argument on public issues, and response to texts. Yet he qualifies his comments by reminding me of the kind of hybrid papers we see in the first-year writing program at BC where elements of personal narrative mix with exposition or argument in the same paper (Tobin, interview).

The misrepresentations of pedagogies that include the teaching of personal narrative are based largely on published writing as opposed to classroom observation. The case against "expressivist" pedagogy derives from written discourse outside the classroom, in such texts as Peter Elbow's *Writing Without Teachers* and William Coles and James Vopat's *What Makes Writing Good*. As Newkirk writes, social constructionists' objections "proceed in an empirical vacuum" (*Performance* 89). Through excerpts from Kathleen Cassity's unpublished ethnographic study of Peter Elbow, who has been placed at the vanguard of "expressivist" pedagogy, and my own observations of two classes at BC, I complicate the assumptions of what can transpire in a classroom identified with this pedagogy.

Why Is the Personal Essay So Controversial?

In the past fifteen years or so there has been an active debate among composition and rhetoric teachers over the merits of teaching personal writing in freshman composition. I want to speculate about why this debate has been happening. In their essay on personal writing in academia, Daniel Mahala and Jody Swilky write, "The social turn in composition research in the 80's can be read as a reaction against earlier process rhetorics, which social turn theorists faulted for inadequately representing the social contexts of writing" (368). (Among those whom they associate with process rhetorics are Elbow, Macrorie, and Britton, as well as those compositionists commonly thought of as cognitivists, such as Linda Flower, John Hayes, Sondra Perl, and Janet Emig.) Mahala and Swilky cite David Bartholomae and James Berlin as "most influential in criticizing 'the process revolution'" (368). I discuss Berlin's representation of "expressionism" later in this chapter, but at this point I want to situate Bartholomae's critique within professional developments in the field of English.

Underlying the criticism of process pedagogy for its alleged lack of attention to sociopolitical matters exists a kind of professional status seeking in an effort to associate the disciplines of composition and rhetoric as part of the cultural studies movement as it has emerged in other fields. To appropriate a phrase Bartholomae himself uses in a different context, behind the social constructionist critique of "expressivism" is "corporate shame" ("Writing" 63).

In 1985, Robert Scholes published *Textual Power*. The chapter entitled "The English Apparatus" cites the split in English departments between the consumption of literature and the production of nonliterature, the latter "perceived as being grounded in the realities of existence" (6). It is precisely this usefulness that makes this form nonliterary; nonliterature "lacks those secret-hidden-deeper meanings so dear to our pedagogical hearts" (6). Furthermore, since academic writing is necessarily cut off "from the exigencies of real situations," the only version of this genre that can be produced in the academy is "'pseudo-non-literature,' which is indeed produced in an *appalling* volume. We call the production of this *stuff* 'composition'" (6, emphasis mine). While Scholes argues that he wants to deconstruct the binary that places "the consumption of literature at the top and the production of pseudo-non-literature at the bottom" (11), his use of the prepositional phrase *in an appalling volume* and the appositive *stuff* would seem to deconstruct his deconstruction.

This hierarchy within English departments is affirmed by Susan Miller in *Textual Carnivals* in her chapter entitled "The Sad Women in the Basement: Images of Composition Teaching." She informs us that, during this century, "as even faint associations with classical grammatical instruction grew dimmer, composition was increasingly diminished and simplified. Concurrently, literary studies grew and became more complex" (128). Because the image of the composition teacher is so low, Miller finds that the teacher of composition may have some of the characteristics of a stigmatized individual as described by Erving Goffman. Goffman discusses their relationship with so-called normals and writes that "the 'central feature' of these relationships is . . . 'acceptance,' which appears to be the primary issue that current composition professionals identify when they discuss accomplished and hoped-for changes in their status" (Goffman qtd. in Miller 129). I see a need for professional acceptance as one of the forces driving the particularly disdainful rejection of "expressivism."

I think it is interesting to examine Bartholomae's critique of process rhetorics in the light of the fact that composition teaching has been viewed as low-status work. The February 1995 issue of *College Composition and Communication* picks up a conversation between Bartholomae and Elbow begun at the Conference on College Composition and Communication (CCCC) in 1989 and 1991. As Bartholomae takes on Elbow, he writes,

> I would also say that our current conversations are very much a product of an important moment in composition in the early 1970s—one in which Peter played a key role. *At a time when* the key questions facing composition *could have been* phrased as questions of linguistic difference—what is good writing and how is that a question of race, class, or gender?—*at a time when composition could have made the scene of instruction the object of scholarly inquiry,* there was a general shift away from questions of value and the figure of the writer in a social context of writing to questions of process and the figure of the writer as an individual psychology. ("Writing" 68, emphasis mine)

The issue of composition's role in the academy recurs later in the essay. "Should composition programs self-consciously maintain a space for . . . the author at a time when the figure of the author is under attack in all other departments of the academy?" (70).

At the risk of reenacting the very error Bartholomae is targeting (i.e., making an individual—as opposed to a social—analysis), I read these comments as reflecting a certain status consciousness. It is as if he is arguing, Don't you see, colleagues? We could have been in the intellectual vanguard of the cultural studies movement and respected as such. Instead we missed out on an opportunity to gain credibility, even philosophical baronetcy, within the English apparatus and now are either left to basement status or running to catch up with our peers in other disciplines.

Historically, the debate Bartholomae and Elbow were engaging in, which has been reduced to the social versus the private turns, was a fallout from the sixties. Let me inject a bit of "sentimental realism" (Bartholomae, "Writing" 67). As a member of Students for a Democratic Society, as well as a member of a self-proclaimed communist party (the Progressive Labor Party, which later became the Party for Workers Power [PLP/PWP]), I was keenly aware of the tension between the social and the individual. Party members were expected to spend just about every waking moment "building a base in the working class." When we began talking about this oppressive atmosphere inside PLP/PWP in the mid seventies, it was clear that many of us felt tremendous guilt whenever we tried to carve out time for family and friends. (These kinds of interactions were not considered to be building a base for the party in the working class or contributing toward building a society that would be humane and equitable.) I hear a version of this conflict in Bartholomae and his representation of what Elbow was promoting. "At a time when" we could have been discussing "race, class, or gender" (68), we were developing new journalism and creative nonfiction, "reproduc[ing] the ideology of sentimental realism . . . [and] a narrative that celebrates a world *made up of the details of private life* and whose hero is sincere" (69, emphasis mine). I find his bifurcation confusing; private lives are lived by individuals with race, class, and gender. Not only is Bartholomae erasing the individuals who make up society, but he is reinforcing a binary between public and private discourse, one I return to in a moment.

I would like to cite one other factor in the etiology of the conflict around personal writing in composition. Given that process rhetorics do encourage the personal narrative in composition classes, and given that there is no concomitant pedagogy for how to respond to these essays, teachers of writing do not readily know how to cope with the discomfort they feel when they get such essays. One common question is, How do I grade these papers?

Let me illustrate the discomfort using an essay written by Bartholomae's student describing her parents' divorce. He reports that the whole class read it. "We've read it because the student cannot invent a way of talking about family, sex roles, separation" ("Writing" 66). Later in the same issue of the journal, Bartholomae responds to Elbow's critique of his dismissiveness of her role as a writer of this essay. Bartholomae declares,

> I begin by *not* granting the writer her "own" presence in that paper, by denying the paper's status as a record of or a route to her own thoughts and feelings. I begin instead by asking her to read her paper as a text already written by the culture, representing a certain predictable version of the family, the daughter, and the writer. I begin by being dismissive. ("Response" 85)

Oddly enough, Bartholomae is not the only one who is dismissive of the essay. Elbow, in turn, replies by telling Bartholomae that he is doing the student's thinking for her. "[Y]ou are telling her that she thought she meant X, but really she didn't. . . . [R]eally her perceptions and experience were a script written out for her by the culture. It feels important to me *not* to do that" (Elbow, "Response" 91). How would Elbow have responded? "[I]f this paper were the first one of the semester, *I would give no response at all*" (91, emphasis mine).

One can respond to personal essays with compassion, with a discussion of a larger culture, and with revision help. It is a model I describe in the conclusion of this book. In the meantime, what stands out for me in this particular aspect of the Bartholomae–Elbow debate is that *both* men are uncomfortable with a student essay about her parents' divorce. My evidence of the discomfort is that neither wants to talk to the student or the audience about it. Why is there not one quotation from the student's essay showing how it reproduces "the master narrative of family life" (Bartholomae, "Writing"

67)? And why would Elbow offer no response? The aversion to the essay is not explained. My problem is not with the aversion, which is widespread and understandable, but with the lack of acknowledgment of it.

Picking Some Theoretical Bones

Before I bring the reader into some actual classrooms in "expressivist" programs, I have a few more theoretical bones to pick. The "expressivist" has become the intellectually limited ingenue to the sophisticated rhetorician of academic discourse and cultural criticism. I call for a sharing of pedagogies and a breakdown of the binaries between the individual and "the social turn" and between private and public discourse. Prior to issuing such a call, I find it necessary to stand up and object to the way some composition teachers have been caricatured. My remarks might seem agonistic, especially for someone who calls for mediation of differences in the field. I am reminded here of a textual interchange between Patricia Bizzell and Nancy McKoski. McKoski calls Bizzell "modernist and reactionary" (334), and Bizzell writes back, "McKoski does not seem to be aware of . . . developments in my most recent scholarship, and she seriously misrepresents some of my views" ("Are Shared Discourses Desirable?" 273). [In a response, or gloss, to an early draft of chapter 8, Bizzell told me, "I was more harsh in my reply to McKoski than I have ever been because I felt she really was unfair and unhelpful."]

The following commentaries on the way Lester Faigley and James Berlin have essentialized "expressivism" may appear harsh as well. Both of these individuals have won awards and are widely respected in the field; they have mentored many people. Nonetheless, I think it is especially important to respond to their writing precisely because they have taken on what Michel Foucault calls "author function" ("What Is an Author?" 267). They are major influences on the way composition and rhetoric scholars all over the country envision the discipline. Their opinions have been a big part of what is now almost a knee-jerk dismissal of anything that hints of "expressivism." As one composition professor says of her past experience at the University of Texas, "The cardinal rule of graduate school is that no one reads Peter Elbow."

Postmodern theorists in English studies often turn to the work of postcolonial writers like Homi Bhabha, Gayatri Chakravorty Spivak, or Edward Said to discuss such concepts as orientalizing, essentializing, or Othering of groups of people who are presented as "less than." (These postcolonialists frequently argue that what we see in the Other is what we wish to deny in ourselves.) There has been an unfortunate Othering of "expressivists" by social constructionists in the field of composition. In fact, I find in the critique of the pedagogy that entails teaching the personal essay an instance of what Marxist Henry Giroux might call "disciplinary terrorism." Giroux complains that, despite an "alleged democratization of knowledge," cultural studies theorists are enmeshed in a "legacy of academic elitism" (6), which propels them to diminish the significance of pedagogy. Similarly, some composition theorists, whom I see as also being enmeshed in "a legacy of academic elitism," are dismissive of a pedagogy that encourages personal narrative. Ironically, the work of such scholars as Berlin and Faigley has prompted other scholars to reexamine the value of the personal narrative. In doing so, we have found it is an even more significant genre than we have thought—not least because it can be an important stepping-stone to activating exactly the kind of social change that Berlin and Faigley have called for.

The social constructionist tendency to view the family-based personal essay as "inconsequential" outside the classroom overlooks the fact that the family system is a site both of individual development and of political consciousness. Rather than some sort of predictable "master narrative," the family is often the place where individuals experience abuse and oppression. Instead of trivializing the social significance of the essays students write about their families or claiming that they are written by the culture, we need to do some difficult psychosocial work. We need to think about the links between the troubling family oppression that some students feel almost compelled to write about and their views about the social oppression of people from other ethnic groups, classes, and genders. We might ask ourselves, for example, Does familial mistreatment establish a tolerance for various forms of social injustice, or does it create individuals who are activists for social change? Or what are the political consequences of divorce? Does it produce individuals who welcome or shun communal, egalitarian ways of living? By disparaging the personal narrative in composition classrooms, I think that some professionals in the field fail to see how the family can function as one of the many capillaries through which power and powerlessness circulate. As Mahala and Swilky point out, the experiential narrative can be a vehicle "to explore the writer's historical location in relation to others and the world" (369). Or, as Chiseri-Strater and Sunstein write, "To understand someone's culture, we often need to understand the person's family, too. Through the individual we come to understand the culture, and through the culture we come to understand the individual" (216).

Let me offer a personal illustration here. Disrespect for people of color and for people of different religions was something I learned from my mother, long before I went to school, watched television, or read the newspaper. By the same token, I learned about gender roles by watching my father go to his retail business seven days a week and my mother work in the home even after there was almost no work left to do there. Similarly, Adrienne Rich tells us,

> [My father] demanded absolute loyalty, absolute submission to his will. In my separation from him . . . I was learning in concrete ways a great deal about patriarchy, in particular, how the "special" woman, the favored daughter, is controlled and rewarded. (650)

Ideology is wrapped up in the family system and, in many cases, these systems are impacted by a variety of unhealthy behaviors, including substance abuse. Those who sever such stories from the political beliefs of their students miss out on their pathos and intellectual energy and fail to help these students make important connections between their personal lives and the society at large. Think of the energy that could be released for social change if our students were able to make these connections.

Social constructionists, according to Patricia Sullivan, "regard knowledge as a function of language, as a product of consensus achieved through communal discourse, and [the theory] locates the 'real' in a web of social interactions and symbolic transactions" ("Social" 950). This emphasis on language and the symbolic may have conservative implications. For example, speaking of the theory's "'linguistic determinism,'" Mary Ann Cain writes, "[S]ocial constructivists, taking their cue from postmodern theories of language, often treat change more as a matter of altering language practices than as a matter of social intervention and emancipation" (24). Even Faigley admits, "Postmodern theory has not produced . . . a broad theory of agency that would lead directly from these critiques to political action" (*Fragments* 39).

In books like *Fragments of Rationality, Rhetoric and Reality,* and *Rhetorics, Poetics, and Cultures,* Faigley and Berlin, respectively, construct an image of "expressivists." For Thomas O'Donnell, these constructs "become unrecognizable (to me at least) as anything expressivist teachers are actually invested in" (425). For example, it is as if "expressivists" are so naive as to believe that the authors of personal narratives are unquestionably writing in propria persona. Somehow we are so passionate in our beliefs that, like the foolish but well-intentioned Maoris in the film *The Piano,* we confuse drama with real life and jump onto the stage to prevent a villainous murder.

The Berlin Wall: Is Writing a Private Vision?

Many composition scholars have been influenced by a taxonomy of the field of composition established by James Berlin. Berlin shapes a history of what he calls "expressionism" beginning in the early part of the twentieth century but with historical roots in romanticism and further back in Plato.[2] "The ideal of liberal culture indirectly encouraged the development of expressionistic rhetoric through its philosophic idealism and its emphasis on the cultivation of the self, both derived from its ties with Brahminical romanticism" (*Rhetoric and Reality* 73). Berlin's reasoning is slippery here. By declaring an indirect link between "expressionistic rhetoric" and "the ideal of liberal culture" with its "philosophic idealism and its emphasis on the cultivation of the self," two characteristics derived from romanticism, Berlin makes these characteristics of liberal culture appear to be attached to expressionistic rhetoric. The indefinite pronoun *its* is used three times in the sentence, further blurring liberal culture/romanticism and expressionistic rhetoric.

What Berlin calls "expressionism" is almost always associated with notions of encouraging the student to develop his or her own "unique self" in writing, writing that avoids and even disdains connection with the material world. This disdain for the external world is nowhere documented by Berlin but is apparently to be taken on the good faith of the implied reader who is willing to accept the connection to Plato. Berlin refines his view over the course of four frequently cited works, sometimes referring to his earlier publications as the only evidence of arguments in later works. These books and articles are "Contemporary Composition: The Major Pedagogical Theories" (1982); *Rhetoric and Reality: Writing Instruction in American Colleges, 1900–1985* (1987); "Rhetoric and Ideology in the Writing Class" (1988); and *Rhetorics, Poetics, and Cultures* (published posthumously in 1996).

The taxonomy was originally presented in his 1982 article published in *College English*. In the same year, Patricia Bizzell published "Cognition, Convention, and Certainty: What We Need to Know about Writing" in *Pre/Text*. She also divides the field into what she calls "inner-directed theorists" and "outer-directed theorists," the former allegedly believing in universal writing processes (77) and the latter assuming that "thinking and language use can never occur free of a social context that conditions them" (79). In the context of the interdisciplinary development and acceptance of cultural studies, as pointed out by Bartholomae, the simultaneous distribution of the two essays worked toward reifying the taxonomy, with Berlin's work becoming more influential. It is unfortunate that Berlin, despite the fact that he disseminated his views over a fourteen-year period, does not seem to have tested his theoretical conclusions against actual "expressionist" classroom practice. If he had, he might have seen a range of pedagogies, some more overtly sociopolitical than others, depending on the comfort level and belief system of the teacher. As it is, Berlin limits himself by not supporting his claims with observations.[3]

Furthermore, Berlin seems either to ignore or to misunderstand the importance of group interaction in process pedagogy. As Elbow puts it in a draft of the introduction to the twenty-fifth anniversary edition of his first book, *Writing Without Teachers,*

> A highly respected scholar and historian of composition, James Berlin, does write briefly of my epistemology, but it's hard to believe he looked carefully at what I wrote. For he says that I am a Platonist who believes that knowledge is totally private, whereas I make it clear that both the teacherless class and the epistemology of the believing game can only function as group processes, and that their validity derives only from people entering into each others' diverse and conflicting experiences. *I argue specifically that the meaning of any spoken or written discourse is entirely dependent on groups and communities.* . . . The teacherless class and the believing game are completely undermined if one tries to function solo. (xxvi–xxvii, emphasis mine)

In fact, Elbow's notion of meaning making discourse communities does not sound so different from what Berlin calls "epistemic rhetoric." Writing in *Rhetoric and Reality* Berlin tells us, "The epistemic position implies that knowledge is not discovered by reason alone, that cognitive and affective processes are not separate, that intersubjectivity is a condition of all knowledge, and that the contact of minds affects all knowledge" (165). Thus, for both Elbow and Berlin, meaning making is a social process.[4]

In *Rhetoric and Reality,* Berlin does discuss group process, but he does so critically. In the section "Subjective Rhetoric," he writes, "For the expressionist, solitary activity is always promising, *group activity always dangerous*" (145, emphasis mine). However, Berlin makes an attempt to undercut essentialism by allowing for "varieties of expressionistic rhetoric" (145), including a few that approach epistemic. "[I]n this view language does not simply record the private vision, but becomes involved in shaping it" (146). But alas, this group of "expressionists" also runs amuck

> because it denies the place of intersubjective, social processes in shaping reality. *Instead, it always describes groups as sources of distortion of the individual's true vision,* and the behavior it recommends in the political and social realms is atomistic, the individual acting alone. (146, emphasis mine)

Among the "expressionists" who follow what he calls the "latitudinarian" view are Ken Macrorie, Donald Murray, Walker Gibson, William Coles, and Peter Elbow (146). Berlin's conclusions are as inflammatory as they are unsubstantiated.

I do not find any evidence in Berlin's book that these five men either view group process to be dangerous or recommend acting alone. There are only two references to the "expressionists" and group processes, or what Berlin calls "editorial groups," in the section. He writes, "[T]he purpose of editorial groups is to check for the inauthentic in the writer's response (Berlin, 'Contemporary Composition')" (*Rhetoric and Reality* 152). The reader can see that his source for this conclusion lies not in any of the five "expressionists" to whom he calls our attention but in his own prior article. (I might add that neither does he offer the reader a page citation from his article, "Contemporary Composition.") The second and final reference to editorial groups is in relation to Elbow or, as he puts it, "Elbow's camp," and it concludes the section.

It is not surprising, then, that Elbow's version of the editorial group was influenced by the methods of group therapy and of the encounter group (121). Finally, at the start of this discussion, I said that Elbow's approach is not overtly political. In the last analysis, however, for Elbow as for other expressionists, the personal *is* the political—the underlying assumption being that enabling individuals to arrive at self-understanding and self-expression will inevitably lead to a better social order. (*Rhetoric and Reality* 154–55)

While Berlin does refer back to one thing he said at the beginning of the discussion, that Elbow's work is not overtly political, he does not refer back to his initial inflammatory remarks, "For the expressionist . . . group activity [is] always dangerous. . . . [T]he behavior it recommends in the political and social realms is atomistic, the solitary individual acting alone" (145–46). Berlin has not provided one shred of evidence of these initial declarations.

That the personal is political has become something of a slogan in various theoretical circles, most noticeably some feminist ones. Berlin does not agree with his own definition of what the slogan means, that individual change precedes social change. Moreover, he seems rather obtuse about the workings of "the editorial group" and the process of meaning making that goes on in it. Of course these groups make meaning and they are, in their own right, discourse communities. Even if he is correct and early "expressionists" saw their purpose as solely to help the individual clarify and strengthen his or her writing, that does not mean that they encouraged an atomistic lifestyle. I find the opposite to be true: by sharing one's work in a safe community where there is both encouragement and constructive, nonshaming critique, individual isolation breaks down.

Even more important, these groups have the potential for creating bonds across racial and class lines. In my ethnographic study of BC, a white teacher develops a relationship with Tanya, the only student of color in her course, that is strong enough to help her workshop an antiracist essay and become an active member of the community. When one of my own students workshopped a very "sensitive" essay about his aging grandmother, he and several other students in the class began to cry (Eagleton 98). Because they were in the same developmental stage, many of the students were facing similar losses, including one student who had just learned the evening before that her grandmother did not have long to live. Berlin advocates "intersubjectivity" (*Rhetoric and Reality* 165) in the construction of knowledge, but "it is important to remember that *inter*subjectivities require subjectivities, and vice versa" (Cassity, "Embracing" 179).

Berlin reduces the dialectic in "expressionist" editorial groups to one function: "to enable the writer to understand the manifestation of her identity in language through considering the reactions of others—not, for example, to begin to understand how meaning is shaped by discourse communities" (*Rhetoric and Reality* 153). What kind of meaning gets credit for being shaped in discourse communities in the Berlin worldview? He never specifies. When students come together to help each other write more forceful essays about racism on campus or about the loss of a loved one, aren't they making meaning within a community? Doesn't this kind of bonding break down the distrust, cynicism, and competitiveness that accrues in academia, a bonding that could carry over to all kinds of collective support, whether for "overtly political" causes, such as organizing to stop the spread of racist graffiti, or for overtly personal causes, such as supporting one another through loss?

In *Romancing Rhetorics,* Sherrie Gradin takes on the false binary personal/political with her neologism "social-expressivism." She tells us that "expressivist theory evolves from a tradition [romanticism] that recognizes the economic, social, and political conditions of existence," but she acknowledges in response to Berlin that "the practitioners of expressivism can certainly fail to incorporate this tradition into their pedagogy" (109). There are, as Berlin himself tells us, "varieties of expressionistic rhetoric" (*Rhetoric and Reality* 145). Perhaps some classrooms are less overtly political than others, depending on the degree to which individual practitioners are comfortable with the potential for heated debate. Individual differences not withstanding, the existence of these classrooms does not constitute a concerted and unitary theory either of avoidance of such issues or of infatuation with "the private vision."

In "Rhetoric and Ideology in the Writing Class," Berlin argues that "the ruling elites in business, industry, and government are those most likely to nod in assent to the ideology inscribed in expressionistic rhetoric" because it reinforces "individualism, private initiative, the confidence for risk-taking, the right to be contentious with authority (especially the state)" (487). Newkirk sees a logical fallacy underlying one of Berlin's conclusions, namely that "expressionism" nurtures the capitalistic spirit in its students. He faults Berlin for making similarity appear to be causation. Referring here to Berlin's restatement of the argument in *Rhetorics, Poetics, and Cultures,* Newkirk writes,

> To paraphrase Berlin, there are attitudes and values fostered in expressionist pedagogies that *resemble* those that a capitalist system seeks to foster in consumers (the self-gratifying enjoyment of "choice") and in entrepreneurs (private initiative). Because of this similarity, expressivist teaching causes students to enter happily and even successfully into that system.
>
> This argument is so loose that it could easily be used against the cultural studies approach [of Berlin and others]. One could easily imagine how corporations could profit from the critical skills students develop when they "problemitize" seemingly self-evident arguments and positions. (*Performance* 89)

Because two things appear to be alike, it does not follow that one causes the other. Newkirk does not see how Berlin has proven that "expressionism" fosters an accommodation to capitalism.

I would add to Newkirk's critique that any pedagogy that results in grading students, ranking them in their class, and providing the basis for records that go out to future admissions officers or employers is part of capitalist relations of power and authority. Grading and ranking trigger competition whether you are teaching the canon, grammar, personal narrative, or some form of cultural studies in which students are encouraged to see how representations of the empirical world in the mass media work to maintain a class system (as Berlin suggests in two model courses in his *Rhetorics, Poetics, and Cultures*). Most teaching in our system perpetuates divisions and hierarchy.

Finally, Berlin does not explicitly debunk "expressionism," but he does come to a surprising conclusion. There is only one reference in *Rhetoric, Poetics, and Cultures,* to "expressionism" and it is indirect. The proposed course "Codes and Critiques" is put forward as a foil to an unnamed but behind-the-scenes pedagogy. Berlin himself uses some coding here that the Berlin reader should have no trouble recognizing. "Unlike classrooms that insist that each student look within to discover a unique self, this course argues that only through understanding the workings of culture in shaping consciousness can students ever hope to achieve any degree of singularity" (124). I am surprised to see Berlin advocating *singularity,* a word that means being one of a kind or having a trait marking one as distinct from others. I find it hard to believe that Berlin's goal, in the end, is for the individual to see him- or herself as "distinct from others" because it seems to represent the "private vision" that this cultural critic argued against over a fourteen-year period.

Faigley: The Dismissal of Autobiographical Writing

In 1992 the University of Pittsburgh Series in Composition, Literacy, and Culture published Lester Faigley's *Fragments of Rationality: Postmodernity and the Subject of Composition*. In 1994 it received the Outstanding Book Award from CCCC for making an outstanding contribution to composition and communication studies. It contains such an impressive body of knowledge about the history of composition, postmodern thought, linguistics, and computer-assisted instruction that, had I been a member of the Outstanding Book Award Committee along with Alice Gillam, Cheryl Glenn, Betty L. Hart, Frank Littler, and Charles I. Schuster, I might have concurred. And I might have done so despite deep reservations about the chapter entitled "Ideologies of the Self in the Writing Classroom," a chapter in which Faigley uses a postmodern orientation to deconstruct the merits of the personal essay in the writing classroom.

According to Faigley, this genre proclaims "the existence of the rational, coherent self and the ability of the self to have privileged insight into its own processes" (111), both of which are questioned by postmodern theory. "Expressivist" writing is guilty of what Catherine Belsey calls "expressive realism," a naive assumption that language is somehow ahistorical and apolitical, that it provides a transparent window into the empirical world (Belsey qtd. in Faigley 112).

Faigley is troubled that the field of composition shows signs of being biased toward personal narrative. Despite a broad range of contributing faculty to William Coles and James Vopat's *What Makes Writing Good* (1985), a collection of what these professors felt to be excellent responses to their assignments, the bulk of the writing samples are personal-experience pieces. "Not one essay resembles the frequently assigned 'research paper,'" according to Faigley (*Fragments* 120). When writing teachers use "authentic voice" as an assessment criterion for these types of essays, they assume that the reader can "distinguish the true self" (122). Because

27

of the unconscious, we cannot know if something is being repressed and, therefore, we cannot assess the sincerity of the writer (127). Additionally, Faigley argues that the apparent freedom that students are given to choose autobiographical topics in writing classrooms conceals "the fact that these same students will be judged by teachers' unstated assumptions about subjectivity and that every act of writing they perform occurs within complex relations of power" (128). The contributors to the Coles and Vopat anthology naively assume that the rhetorical situation is neutral and that the pressure of representing oneself to an authority figure has no impact on the content of these essays.

In spite of this avalanche of arguments, it is to Faigley's credit that he sees some value in personal-experience essays. He tells us, "The many varieties of autobiographical writing have provided sites for resistance to dominant discourses" (*Fragments* 129). However, I am surprised that, given his support for cultural studies, Faigley does not elaborate on the phrase *resistance to dominant discourses* or provide any examples of such writing. Personal narrative has been historically associated in this country with African Americans and with women who are writing against oppression and producing what Foucault has called "subjugated knowledge" (*Power* 82).

I will limit my objections to Faigley's critique to two points. There is a problem with his notion of the self in personal and expository essays. Furthermore, gender bias is manifested in Faigley's lack of intellectual respect for a particular student essay. I read Faigley as issuing a blanket dismissal of 62 percent (thirty out of forty-eight) of the Coles and Vopat essays as simply personal experience, either directly autobiographical or "writing about the writer." Why is Faigley so intellectually unhappy with personal narratives? His thinking rests on one of the now almost foundational "truths" of postmodern thought: a rational, coherent, and unified self, the persona that is always already in personal narrative, does not exist. Personal essays that exhibit rational, coherent, and unified selves constitute a naive ignorance of both the complex human consciousness and the social context of the writer and his or her persona.

Faigley seems to hold an unstated double standard, perhaps along the line suggested by Newkirk. In *The Performance of Self in Student Writing,* Newkirk comments on a contradiction, or what he calls "a strange schizophrenia," regarding narrative in English departments.

> On the one hand, [English departments] are built upon the narrative—it should come as no news that students become English majors to get academic credit for reading narrative fiction. Yet in writing classes there is a sense that narratives are relatively easy to write and academically suspect. (20)

Nowhere does Faigley object to the reading of narrative in the genre of fiction.

Although Faigley devalues the rational, coherent, and unified self in student texts selected as examples of good writing by many of his colleagues, he apparently values such a stable persona in academic writing. More specifically, nowhere in *Fragments of Rationality* does the narrator, Lester Faigley, actually present a fragmented consciousness. The argument and point of view are consistent and clear throughout. (Of note here is the fact that nothing of the author's personal life is woven into the text other than the epigraph from Ian Faigley, "Face it, Dad. You're totally out of it. Your last good year was 1976, the year you had me.") Faigley celebrates the postmodern notion of the self in his title, yet the celebration is not actualized in his writing. Why is it permissible to present oneself as rational and coherent in one mode of discourse but not another? Why may Faigley present a rational, unified, coherent persona in an expository book on composition, but students who do so in personal narratives and professors who affirm these essays are missing the latest boat in terms of theory? Eleanor Kutz, who offers ethnography as an alternative to the traditional research paper we assign our students, describes the voice in one student's ethnography. "This is not a distanced academic voice, and it does not pretend to an objectivity that would always remain unrealized" (355). The presumption of objectivity in Faigley's *Fragments of Rationality* is troubling.

A related problem stems from our culture's conversation about "authentic self." I do not agree with Faigley that respect for a voice that has integrity necessarily implies belief in "the true self." Rather, such respect can demonstrate the persuasiveness that accrues to a narrator who achieves ethos.

Faigley writes that the compositionists who appear in Coles and Vopat's *What Makes Writing Good* assume "that individuals possess an identifiable 'true' self and that the true self can be expressed in discourse" (*Fragments* 122). His proof comes from James Vopat's student, Peggy Bloxam, who writes of "true selves" and "a real self" in her essay on Studs Terkel's *Working*. Faigley concludes, "The question that remains for both traditional Marxists and 'authentic voice' proponents is how do we distinguish the true self?" (122). A subtle slippage occurs in Faigley's paragraph. He takes Bloxam's worldview and claims that her teacher, James Vopat, Marxists, and authentic voice proponents in general all believe in "the true self." I simply do not see the worldview of Bloxam and Vopat (who is made to represent traditional Marxist and "authentic voice" proponents) as one and the same.

Bloxam complains about being forced to write a paper on degradation because if she does not she will be "punished." She uses her own response to the task environment as a segue into talking about workers' experiences of feeling degraded, essentially being forced to adopt subject positions they would rather not. Or, as she puts it, "[A] false self possessing characteristics totally divorced from those of the real self has taken over" (Coles and Vopat 351). Vopat's commentary follows the reproduction of Bloxam's essay. He affirms the student's frustration.

> Writing is a loss of identity, *another loss of self.* . . . This is my idea of political writing: seeing the implications of experience, the 'I' as both personal and representative. The writer is also the worker; the "I" literally becomes part of the "we." (353, emphasis mine)

I do not read Vopat as fitting Faigley's construction of the "expressivist," namely, a proponent of the one-true-self theory. Instead I see Vopat valorizing the notion of changing selves, of one becoming another, of one's separate story becoming the story of a group of people. If he were an advocate of the one-true-self theory, he might, for example, argue that when the student's *I* becomes *we* she either loses or finds her true self. He does not. For that matter, in her understanding of the difficult subject positions that we are forced to adopt in our working lives, I would argue that, despite her belief in "the real self," Bloxam actually sees the self as multiple.

There is another matter here as well. It is a staple of Aristotelian rhetoric to have the speaker convey ethos (i.e., to appear credible, moral, honest). When an evaluator labels a text "honest," "authentic" or written with "integrity," in my opinion it is a strong indication that the narrator has convinced the audience of his or her reading of a situation. The narrator has persuaded. In fact, I would argue that *the logos of expressive discourse, of personal narrative, is its ethos.* As Aristotle puts it, the speaker's "character may almost be called the most effective means of persuasion he possesses" (1329). I read Aristotle as saying that the audience is persuaded because of the credibility of the writer. When Faigley dismisses the notion of "authentic voice" as a belief that the author is writing in propria persona, he is confounding an alleged naïveté of the "expressivist" reader with the ethos of the writer or the narrator.

Yet how can we determine the credibility of the author when we have author-evacuated prose, the kind of prose that is currently the standard of credibility in academia? If we take into consideration Faigley's approval of Greg Shaefer's essay, "Thucydides: The Historian as Creative Artist" (Coles and Vopat 306–9), along with his disappointment with personal-experience essays, we can conclude that Faigley prefers author-evacuated prose. Faigley compares Shaefer's well-written expository piece with Norma Bennett's personal narrative about her family (Coles and Vopat 158–60). Faigley asks his audience,

> [W]hy is writing about potentially embarrassing and painful aspects of one's life considered more honest than, say, the efforts of Joseph Williams' student, Greg Shaefer, who tries to figure out what Thucydides was up to in writing about the Peloponnesian War? (*Fragments* 121)

When I read Shaefer's lucid and well-argued essay, I find that it involves no risk taking. He has been directed to "compare and contrast the first two speeches in Thucydides' *History*" (Coles and Vopat 305), and that is precisely what he does. He ventures no opinions. Schaefer writes, "The Corinthian argument failed because for an imperial power like Athens, justice is not a very strong controlling force" (309), but we do not know where he stands either in regard to the dispute brought before the Athenians or in regard to Thucydides's representation of speeches he never heard. He writes a safe essay because he does what he knows his teacher wants him to do. Schaefer can put aside any positivistic tendencies and write about representation.

Norma Bennett, on the other hand, does take a risk. She chooses to write an essay that exposes her family to the public eye in response to an assignment by Erika Lindemann that does not ask for any kind of exposure. "The assignment asks you to write an essay that is primarily descriptive but that makes its point by comparison and contrast." When I read Faigley's summary of Bennett's essay before reading the essay itself, I imagined the piece to be maudlin and self-pitying, and I imagined that the narrator was so upfront with her emotional pain that I would feel embarrassed reading it. I felt contemptuous toward her mother and repulsed by her father from Faigley's reconstruction. After reading the essay itself, however, I no longer feel any of these things. Here is Faigley's summary:

> Norma Bennett's paper is a narrative of a summer vacation spent with her two divorced parents who now go to different resorts. Her mothers [sic] wears her PTL ("Praise the Lord") jacket (in the days before Jim and Tammy Bakker's fall) and spends much of her day sleeping or sobbing. Her potbellied father also spends much of the day sleeping—passed out drunk on the beach with a twenty-five-year-old woman in a white string bikini while Norma babysits for the woman's young child. I have a great deal of sympathy for students like Norma Bennett, who must cope with difficult family situations as well as the pressures of college. (*Fragments* 121)

After reading Faigley's representation of the Bennett essay, I have negative feelings toward her mother, a member of the religious right who sleeps and sobs most of the day. Yet my experience of this woman is different when I read Bennett's own account. While her mother's religious affiliation does emerge in the text, the description does not play on a reader's potential antifundamentalist bias. Norma's mother rises before dawn each morning to walk to the beach and collect shells. "My mom . . . praises God for his magnificent creation, and photographs her favorite sanctuary" (Coles and Vopat 159), activities that feel decidedly ecumenical to me. Moreover, I find no indication that, as Faigley puts it, "she spends much of the day sleeping or sobbing." Norma tells us only that, when her mother returns from the beach, "her eyes are watery, her cheeks are red, and her nose is runny. I'm not sure if it's because of the cold wind outside or if she's crying about my dad again or if she's been overwhelmed by the presence of the Lord. Maybe it's all three" (159). Faigley condenses Norma's speculation to one word, *sobbing*, thereby reducing the representation of the mother from a spiritually active person, who is experiencing an appropriate grief reaction, to an emotional mess. In doing so, he short-circuits the kind of compassion we feel for her after reading Norma's account.

Nor do we have any evidence that she spends much of the day sleeping. Norma writes,

I give her a hug and grumble about getting up. She laughs and teases me about being lazy. My mom won't go out on the beach in the middle of the day. She goes back to bed while I go lie with my friends. Late every afternoon, just before dinner, we go out on the beach together, carrying sand buckets and shovels. Like a couple of kids, we sink down in the sand and start building a castle. (Coles and Vopat 159)

Because Norma's mother goes back to bed and does not go out on the beach in the middle of the day, Faigley assumes she is the "lazy" one. In the absence of any account of her activities, probably something that Norma herself is not privy to, he concludes that the mother sleeps away the day.

I am troubled by Faigley's representation of this woman. It leads me to identify against myself as a woman. Drawing on a theory of Judith Fetterley, Patrocinio Schweickart puts it this way: "Androcentric literature . . . does not allow the woman to seek refuge in her difference. Instead, it draws her into a process that she uses against herself" (42). After reading Norma's essay, I realize I had been drawn into collusion with Faigley, that I had adopted a contempt for Norma's mother and other women who are working through losses, a contempt that borders on misogyny.

Faigley reads Norma as writing about "potentially embarrassing and painful aspects of [her] life" (*Fragments* 159), but I do not feel her embarrassment; I do not think she burdens the reader with her pain; and I do not think she asks for our sympathy. She treats both of her parents with respect, something that may be hard to do in relation to a father who does appear to "spend much of the day sleeping—passed out drunk on the beach with a twenty-five-year-old woman in a white string bikini" (121). Yet Norma does not display this kind of contempt for her father either. She concludes her essay:

My Dad yells and says for me to look after David [his girlfriend's son]; they'll be back late. Tears come to my eyes. Dad has *lost his sobriety,* his family, and his God. I wonder how long it will be before his foundation is washed away, and his castle is level with the sand.

I love my mom and my dad both. My dad has many friends and many good times, but he is too miserable to enjoy them. My mom is a loner. She has quiet times and peace of mind. As I look at my own life, I search for a castle—up high, away from the shoreline—far away from the destruction of the tide. (Coles and Vopat 160, emphasis mine)

I feel the narrator's pain here but I do not feel her reaching out for pity from the audience. There is maturity and an ethos evident as she stands apart from her parents, wanting none of the "destruction of the tide" in her life. She writes that her father has "lost his sobriety." Faigley and other readers may be unaware that she is using what ethnographers call "insider language" from Alcoholics Anonymous, bringing not embarrassment to the story but a view of her father as a man with a disease who has gone into relapse. What *lost his sobriety* means in this context is that he was abstinent from alcohol for a period of time in AA but that he lost that abstinence and the peace of mind that can come from working within the program's suggested steps. I feel only her sadness at this relapse.

Perhaps it is Faigley who feels embarrassed by the story. The absence of any sort of self-reflexivity in this particular chapter further weakens his arguments against autobiographical writing. Edward Said advises theorists to declare their personal investment in critical projects. Influenced by Antonio Gramsci, Said suggests that we develop a consciousness of who we are as products of "the historical process to date." These processes have left many marks but no inventory. "'Therefore it is imperative at the outset to compile such an inventory'" (Gramsci qtd. in Said 25). I wish Faigley had done so.

Thus far, I have faulted the social constructionists both for weak theoretical criticism and for ignoring classroom practice as they problemize "expressivism." In the next chapter I turn to representations of the "expressivist" classroom, including an ethnographic study of Peter Elbow by Kathleen Cassity.

2 ⇒ IN SITU
The Political Elbow

Many accusations have been made about "expressivists," but they have not been based on classroom observation. With the exception of this book and Kathleen Cassity's unpublished study of Peter Elbow's class in Hawai'i, the published ethnographic research on these college-level writing classrooms is limited. Cassity's research in no way demonstrates that Elbow has any particular fascination with the personal narrative or that he elevates the writer's private endeavors or intent over social issues. In fact, in his CCCC presentation in 1999, "Revisioning the Personal," he argued that writing on personal topics eventually brings out nonpersonal issues with larger dynamics. Before taking a look at Elbow's classroom, I discuss a few case studies, ethnographies, and examples of teacher research on primary and secondary school practices.

Through Teachers' Eyes: Portraits of Writing Teachers at Work by Sondra Perl and Nancy Wilson (1986) is the result of a three-year-long follow-up study of high school teachers. Glenda Bissex and Richard Bullock draw upon teachers' self-reports in *Seeing for Ourselves: Case-Study Research by Teachers of Writing* (1987). In *Listening In* (1992), Thomas Newkirk (with Pat McLure) looks at McLure's elementary-level classroom.

To my knowledge, the first ethnographic study of a college-level "expressivist" writing classroom is Elizabeth Chiseri-Strater's chapter "Anatomy of a Discourse Community: Prose Writing" in *Academic Literacies* (1991). Chiseri-Strater describes Donna Qualley's advanced writing and reading classroom at the University of New Hampshire during the fall of 1987. Instead of making student writing the major reading in the course, Qualley used an outside text. Compositionists exposed to the Berlin taxonomy of the field who might expect to see her syllabus highlighting the work of "expressivist" Donald Murray will be surprised to find that the only text is *Ways of Reading* by Bartholomae and Petrosky. Chiseri-Strater tells us that when Qualley

> combines open paper topics with a series of triggering texts, what results is that many students "choose" to use the readings to help them frame and reframe their own experiences. The students' lives, their personal and/or intellectual experiences remain the central view displayed in the writing; the new addition is the frame of published readings, which adds further support to that window. (23)

Thus we can see that, while respect for students' lived experiences remains high, the teacher in this classroom encourages her students to re-view them through a wide-angle lens that incorporates the experiences of others. The researcher does not see Qualley as someone encouraging "the private vision," as Berlin would have it.

Additionally, Chiseri-Strater notices that whole-class and peer-group discussions are characterized by a "narrative conversational style [that] contrasts dramatically with the interrogative model that dominates schooling" (13). While the interrogative style assumes the existence of one right answer, the narrative style involves the practice of asking open-ended questions and the belief that students have much that is worthwhile to contribute to discussions about literacy. In fact, most of the students in the class said that, other than freshman composition, this was the only college class that had encouraged them "to talk in an unstructured, conversational way" (16). Chiseri-Strater finds that the talking "helps shape students' ways of thinking and eventually shape what they will write" (16). The class rapidly becomes a discourse community.

One indication that Qualley "assumes that knowledge is socially, not individually, constructed" (Chiseri-Strater 24) is the assignment of the collaborative writing project. Rather than encourage solipsistic writing, Qualley tells her students, "A good part of the writing done outside of school, especially in an organizational setting, is collaborative. Members work together to produce reports, recommendations, policy statements, business plans, rules, and other documents" (Chiseri-Strater 177). Many students in Qualley's class found such writing to be difficult, as there was so much negotiation involved. Chiseri-Strater concludes that the collaboration "fosters risk taking and fresh understandings of the thinking process" (31). It would appear that meaning is being made in this interactive writing process.

Roskelly and Ronald offer more recent vignettes of what might be labeled "expressivist" classrooms in *Reason to Believe: Romanticism, Pragmatism, and the Teaching of Writing*. In an effort to reunite theory and practice, a separation that has come about because of "the privileging of what Cornel West calls 'grand theory' over pedagogical practice" (qtd. in Roskelly and Ronald 2), the authors stitch together a history of "romantic/pragmatic rhetoric." Such a rhetoric enables teachers to have "a philosophy that embraces both idealism and practicalism, individuality and social responsibility, inquiry and faith" (3). The authors are explicitly deconstructing the unfortunate binary that has been built up by the social constructionist taxonomy between teachers allegedly focused on individual issues and those who take a "social turn." In the book's final chapter, subtitled "Romantic/Pragmatic Rhetoric in Action," we are treated to Roskelly's observations of some teachers she appears to be supervising whose practice does not fall solely into either focus.

We see high school teacher Bill Buczinsky teach a class of students who are usually labeled "at risk." They are poor and largely black. Some speak English as a second language, and others have obvious physical impairments. Buczinsky is an energetic young man, apparently able to do several things at once with an attitude that is both jovial and respectful of his students. While passing out a poem they will be discussing (Paul Laurence Dunbar's "Sympathy"), he puts on classical music. Buczinsky tells his students,

> You may know what the poet feels like. Before we do anything else, I want you to take five minutes and think about it. Write for five minutes. Do you ever feel trapped like the guy in the poem? Do you know why the caged bird sings? (Roskelly and Ronald 141)

Roskelly sees a great deal of theory informing Buczinsky's practice, as well as the belief that reading is powerful and "relevant to students' experience." "There is learning theory. Reading and writing are acts of interpretation; students have knowledge to share. . . . And there is a pedagogical theory that values the social, the interactive, the dialogue between teacher and student" (141).

After the writing exercise, some students share their responses; they describe the ways in which they feel imprisoned by rules and codes at home and in school. Mixed in with their responses, Buczinsky manages to teach the students about rhythm and rhyme, structure, mood, persona, and metaphor (143). Translating the data from Buczinsky's class back into theory, Roskelly writes, "Multiculturalism is . . . not simply an educational buzzword for managing students. . . . [Buczinsky's] class forces an examination of uncomfortable truths about our society" (143).

Elbow in Hawai'i

I turn now to the only ethnography, to my knowledge, of the work of Peter Elbow. In doing so, I do not mean to reinforce the binary in composition studies between this one practitioner (labeled "expressivist") and Berlin or Bartholomae. The problem is that there do not appear to be any published observations of the teaching of other more or less well known "expressivists."

Cassity takes strong exception to the strict individualist, apolitical bent attributed to the "expressivists" by some contemporary theorists. Reading her study is a way to get a sense of the culture of Elbow's section of English 100, Expository Writing, a required course for incoming students; it brings us closer to lived experience than either critical commentary on texts or generalizations about imagined classrooms. The study was conducted at the University of Hawai'i in Manoa during the spring of 1996, the year Elbow was a visiting professor. As a master's student, Cassity had an opportunity to take a class with Elbow and then observed his Expository Writing class as the basis for her thesis. He had been looking for someone to give him feedback on a new grading contract he was implementing that semester.

Cassity is troubled, as am I, by the association of "process/ expressivist" approaches "with rugged individualism, with naïve and simplistic concepts of 'self,' and with epistemological frameworks that shortchange social, cultural and historical contexts" ("Embracing" 15). She ultimately finds in Elbow's teaching something that looks like the radical approach of Henry Giroux, "border peda-gogy." Giroux believes that we should give students more opportu-nity to write about their own personal experiences with and emo-tional reactions to issues, such as race, rather than have them only "articulate the meaning of other peoples' theories" (Giroux 11).

The focus of Cassity's ethnography is Elbow's grading contract. In this contract, the student could choose what grade he or she wanted, a grade based on workload. Many students found the work-load necessary to achieve an A to be burdensome, even after he modified it twice. My interest in her study, however, is not in the contract but rather in the evidence Cassity provides for her initial statement that the representation of "expressivist" pedagogy as shortchanging social, political, and historical registers is false.

Let me comment first on issues of race and ethnicity. Of the nine-teen students in Elbow's class, fifteen were of Asian, Pacific, or mixed ethnicity; four were Caucasian (Cassity, "Embracing" 9). Six of the fifteen students raised in Hawai'i indicated that their primary lan-guage was Hawaiian Creole English, or pidgin (7). In one of many lively group discussions observed by Cassity, the students com-plained about the perception of Hawaiians by outsiders. "'People are so stupid, they actually think we live in grass shacks and stuff.'" "'You tell them you go to the University of Hawai'i and they're, like, surprised that people in Hawai'i even *study*'" (65). Their discussion reminds Cassity of her graduate seminar in colonialism.

In disagreeing with Berlin's characterization of these groups in Elbow's pedagogy, Cassity writes,

> The small groups were not designed for the purpose of assessing any writer's "authenticity" or "sincerity"; instead, the techniques of show-ing, telling, summarizing, pointing, and relating "movies of the mind" (all described in [Elbow's] *Writing Without Teachers*) allowed for reader response and negotiation of meaning between readers and writers. ("Embracing" 171)

In short, they were dialogic.

The first assignment began with a freewrite on "'any aspect of your group identities'" (70). Of note is the fact that the assignment did not encourage students to write about their individual, unique identities. After the freewrite became a homework assignment, it was then to be revised into a more public form. Students would pair up, and their collaborative projects were to include library research. Sue, a shy eighteen-year-old Chinese American, read her paper aloud in conference. When asked to write about her "group identities," Sue selected the topic of racism toward Chinese people.

> She discusses the slurs used against those of Chinese descent in Hawai'i and recites one of the derogatory rhymes she heard other kids chanting when she was little, rhymes feeding into the stereotype that the Chinese are "cheap." Breaking away from her text, she tells Peter as an aside, "I don't really believe it, you know."
> "Right," says Peter. "But it's sort of like some of the rhymes black kids have had to hear—some of the slurs—nowadays it's outlawed, but you've still heard it. It's still in there." ("Embracing" 70–71)

Elbow expands on the student's observation about racism toward Chinese people to include other people of color.

The use of Hawaiian Creole English, or pidgin, surfaces in the class. Cassity does not address the theoretical influences on Elbow here, but from what I can see of his pedagogy, he is in line with suggestions made by both Lisa Delpit and Eileen Oliver. Delpit tells us that "each cultural group should have the right to maintain its own language style"; however, we must tell students that "there is a political power game that is also being played, and if they want to be in on that game there are certain games they too must play" (292). They must learn the dominant register both to understand and to change the power realities (293). As Oliver puts it, "Students should have an opportunity to become exposed to an alternative dialect . . . a dialect commonly accepted by people in economically advantaged positions" (200).

Elbow apparently values both the native and the dominant dialects. Cassity demonstrates the pedagogy here through Elbow's work with Kerry. Kerry was worried because her primary language was nonstandard English. Here are some excerpts of either oral or written dialogue between student and teacher on the subject.

Kerry: I'm afraid my pidgin English will get in my way. You didn't write anything about pidgin English on your contract.
Elbow: Feel free to write in pidgin. . . .
Elbow: [Responding to an essay written in multiple linguistic registers] I like the pidgin section a lot. In my view, it's important to learn to write in it. As you say, it's YOUR tongue, your "mother tongue"—and so it's got the most "juice" in it—and you can put the most of YOU in it. You need to write in Standard English; but it's my belief that your Standard English might improve if you let yourself sometimes write in pidgin.

Kerry: [Responding in a process letter] I am very pleased that you don't discriminate against my language. (Cassity, "Embracing" 136–37)

Cassity tells us that Kerry received an A in the course, even though she had said at mid semester, "I give up." "The more Elbow not only accepted but encouraged Kerry's 'mother-tongue,' the more she wrote in both Standard English and pidgin" (141). Language is clearly an aspect of group identity for Elbow and his students.

The issues of ethnicity and gender emerge with an apparently defiant young man named Gary. Cassity describes a conference:

Gary interrupts again, launching into another monologue. Peter urges him to talk to his collaborator. "If you want to make these arguments about gender and ethnicity, if you want to say all these don't affect who you are, I want you nevertheless to take account of the fact that it looks to a lot of people like they do. I want you to take into account the opposite point of view." . . . I wonder if [Peter] feels [as] frustrated as I do. If so, he doesn't reveal it in either his facial expressions or [his] body language. (74)

However, I do read frustration in some of Elbow's written comments as he challenges viewpoints he disagrees with. He writes to Dave and Brad: "'When you talk about the rise in wages for women compared to men, you forget to mention one little fact: that women still get paid MUCH LESS than men for the same work!'" (89). To Karen and Gary he writes,

"There's something quite weird about your paper. EVERY EXAMPLE of racism that you talk about is an example of thinking or behavior by members of a targeted group, blacks or Hawaiians. NOWHERE IN YOUR PAPER do you ever give an example or seem to acknowledge the more pervasive racism of groups with more power . . . as though you think only blacks and Hawaiians are racist. Did you mean to do that?" (89)

To Adam and Mark he notes,

"You make a bunch of statements that are kind of illogical—that no one you know is gay. (You better not be so sure.) That everyone you know who is gay is messed up. (I thought you didn't know anyone.) That once someone is gay you can't see them the same. (Well how can you trust your perception when you know you go into this gear?)" (90)

In spite of Elbow's disagreements, he is still able to make positive comments on some aspects of each of these essays whose perspectives clearly trouble him. However, Cassity informs us that, with

Adam and Mark (who wrote about homosexuality), "[T]he best he can come up with is 'I'm glad you enjoyed working together—and that you did substantial re-arranging and changing'" (90). From her perspective, Elbow was struggling to find something positive here.

Let us recall that Elbow and other white people were in the minority in this classroom. After reading the first draft of my summary of her work, Cassity, who is herself of mixed ethnicity, responded,

> Obviously, if you come cruising in here with a white superiority attitude, you will soon be cruising back out, probably with a black eye. Peter was well liked by his freshman students so I think that says a lot about what kind of attitudes he displayed in class toward differences. (E-mail)

After having had this privileged peek at a small slice of Elbow's teaching practice, I can only conclude that race, gender, and sexual orientation are fair game for this "expressionist's" classroom. Not only does Elbow appear not to find the last word in any private vision, as Berlin has repeatedly told us, but he seems to have no inhibition whatsoever about challenging these visions when he disagrees with them.

In an effort to encourage a larger project in composition studies, where theorists take a look at the "opposition's" classrooms before publishing critiques that then become hypostatized as truths, I borrow from the ethnographic work of Chiseri-Strater, Roskelly and Ronald, and Cassity. As Cassity puts it, "In the specific case of Peter Elbow, the term 'expressivist' does not even begin to describe his approach" ("Embracing" 187). My intent in this chapter is to disrupt the essentialized misrepresentation of those teachers who encourage writing and classroom tasks that mix the personal, the social, and the academic. My own study of two teachers at Boston College follows.

3 ❧ ETHNOGRAPHY
A Postmodern Way of Seeing the World

After having been repeatedly assigned the works of James Berlin, Susan Miller, and Lester Faigley in doctoral seminars in two different graduate programs, I decided to attempt to fill what Thomas Newkirk calls "the empirical vacuum" in their work (*Performance* 89). I wanted to offer some local evidence that would speak more directly to the teaching practices of "expressivists." In short, I felt that it was time for the Other to speak to its critics, to say that it is not true that all of us avoid serious political issues in the writing classroom or that we encourage our students to think of their selves as unified and coherent or that we elevate "the private vision" of the writer cut off from the social.

The central research question I formulated is, What does it look like when composition faculty invite their students to write autobiographical essays? There are two related questions: Are faculty able to maintain their role as writing teachers without crossing over into the territory of the psychotherapist? Do skills learned in producing personal narrative transfer to expository or persuasive writing?

In my study of two writing faculty at BC, I did find enough evidence to question the ways in which "expressivist" programs have been dismissed by important theorists. I also found that there were noticeable differences between the two faculty members and that some of their work with students and their texts was troubling to me. Before describing the access to my field site and introducing my first subject, Helena, I discuss some of the problems that can emerge in conducting an ethnographic study.

Postmodern Features of Ethnography

Elizabeth Chiseri-Strater and Bonnie Stone Sunstein define ethnography as "the study of people in other cultures and the resultant text from that study" (43). Linda Brodkey calls it "the study of lived experience": "[T]he point of ethnographic research is to examine how, in the course of fabricating their lives, individuals also weave their material cultures" (25–26). Emerson, Fretz, and Shaw flesh out what such a study can entail.

> Ethnographic field research involves the study of groups of people as they go about their everyday lives. Carrying out research involves two distinct activities. First, the ethnographer enters into a social setting and gets to know the people involved in it. . . . The ethnographer participates in the daily routines of this setting, develops on-going relations with the people in it, and observes all the while what is going on. Indeed, the term "participant-observation" is often used to characterize this basic research approach. (1)

In fact, it is not possible to observe without, to some degree, participating. Just as taking the temperature of a substance can change the temperature, the presence of an observer can change the unfolding of events. A new layer of performance forms when people know they are being watched and written about. Then there are more problems when the observations are written up.

Compositionists conducting ethnographic research draw on the work of the postmodern anthropologist Clifford Geertz, who has intensively studied Javanese, Balinese, and Moroccan societies and who helps us to remember that ethnographic texts are rhetorical. These texts are interpretations, not exact replicas, of the phenomenological world. Or, as Geertz puts it, ethnography neither offers an occasion "for revelatory make-believe" nor represents its material "as naturally emergent from an absolutized world" (*Works* 142). Ethnographies are neither wholly subjective nor wholly objective but what might be called *self-reflexive re-presentation*. The researcher is very much aware that, even as he or she tries to bring the reader to the field site through descriptive prose as if it were an "absolutized world," the very words the researcher chooses and the situations he or she reports reflect the researcher's own values and subjectivities.

I find a rich image for this mix of quasi-positivist research and interpretation inherent in ethnography in the novel *Louisiana* by Jamaican sociologist Erna Brodber. The story takes place during the Depression as the Work Projects Administration hires the protagonist, Ella Townsend, at Colombia University to study a woman who knows much of the labor history of New Orleans. The informant, Mammy, dies before the project is completed. After Mammy dies, Ella has an episode of violence and shouting "consistent with the transfer of souls" (38). It seems as if the informant has inhabited the mind and spirit of the ethnographer. Ella spends most of the rest of her life relistening to the transcripts. She finds that she herself had shouted sentences during the interview. Even stranger, "[W]hen I listened I heard Mammy's voice in more places than I had known her to speak" (43). Ella realizes she has become a medium between the world of the living and the dead. Eventually a need for the tape disappears, because the voices just speak inside her head.

I see the psychic fusion of selves between the live researcher and the deceased subject as a metaphor for the practice of ethnography. Specifically, despite the scientific recording of their conversations and verbatim transcriptions of the same, the researcher's interpretations keep revising themselves. The more we examine the data, the more complicated the conclusions become. Nothing is self-evident.

Perhaps the most well known composition ethnography is Shirley Brice Heath's *Ways with Words*. During a period of wide-scale school desegregation in the South, Heath was an instructor in anthropology and linguistics at a state university (1). From 1969 to 1978, she studied two small communities in the Piedmont Carolinas, the white working-class community of Roadville and the black working-class community of Trackton. The primary question that guided her research was: "What were the effects of preschool home and community environments on the learning of those language structures and uses which were needed in classrooms and job settings?" (2). Heath's longitudinal study has set a high standard for ethnographic research in literacy and pedagogy.

Despite the success of Heath's book, ethnography has not yet become a widely studied genre among the English professoriat. Linda Brodkey tells us that the academy has traditionally demonstrated a limited tolerance for lived experience, which it easily dismisses as "anecdotes" or "stories," and in some quarters the intolerance is so great that any ethnographic narrative would be an affront to scholarly sensibilities. (40)

She reasons that the intolerance emerges because, where ethnography narrates the story of its production, traditional academic prose works to "submerge the means of production, that is, [works to] disguise the processes by which individuals arrive at original interpretations" (44–45).

To work in the genre of ethnography in an academic discourse community is to take a risk. In her essay "The Perils, Pleasures, and Process of Ethnographic Writing Research," Wendy Bishop reports that at the time she was writing there were only four book-length composition ethnographies, although many books on composition methods include discussions of ethnographic methods in classroom research. Ethnographic methodology is both perilous and pleasurable. Bishop tells us that the experience of conducting composition ethnography has been decidedly mixed for her.

> After several years of "doing" and teaching ethnography, I have come to feel that it is possible that everything about ethnographic writing research is perilous. At the least, ethnography resists definition. It is difficult to learn to do, seemingly impossible to evaluate, inappropriate for publication in traditional formats, and complicated to teach. Ethnography is also intellectually and physically exhilarating, and naturalistic research, overall, is pleasurable in the way writing and reading and talking and learning are pleasurable. . . . For me, then, doing, theorizing, and teaching ethnography remains the most engaging and frustrating process I've ever undertaken. (263–64)

I too have wondered about the use of ethnography in an academic setting simply because it seems so brazenly subjective. When I first drafted this chapter, I was also teaching ethnography to a group of freshmen at BC. Using the text *Field Working: Reading and Writing Research,* coauthored by Chiseri-Strater and Sunstein, I assisted my students as they observed sites and subjects as varied as an established brokerage firm, law school students, a Division I varsity football team, a Latino student organization, and transit commuters. Before that semester, I had never done much soul searching about the extent to which I teach my students traditional academic discourse, but I began to do so in the early weeks of the course.

Was I really teaching writing? Eventually it occurred to me that ethnography is a rather unique mix of all the modes of discourse. There is *exposition* as the study is enriched by library research. To conduct this research, students have to see their local field site in terms of broader social or political issues. The issues that emerged that semester for my students were the glass ceiling for women in corporate America, class tension between college students and cafeteria workers, and cultural analyses of the current fitness revolution. The student begins the project with specific research questions and eventually takes a position and writes a convincing *argument*. Using assignments like Chiseri-Strater and Sunstein's "verbal snapshot" (110) students learn to write *description* compelling enough that the reader can feel present in the field site. Finally, as students write up both their entries into the site and their experience there, as well as the subjectivities they perceive along the way, they are writing *narrative*. When they reflect on aspects of a culture that is not familiar to them, I prompt them to examine the ethnic, gender, and class biases that they bring to the work. Thus they have practice in all of the modes and, as they draft and revise their ethnographies, they develop skills in making transitions between the different registers. It is this tolerance of multiple modes, registers, and genres that any ethnographer asks of the audience.

Accessing the Field Site: When Colleagues Become Subjects

I wanted to be a participant observer in a writing-field site that is regarded as "expressivist." As it turned out, I did not have far to go. During the spring semester of 1997, I conducted an ethnographic study at BC, where I had been working as a part-time lecturer for four years. I observed the classes and one-to-one student-teacher conferences of two faculty members ("Helena" and "Debby") while I was teaching my own core literature class on the theme of love and the construction of women. I also read student texts, interviewed the instructors and their students, and did volunteer work in a homeless shelter with one student. During this time, I made twenty-eight sixty-minute audiotapes.

Both my informants had also been my coworkers for four years. We attended staff meetings (and rolled our eyes synchronously when appropriate), laughed at each other's jokes, grimaced over politically unsavory situations, and maintained and built collegial friendships.

During the course of my ethnography, we spent a great deal of time together, and I often lost a sense of being involved in a research project. Sometimes this change took the form of speaking in their classes as if I were "a second professor," as one student called me. At other times, we talked informally about campus dissent, our divorces, and my own teaching. At one point in the semester, Helena and I wrote a letter to the campus paper protesting the failure to tenure a lesbian in the English Department. The same student who saw me as a second professor also said that she "forgot I was there." The point I am making is that I too often forgot I was there as a researcher. In short, I had dual relationships with my two informants. As ethnographer Jennie Dautermann puts it, "[W]e must recognize that the autonomous researcher, like the autonomous author, is dead" (257).

While there was a certain level of comfort in our having known each other from the workplace, there was some discomfort as well. In changing my own subject position from fellow part-time BC faculty to ethnographer I was, in a sense, pulling rank on my colleagues. David Bleich calls it "observational privilege" in his frequently cited essay "Ethnography and the Study of Literacy: Prospects for Socially Generous Research." Bleich quotes Frances Mascia-Lees: a "'problematic social disparity [exists] between the researcher and the research'" ("Ethnography" 179). Throughout the project, I was aware of a steady but unpronounced tension in our collegial relationship as a result of the more formal research relationship.

Sensitive to the notion of observational privilege and disliking the feeling of being some sort of colonizer, I invited Helena to observe a session of my class as well. Or, as Ella Townsend puts it in Brodber's *Louisiana,* "Let him feel what it is like to have the scales turned on you and the field interrogate you!" (72). I was teaching Gloria Naylor's *Women of Brewster Place* for the first time, and Helena had just taught the course Black Women Writers. I had a deeper sense of the meaning of "observational privilege" when I had trouble sleeping the night before her visit. I worried that my lack of experience with the work would show.

In my first visit to each class, I gave a short speech to the students that described the focus of my research interest as the way writing is taught in college. I did not specify any particular type of writing. I told them that participation was voluntary, that I was merely the guest of their teacher, and that their decision to work with me or not would have no impact on their grade. If they chose to participate, I would want to sit in on their conferences, although they could deny me access to particular meetings if they wanted to, and I would use pseudonyms. I described Janet Emig's study of high school students' writing and the impact that study had had on the field of education and said that their work might have some impact as well. My immediate goal was to produce a doctoral dissertation, but I hoped to use material in the study for professional conference presentations, for articles, and later for a book. All of the sixteen students in Helena's Freshman Writing Seminar (FWS) and eleven out of fifteen in Debby's advanced writing class signed up to participate the first day.

Helena Receives a Teaching Award

I had many more opportunities during the semester to observe Helena in the broader context of her professional life than I did with Debby. Helena is half African American and half Puerto Rican but at the time of the study identified herself as primarily African American. (In an interview several years later, she told me that, as she spends more time in Puerto Rico visiting members of her family, her ethnic identification is "evolving.")

At the time of my study, Helena was a twenty-six-year-old doctoral student in a majority white department and college. She had an attractive, smooth complexion and a quick and easy laugh; she had straightened hair midway between her ears and her shoulders.

I came to see that she had a particular way of negotiating with the world, particularly in regard to racism. As she rarely directly challenged what she heard from her students, there was no confrontational pedagogy. Instead she worked to get them to be open with their opinions on controversial issues, and then she placed her opinions alongside theirs. Most of the time I admired her approach, but sometimes it frustrated me. I wanted her to more vigorously challenge the views of her student Janet in regard to the homeless. "I choose my battles," or "Maybe it's my Catholic upbringing," she told me. Thus, when her students disagreed with what she said or with what was written in a text they were reading and seemed to expect her to take up the gauntlet and perpetuate the disagreement, she would surprise them by finding ways to support their arguments. In one class, after a student had critiqued something Helena said, her response was, "You got me. I love it when that happens." Instead of stating or implying that certain ideas expressed by white students were racist, she continued to work toward helping these students become more aware of the problems faced by people of color.

As I have said, during the time of my study Helena was a doctoral teaching fellow. She was working on her doctoral exams by revising a paper on a nineteenth-century book by a black butler named Robert Roberts, *A Household Guide for Butlers*. The book has been classified as a cookbook, but Helena saw it as a treatise on surviving in the white mainstream. She had just taught an elective called Black Women Writers the semester before my observation. Near the end of my study, we both learned that Helena had won the Donald J. White Teaching Excellence Award for this course. The opportunity to observe her in the awards assembly was a fortuitous gift for me as an ethnographer. Helena was the only one among the recipients to be asked to give a speech at the ceremony.

All of the top officials at this Jesuit college, all of them male, constituted what I, as a Jew, experienced as an intimidating presence on the platform behind her. They included the university president, the dean of faculties, and the dean of the School of Education. On the program, all their names began with "Reverend" and ended with "S.J." Sitting in the audience, I really felt the meaning of the Foucauldian phrase "institutional power." However, Helena was quite composed throughout the assembly and during what could have been an awkward interaction with the college president in the reception that followed. Despite her potentially low status as both a black woman and a graduate student in a predominantly white institution, the powers that be had sought her out for recognition. Her speech would prove that she was adept at being gracious about this recognition without letting it stifle any concerns she had about the institution.

The assembly itself took place during a month-long period in which there had been several campus demonstrations, including a march on the president's house, as well as many petitions and letters to the editor of a student newspaper. The local media had covered much of the disturbance. Black and white students were disgruntled about many issues: racism against students of color on campus, represented by a tasteless cartoon in a right-wing newspaper funded by the college; the failure to tenure faculty of color and to provide sufficient core courses in non-Western thinking and literature; the refusal of official recognition of the gay, lesbian, and bisexual student organization on campus; and the denial of tenure to a lesbian in the English Department.

Helena's acceptance speech demonstrated the gentle style of what I came to see as her "cooperative resistance." On the one hand, she shared a somewhat self-mocking narrative about the seeds of her teaching career in elementary school. On the other, she did not allow the administration the luxury of sidestepping the serious problems with racism on campus by simply presenting awards to some promising teachers of color. She adopted both personal and political rhetorical stances. Because of this concurrent focus, we can see Helena as an example of what Gradin has called a "social-expressivist."

Helena began by locating her success in the community of scholars in her department, naming many of us. Then she returned to her past.

> In elementary school the women who taught me were so great, so smart, so charismatic, that I knew *then* I wanted to be a teacher. . . . In the third grade I used to get in trouble all the time with my teacher, Miss Delay, because I'd finish my work early and get out of my seat to "assist" the other kids in class. Every single report card I received from first through eighth grade read that I was a good student but I needed to cut down on my chatting, socializing; I was a "busybody." *Now* my elementary school teachers understand that I was not socializing, but preparing for the path that I currently pursue at Boston College—and they approve. (Speech)

The dean of faculties picked up on Helena's elementary school story when he spoke. Clearly he was pleased. In the reception that followed, the president of the college came over to Helena, ignored the two of us who were standing with her, and began to describe his daily walks to a one-room schoolhouse. After Helena told him she was still in contact with her former elementary teachers, he said, "Maybe some day you will go back there." I took the remark to be an insult: that after she finished her Ph.D. she would be qualified to teach in elementary school. I asked Helena about it and her response was, "I have to choose my battles. I didn't respond because I simply did not wish to engage with the man."

None of the administrators saw fit to comment on the explicitly political remarks she made in her acceptance speech.

I have learned a lot from my students, and am committed to establishing an environment in the classroom where everyone feels safe enough to take a risk and hash out what really matters to us. It is my hope that, on occasion, the classroom is a space where we wrestle intellectually with the more difficult and sensitive issues of the day, like race, gender, and class relations among the people on our very own campus. (Speech)

Helena had shown me this speech beforehand and asked what I thought. I wanted her to sharpen up this last point and be more specific, knowing that she would not because it was not her style. Hearing the text spoken in the context of the assembly against the backdrop of Jesuit administrators in habit, I realized that her way of stating the issues was powerful precisely because of the absence of specifics or blame. I also concurred with the description of her own classroom as a place safe enough to hash out sensitive issues.

The semester of my observation Helena was teaching freshman writing for the third time. She had not had an opportunity to take the required graduate composition theory course offered by Lad Tobin when she began teaching the class because she had been hired at the last minute to fill a sudden vacancy. Instead Tobin held several tutorial meetings for Helena where they discussed works by compositionists, such as Donald Murray and Peter Elbow.

Early in the semester of my observation, she experienced difficulty working with a student whose personal narrative was an unfocused display of a "typical" weekend on campus and included discussions of smoking marijuana and of masturbation. His "revision" was a resubmission of the first draft. Helena immediately sought out Tobin to discuss how to work with the student. Tobin was quite accessible to those in the program who wanted his help, and he thoroughly enjoyed hashing out issues related to practice. Their talk helped to defuse any potential animosity toward the student and to figure out a way to work with him.

The class-size limit for the FWS was fifteen students, but Helena signed an override and had sixteen. Of this number, four were male, and five were people of color: two black women (one Jamaican and one Nigerian), one Asian woman, one Hawaiian male, and one male who described himself as "part Native American but my grandmother is off the boat." Three of the nine white women were the most frequent contributors to class discussion.

There was no particular emphasis on autobiographical writing; in fact, like many freshman writing courses, the personal narrative was only one of four required papers for the class. Despite the representation of "expressivist" pedagogy as not dealing with important cultural and class issues, the course packet she put together was inundated with essays dealing with such issues as race and poverty by largely "ethnic" writers. Despite this focus in the assigned reading, the course description highlights writing skills.

> Our priority during this Freshman Writing Seminar is to hone writing skills through in-class writing experiences, drafts and revisions of drafts of papers, reading, class discussion, group workshops, and individual conferences. Students will create a portfolio based on at least two drafts of four separate writing assignments: Personal Narrative, Analysis, Argumentation-Persuasion, and Research. (Syllabus)

The only two books she assigned were the *MLA Handbook for Writers of Research Papers* and the McGraw-Hill Primis reader, *English*. The latter is a course packet whose contents Helena selected from options provided by McGraw-Hill. Six out of the twenty-four essays addressed the rhetorical modes or writing per se. Questions and annotated student writing samples accompanied some of these essays. I found the expository essays on rhetoric to be flat and lifeless prescriptions that would reproduce themselves in kind. They are entitled "The Characteristics of an Essay," "Narration," "Cause-and-Effect Analysis," "Argumentation-Persuasion," and "Classification-Division." The excerpt on freewriting from Elbow's *Writing Without Teachers* could have been read against the didactic nature of the other pieces, but Helena discussed it as a discrete essay. For example, the first piece, "The Characteristics of an Essay," smacks of the how-to genre. One of the guidelines is "The thesis should not be a formal pronouncement" such as, "This paper will discuss the reasons the United States needs election reform" (2). The essay gives much advice about supporting details, topic sentences, and writing interesting introductions and effective conclusions. It attempts to provide a formula for writing "a good essay." However, such didactic exposition can become a formula for killing the inventiveness, vivacity, and passion of the writer and the text. It elevates one of Aristotle's artistic proofs, logos, over the other two, ethos and pathos. Or, as Elbow puts it in the next selection as he advises the reader not to edit while producing:

> The editor is, as it were, constantly looking over the shoulder of the producer and constantly fiddling with what he's doing while he's in

the middle of trying to do it. No wonder the producer gets nervous, jumpy, inhibited, and finally can't be coherent. ("Freewriting" 17)

A student writer who tries to keep all the advice in "The Characteristics of an Essay" in mind while writing would be horribly constrained. (In a memo to me, Helena objected to my point here, telling me that she included the essay "in case a student gets super stuck.")

The rest of the Primis reader is made up of many essays under categories entitled "Readings in Sociology" and "Readings for Writers." They are highly politicized pieces that deal with the now popular issues of race, class, and gender. If one were to accept the bifurcation between the "expressivist" and social constructionist classrooms, it might come as a surprise to find such essay topics in an "expressivist" program. Among them are Jack Agueros's "Halfway to Dick and Jane: A Puerto Rican Pilgrimage"; Kenneth Kohler's "How I Came out to My Parents"; Clara Spotted Elk's "Skeletons in the Attic"; Peter Conrad's "Social Meaning of AIDS"; Etty Hillesum's "Letter from a Concentration Camp"; and Peter Rossi and James Wright's "Urban Homeless: A Portrait of Urban Dislocation." During the semester, Helena supplemented these selections with handouts from the popular media on the multiethnic Tiger Woods, on lesbian comedian Ellen DeGeneres, and on the media coverage of the O. J. Simpson trial.

The first writing assignment was a personal narrative. The two samples of the genre in the anthology were both essays in which the individual was contextualized in the social and the emphasis was on the social problem. Jamaica Kincaid's essay "On Seeing England for the First Time" points to the narrator's irritation both with seeing everything in her country of Antigua stamped with "made in England" and the fact that she was only taught the history of the colonizer and not of her native country. The other personal narrative was written by Agueros, who tells us that his life changed after his family moved. His "clean and open world" (30) closed up because of overcrowding and prejudice. As far as we know, there were no intrafamily problems with either author. While this may surprise those who have accepted Berlin's representation of the "expressivist" classroom, the Primis selections do not encourage writing about intrapsychic conflict, past or present individual trauma, or family problems, such as selections from Toni Morrison's *Bluest Eye* might have. A student essay included in the reader, "How I Came out to My Parents," was the most personal, in the sense that I am using the word, but it was critiqued by Helena, and rightfully so, as having "a nice, tidy ending" that sealed over the real lack of resolution indicated in the narrative.

On the day the Kincaid essay was assigned, some class discussion ensued regarding the nature of prejudice, with one white student arguing that "prejudice cuts both ways emotionally" and another white student implying that racism against black people is worse. Helena made a strong statement but without putting anybody on the spot. "Prejudice in the hands of those in power is lethal." She concluded, "We all have prejudices. We can't deny that we will have. It's what you do with the prejudices you have." Without ever calling attention to any preconceptions her white students might have had about a black teacher, the issue of racial prejudice was brought out early and often during the class. At times I sensed that the majority white student body challenged Helena more precisely because she was a person of color who chose to foreground race.

Helena's notion of what constitutes the personal in a FWS, as represented through the reading selections, weighted the cultural community over the individual and the family. Yet despite this emphasis, some students wrote personal narratives that examined aspects of their families in isolation from the rest of society. Janet wrote an essay about being abandoned by her grandmother, and Catherine wrote one about her father's alcoholism.

My description of Helena's class in the next chapters includes excerpts from student texts and from transcripts of class discussions, student-teacher conferences, and interviews with Helena and with her students. Geertz might remind us that such inclusions are just part of the work. The textbook definition of ethnography is limited to "techniques and received procedures," such as "establishing rapport, selecting informants, transcribing texts, taking genealogies, mapping fields, keeping diaries" ("Thick" 6). To help us see what else ethnography consists of, he borrows both a phrase from Gilbert Ryle, "thick description," and an example, a wink. To write that a wink is a contraction of an eyelid is only thin description. To interpret that gesture as "'practicing a burlesque of a friend faking a wink to deceive an innocent into thinking a conspiracy is in motion'" (qtd. in Geertz, "Thick" 7) is to offer thick description. It is clear to me that, to become a responsible and credible witness, one must first offer thin and then thick description, which is the way I intend to proceed in the following ethnographic chapters.

4 ✤ CONFRONTING BIAS IN STUDENT TEXTS

A Word on the Researcher's Biases

In his foreword to a long-term classroom ethnography conducted by Sondra Perl and Nancy Wilson, *Through Teachers' Eyes,* James Moffett explains the value of ethnographic research in literacy. "[A] myriad of factors go into [the] writing [process] that only an ongoing, flexible, and pluralistic sort of research can do justice to" (x). Writing about the "web of factors and circumstances" (x) involved in the interaction between student and teacher makes the work of the ethnographer complicated. I found it especially difficult to be "flexible and pluralistic" when my biases came up against those of a student I met in Helena's class.

Two pedagogical issues emerged in Helena's work with a white middle-class student whom I will call Janet. In chapter 1, I discussed Faigley's argument that "expressivists" collude with students on the creation of coherent, unified selves in autobiographical writing. To the contrary, I demonstrate how a teacher in an "expressivist" program responded critically to the presentation of a tidy ending to a personal narrative in which all conflicts appear resolved. Furthermore, my study shows an inadvertent extracurricular benefit to writing about a family-based matter when one student decided to take her text back to the family from which it emerged; the process prompted apparently much needed discussion.

The other pedagogical issue I discuss is the difficulty of interacting with a student whose conception of the poor differed from that of the teacher, a difference that came out when students were encouraged to write about issues beyond the self. These kinds of political differences between teacher and student are not uncommon. What is uncommon is the student's willingness to express them despite the risk of a grade penalty. Janet's father was an engineer, her mother a manager in a lighting business, and her sister a graduate student in public health at an Ivy League school. Despite her own unearned class and racial privileges, she felt free, for example, to question the honesty of panhandlers. Many teachers report discomfort with evaluating essays about intimate topics, but there is also the vexing issue of assessing essays informed by a different worldview of poverty. I illustrate how one teacher handled the problem.

Gesa Kirsch and Joy Ritchie lament,

> In composition there are few published accounts in which researchers reflect on the knowledge they gained about themselves and their relations with others due to the research they conducted. But we have anecdotal evidence from colleagues and friends who have discovered that interactive, collaborative research leaves them with a changed attitude toward themselves. (15)

As a result of my research in Helena's classroom, I have come to take many exceptions to a prior concept of myself as someone who "knows" exactly what is going on and who can report events "objectively."

In the early part of the semester, when Janet was working on a personal narrative about her estrangement from her grandmother, I felt a great deal of compassion for her, and I valued her writing. As she turned her attention to more explicitly political issues, I developed an opposite feeling, one that I can only describe as an aversion. It was not until after I had completed the first draft of this chapter that I had an insight into these negative feelings.

One day a friend asked me how my writing was coming along. I told her that the chapter on Helena and Janet was going fairly rapidly but that I felt tortured by my attitude toward the student. Driving home, I had a memory of myself as a sophomore at the

University of Rochester in 1967. My boyfriend at the time, and future husband, had a teaching assistant in his history class who was an avowed communist. Alan S., the teaching assistant, had prompted my boyfriend's involvement in Students for a Democratic Society and was trying to recruit him to the PLP/PWP, an offshoot of the American Communist Party. Apparently my lack of interest in politics was an obstacle to his recruitment. In my flashback, I saw myself once again in the living room of Alan and his wife, Carol, as they argued with me that the correct slogan for the antiwar movement should be "U.S. Out of Vietnam Now! No Negotiations." And I recalled myself, budding New Critic, saying in response, "Yes, but you just can't walk out of someone's house without saying good-bye." While this statement probably was indicative of my own ambivalence about being in their home and participating in the heated discussion, it also represents to me the embarrassing naïveté of a former politically unconscious self, a self that saw class and national conflict in terms of manners. My insight was that I had been impatient with Janet because she reminded me of a self I would just as soon forget. Today I see Janet's attitude toward the problem of homelessness as just as politically unsophisticated as mine was toward U.S. involvement in Vietnam. We both focused on individual culpability as opposed to what I see now as political and economic oppression. Because of this denied aspect of myself, I also grew impatient with what I saw as the teacher's pedagogical generosity toward this student.

Helena's approach to Janet changed during the course of their work together. In the beginning of the semester, as Janet worked on a family-based narrative, Helena was fairly directive and did most of the talking in their conferences. As the semester progressed and Janet worked on two essays dealing with homeless people, Helena became less directive, allowing her student to dominate extended conferences with anecdotes about homeless individuals whose life stories she claimed to know. Helena often allowed Janet's monologues to continue to the point that Helena's next student had to wait for as long as fifteen minutes beyond his regularly scheduled appointment time. I was often frustrated both by the way that Janet presented herself as an expert on the subject of the homeless and by the way that her teacher allowed her to maintain that subject position. Janet reminded me of Sharon, a student in Wendy Hesford's teacher research. "If she did conceptualize the prostitutes, for example, from a more socially oriented perspective, then prostitution would be criticized as economic coercion, rather than framed as an issue of individual power and choice" (175). Janet viewed homelessness as a result of an alleged bad culture of working-class families.

Because of the unresolved impatience toward my undergraduate self, I wanted Helena to interrupt Janet's monologues and challenge her views more strongly. Reviewing the transcripts after having had my memory, I see many moments when Helena did question Janet's preconceptions about the poor, moments I had minimized earlier in the research process.

Helena told me that Janet was "at the beginning of a budding consciousness," not unlike the self that I just described during my first exposure to anti-imperialist politics. Helena believed that it was better to "plant seeds" of a new consciousness in Janet than to strong-arm her into some sort of ideological compliance. Yet Helena did acknowledge my frustration. "Yes, Janet takes a great license in talking about [the problems of the homeless]." Throughout this chapter, I incorporate Helena's comments about my work. These comments emerged in glosses on the chapter drafts (given here in square brackets), e-mails, taped interviews, and informal conversations.

The Self in a Personal Narrative

The first assignment in Helena's FWS was the personal narrative. Many theorists have questioned the propriety of teaching personal writing in the academy (Swartzlander et al.; Faigley, *Fragments;* Gibson; Bizzell, "Theories"; Summerfield; Barnes et al.; Morgan; Valentino). Some question the ethics of requiring students to self-disclose; and others, like Dan Morgan, are simply at a loss about how to respond when their students write, for example, about having committed a murder. He asks, "What *is* the nature of our 'contract' with students, exactly?" (320). Suffice it to say that many teachers feel out of their element when reading unsolicited personal trauma from their students. I discuss these ethical issues more fully in the conclusion.

At this juncture, I want simply to state that it has been my experience that students feel most connected with the culture of the academy when they are invited to use personal experience in their writing and when the narratives they produce are treated responsibly and valued by their teachers. Whenever I ask students to discuss what they have disliked in prior writing classes, frequently they complain about having to write about "boring topics." When writing about their own experiences, either as individuals or in the context of family or wider cultural arenas, students feel some authority and they display confidence (Sommers, "Between" 29). As David Bleich puts it in his essay "Collaboration and the Pedagogy of Disclosure," "[M]odes of self-disclosure are what many students have longed for since I have been in school but were taught to confine to ultra-private, often unsharable social locations apart from school" (48). He invites us to counter the teaching-to-the-test mentality that has filtered through all levels of education by "mak[ing] schools feel more like sites of cultural generosity, where students are honored by having their own histories and cultures recognized in the classroom and in the curriculum" (49). Students do feel pleasantly surprised when we value their lived experiences enough to invite them to put them into writing. I think the appreciation of and eagerness to respond to these assignments happens no matter what the emotional intensity of the essay the student decides to write. The point is, the topics that are close to the self stimulate inventive energy.

One reader of this book commented that he was surprised that all the examples of the students' personal essays I use here are rather extreme. The reviewer more commonly sees essays that are rather easy to respond to, essays such as those about positive events in their students' lives, surprise discoveries, or tributes to those people who have changed the students in some way. I think teachers who assign the personal narrative send either direct or subtle messages about what they are open to reading. I would have to say that these so-called extreme essays were not rare at BC where I taught writing for six years. Their presence may have been continually fueled by the annual collection of strong first-year essays in the program's journal, *Fresh Ink,* which usually included a few essays on a disturbing experience. So in this community, students came to realize that it is acceptable to write either troubling or humorous essays about the self. While both of these styles encourage students to develop their rhetorical skills, I focus here on the more extreme examples, as they are precisely the essays that are difficult to respond to and whose content has been used to drive the argument against having such writing in our classes. In fact, when I distributed an essay about one student's alcoholic family at a training session of teachers of first-year writing, one person announced, "The main thing we should be discussing here is how to prevent such an essay from being written in the first place."

Janet chose as the subject of her personal narrative a rupture that had occurred in her family. She had been very close to her paternal grandmother. As a result of some conflict that had taken place between her parents and her grandmother, Janet was cut off from this woman and she died before there was any reconciliation. Janet was still struggling with anger at having been abandoned by her grandmother when Janet was seven years old. The narrative she wrote was neither simple nor chronological; it was complicated by the use of flashback. When I first read it and sat in on her conferences, I felt the pain of her loss. However, after the semester was over and I began to write up my data, I felt troubled by the production of the text and by the way Janet negotiated revision with Helena. This was a paper she had submitted in high school (as was the research paper she did later in the semester). Despite my reservations regarding Janet's academic honesty, I also came to see that writing the paper and sharing it with her family had some important repercussions outside the initial task environment.

Janet was a vivacious woman who often spoke rapidly and with no sign of emotional pain even as she described what she referred to as troubling events in her life. In my first observation, I heard Janet quietly announce, "This is my first conference." She proceeded to eat a dry, sliced bagel and drink something cold from a pink and orange Dunkin' Donuts cup while Helena read the initial draft of Janet's personal narrative. As she fleshed out the events that informed her essay, I felt compassion for her. Afterward I wrote in my journal,

> Nice day. Felt close to Helena. We talked after Janet's conference. I said how I had felt sad [during the conference] and Mike[her officemate, who was within earshot on the other side of the partition] said he had felt sad too. We cannot feel these feelings as teachers, or at least not in the conference.

Janet's untitled essay was a fairly sophisticated piece of writing. Eventually she would select it to represent her work in the class magazine. I was initially confused by the chronology in the narrative until I realized she was using a flashback within a flashback to tell the story of how she had once been close to her grandmother but was separated from her by a rift in the family. The first drafts concluded with what might be seen as a false resolution to the conflict.

Because the narrative was somewhat confusing, in the first conference Helena worked with Janet on clarity. Their discussion demonstrates a way to work with a traditional rhetorical issue when the subject matter is quite personal. As Helena tried to help the student make the essay clearer, she also invited Janet to let her know if she was asking questions that were too personal. Janet explained that there were "internal family problems" and described her grandmother as stubborn. She told Helena that she never had the opportunity to ask, "How could you abandon me when it was my parents you were angry with?" Helena repeated back to Janet what she said while protecting her right to privacy.

> You don't have to go into the details of the family argument . . . but I think it might be important for us to know that you feel abandoned and you feel that, despite the fact she wasn't speaking to your parents, she could have still spoken to you. That much I think the reader could stand to know.

Helena also worked against some clichéd expressions without insulting the student by labeling them as such. She felt that the text was "vague" in places and, instead of writing something like "The memories came rushing back," Janet could have described the move to Maine in more detail. Helena used the word *vague* to indirectly inform her student that she had not yet made the events as important to the reader as to the writer. She affirmed Janet's commentary but continually tried to elicit more information to "help [the reader] further understand the pain of the break." In this conference, she also hinted that there was a problem with the conclusion but did not say much other than that the dearth of details made it seem like Janet was "trying to make it neat and more pleasant."

Their discussion of the conclusion in the next conference offers us a glimpse of how a writing teacher may try to help a student reexamine what appears to be a facile textual ending to an emotionally complex experience. Despite Faigley's representation of the "expressivist" program, Helena actively discouraged the presentation of a rational, unified, coherent self. What follows is the initial concluding paragraph to Janet's personal narrative. Janet had described a spontaneous visit to the house where she used to visit her grandmother. Two little girls, the same ages as Janet and her sister before the family feud, were among the inhabitants.

> I waved good-bye to the family that had made a home out of my Nanna's house. I smiled fondly, the familiar image of the house replacing my hazy memory. I turned my back on the family and the house. Behind me, a door shut on the darkness of my past. I skipped down the stairs and splashed through a puddle, shattering the stillness of my soul. The night was rainy and dark, the house aglow now from an internal warmth. Memories of smiles and laughter overwhelmed me and I paused to reflect on the past. Slowly, the rain faded away, and I could almost feel the sun at my back. A small child ran with a careless countenance, her contagious giggle bringing a smile to my frozen heart. In one of the windows an old woman watched the child with a look of tender love and concern caressing her aged face, she called something to the girl and turned away from my view. I restrained my arm from reaching out to her, instead allowing the child to run to her call. The scene faded and the rain once again fell on my face. Good-bye, I said aloud[,] Good-bye.

Social constructionist Bartholomae would probably find in this ending the chaff of "almost two hundred years of sentimental realism" ("Writing" 67). I would have to agree that this ending does seem almost intolerably syrupy. In their second conference, Helena did a fine critique of the ending, focusing on its lack of consistency with the conflicted tone in the rest of the piece. She talked quite a bit with little response from Janet until the issue of revision and her grade came up. I think this example clearly belies the picture of the "expressivist" teacher as encouraging belief in a fully integrated self.

During her critique, Helena paused frequently and appeared to be sensitive to the student's feelings when she told her that the ending was not consistent with the middle of the paper, where she had "depicted a complicated relationship."

> I'm not saying, "End on a negative note." . . . [Y]ou have to get us from this difficult moment in the hospital, you know, where you're struggling between looking at this fragile individual and that MAKES you feel sympathetic toward her, but at the same time you are very angry with her. That her fragility in that situation doesn't ERASE, you know, the problems that you have with her. You at least have to get us from that to this ending, if you want to KEEP this ending. . . . [I]t's dealing with something EXTERIOR, when all the while your narration has been concentrating on something INTERIOR.

Helena was explicitly directive about what she thought Janet needed to do to revise the paper. The teacher wanted the student either to maintain the conflict at the end or to help the reader make a transition from the subject's anger in the middle of the text to the quick resolution at the end. Helena waited until after she had offered extensive feedback before asking the student what questions she had. Helena appeared confident of her assessment.

Janet did not participate in the discussion (other than clearing her throat or softly responding, "Yeah") until the subject of revision and grade change came up. Even though Helena had told her that she was only making "suggestions," Janet commented, "If I were to go back and do all the revisions. . . ." Clearly, she saw the suggestions as necessities if she wanted her grade to go up. If there were a chance of her grade going up and not down, then she would invest time in revision. Rather than reexamine the experience for her own sake or to get the audience to see her point of view, Janet revised for an external reward. Helena saw Janet's response to her comments as typical of freshmen in the FWS. "What we introduce to them in FWS is almost the exact opposite of what they've learned their whole (grade-driven) lives; the grade concern isn't unusual or surprising." She cautioned me not to "demonize" Janet. Here is the revised conclusion turned in subsequent to their second conference.

> I splashed through a puddle, shattering the mirror stillness of my soul. Memories of smiles and laughter overwhelmed me and I paused again to reflect on the past. I wanted so badly to replace the pain with happiness. I staggered under the opposing forces in my heart and for a moment, the old familiar pain began to eat at the happiness I had found. However, I fought the urge to forget, willing a final memory from my mind. Good bye, I said aloud, Good bye.

It was difficult to sustain both happiness and "the old familiar pain" without one suppressing the other. Helena affirmed Janet's ability to do just that in their final discussion of the paper. "I think it nicely reflects the tension. . . . [A]lso you nicely describe your effort to will away the bad feelings but they continue to reoccur. So I think you got more of the complicatedness of the whole situation down." Or, as she said to me, "The paper even fights with itself. . . . She's still fighting with herself." I see the author here as torn between her desire to master past trauma and her desire to raise her grade, which meant relinquishing some control.

Janet reported that she learned some things about writing through her work on this essay; she learned that audience matters. As she told Helena,

> I was sure that there would be some areas that still made sense to me because I know the whole story. I have the advantage over my readers in that if I say "she" and go on, I know who "she" is. Nobody else knows who "she" is. [There were] some assumptions on my behalf that you would understand my life . . . which, of course, you won't.

While Janet might have also been hinting at some version of "You just don't understand me," it seems equally likely that she learned that it is her responsibility to help the reader understand the text. She is catching on to the difference between what Linda Flower calls *writer-based prose* and *reader-based prose*. The former is written "by a writer for himself and to himself" and "reflects the associative narrative path of the writer's own confrontation with her subject"; while the latter "offers the reader an issue-centered rhetorical structure rather than a replay of the writer's discovery process" (126). It elevates the purpose of the writer's thought over its process. Throughout the conferences, Helena was pushing Janet to describe and explain more, so that the experience would matter to the reader, as well as to the writer.

There was also an extracurricular benefit to this exercise in writing personal narrative, and I think it is important to acknowledge that such assignments may spill outside the classroom. Janet decided to read drafts of the paper to her mother; the process brought back some more memories of the initial family conflict, and it led to good discussions between them. I actually had an opportunity to meet her mother when she volunteered in a homeless shelter with Janet, and she informed me, "I just never knew how upset she was about that whole experience." Certainly, increased family communication was not in Helena's plan for the assignment, but it was one of the unintended side effects.

Finally, while I have framed Janet's motivation to revise in terms of a personal characteristic, obsequiousness, the desire for a good grade is present in most of our students. The issue of appealing to the teacher as opposed to a wider audience is the subject of an ethnographic study by Robert Brooke and John Hendricks. The question that initially informed their study was, "How can we teach 'writing for an audience' in an institutional setting where students know that the teacher, not the addressed audience, assigns the grade?" (xv). Is the student writing for some larger group, such as potential guitar buyers, or just for the teacher? After the completion of their classroom ethnography, they felt that it was the wrong question. "The question should have been 'what sort of person will learning the concept of audience help students become'" (56). According to Brooke and Hendricks, no matter the goals of our first-year writing seminars, what they come down to for the students is the development of their individual identities in a new and complicated social environment, the university. That Janet was struggling with her social identity, specifically the wish to be seen as an authority, would become evident in her work on the topic of homelessness.

The Pedagogy of Political Differences

For the analysis and research paper assignments in her FWS, Janet chose to write about the homeless. She derived the topic from her experience as a volunteer in a shelter for homeless women that year, as well as from a study she conducted as a high school student. Janet initially appeared to be sympathetic toward this population, and Helena accepted her rhetorical purpose: to dispel stereotypes about the homeless. Eventually it became apparent that Janet had herself internalized some powerful stereotypes.

Before exploring the development of these essays, I want to highlight the link between Janet's interest in this population and the culture of her family. In fact, I think it is an example of Lopate's image of the personal essay as the reverse of the Chinese set of boxes; instead of getting smaller, the focus of the personal essay can open up onto the larger world. In Janet's sequence of assignments, there was an unacknowledged identification between what she experienced psychologically within her family system and the social and material conditions of the homeless. In her essay, when Janet was no longer welcome at her grandmother's house, she described herself as "abandoned and forced to go out on her own." She was emotionally homeless. Unfortunately, the compassion she felt toward herself did not always translate into compassion toward the subjects of her later written discourse, the people whose homelessness was a material condition of their lives.

Janet had conducted a project on the homeless near her hometown for a class on the American Dream in high school. At BC, she became involved in the PULSE program, which combined course work that included sociopolitical readings with a volunteer field placement. I had had several PULSE students and, as Helena also observed, there seemed to be a heavy missionary purpose in the work; the goal was to take something to "these poor people" with no mention of what the student could learn from them.[1] My perception of BC students' attitude toward their subjects is different from what Bruce Herzberg reports about students' community-service work at nearby Bentley College. "[N]ow they see that the homeless are people 'just like themselves.' This, they like to say, is something that could happen to them: They could lose their jobs, lose their houses, even take to drink" (308). However, the students I worked with, and Helena's student, Janet, "Othered" the people they sought to help. I never heard any identification. One student of mine made unsubstantiated assumptions about parents that he had never met from the behavior he saw in children in an afterschool program.

Janet and some other students I knew did not seem consistently able to make use of the theoretical material they read in the PULSE program, even material as compelling as Jonathan Kozol's *Rachel and Her Children,* and they wound up seeming to blame poverty on the poor. Here I do agree with Herzberg. "The students tend to see their learners, quite naturally, as individuals with personal problems—alcoholism and drugs, mental breakdown, family disintegration, or some nameless inability to concentrate and cope" (311). The problem is that "if our students regard social problems as chiefly or only personal, then they will not search beyond the person for a systemic explanation. Why is homelessness a problem?" (309). Janet saw each person's plight as the result of a breakdown in the family and eventually invented causes based on information she had garnered from conservative books about the poor. [Helena took a more moderate view here. "This is the trend of our country and its leaders—every aspect of all parts of Janet's world are rife with this conservatism. Therefore, if Kozol's essay and our course made a dent, that is not a small feat."]

I think about different causes of homelessness. One obvious cause is "urban renewal," where reconstructed properties are out of the price range of the former residents. It is also in the interest of big business that there be an unemployed or underemployed class to hold down the wages of those who are employed. The employed can always be replaced by this underclass who are not unionized and who will work for lower wages. Some critics have pointed out that such replacement is precisely what is happening in the various welfare-to-work programs in which previously unemployed people are being trained to take over jobs in the hotel industry, for example, that once paid more money. However, unlike Herzberg, other social constructionists, and Marxists, I do not separate family or personal problems from "systemic" ones. Those of us who have untreated alcohol, emotional, or family problems are especially at risk of losing whatever class privileges and protection we have and becoming homeless. The personal and the economic are tightly linked.

There was a noticeable difference in their conferences as Helena and Janet made a transition from working together on Janet's personal narrative to her more overtly political assignments. Whereas their early conferences had been characterized by a preponderance of teacher talk, the later ones were just the opposite. Janet often spoke nonstop and with a considerable amount of energy about homeless individuals she had encountered. She claimed to know her subjects well, frequently informing Helena that they had told her all about themselves as if she could just transpose this oral information into written discourse sans bias. "I go [to the women's homeless shelter] every Wednesday and Thursday nights and I've been going for a semester and a half now and I know women and I know their life story." Referring to her high school project in which students were taken in vans to tour the shelters for two days, she said, "We lived as if we were homeless." She also displayed a great deal of pride when telling Helena that as a high school student she had been a student representative for United Way. According to her self-report, the United Way's Board of Directors had turned to her to provide firsthand information about homeless teenagers, as well as about the agencies that they were funding. Janet would often deflect even the most moderate criticisms about her writing from Helena with another series of stories derived from these experiences.

I went to the shelter with Janet on two occasions and indeed found her to be quite comfortable preparing meals, cleaning up, and interacting with the women and children who were present. We had several opportunities there to discuss her perceptions and the drafts of her assignments. In one conversation, I indicated that the women might have been managing the information they gave her because they associated her with the administration of the shelter and they wanted to receive the most benefits they could get there. (While there were certain rules, volunteers had some leeway around giving out sanitary items and food portions.) She disagreed: "Well, they may not tell *you* everything because they know *you're* a professor and you're established, but they know I am just a student." Janet was adamant about her own insider status. [Here Helena commented in the margin of a draft of this chapter, "This is the youthful naivete you described earlier."]

In contrast to my increasing sense of exasperation with Janet's presumption of knowledge, in their conferences Helena showed remarkable patience in listening to Janet speak about the different people she had met, even when her descriptions were condescending. However, in their first conferences on the topic, it did appear that Helena and Janet were seeing eye-to-eye about the homeless. In fact, Helena showed a great deal of interest in Janet's reports of individuals whose behavior did not seem to fit stereotypes. Janet did not display any of the "symptoms" I had heard in her conferences on the personal narrative, such as coughing or repeating the phrase *not at all* when there was a difference of opinion. Aside from occasionally running her left hand through her hair, she sat, as before, to the side of Helena's desk, with her right forearm on the chair, her right palm up with fingers either loosely curled or clasping her left hand.

Helena read Janet's analysis paper for the first time in conference. The paper described an experience of meeting a young girl in the shelter. In parts of their talk, Janet did appear to be aware of her class privilege as a college student. She reported that she was at the shelter complaining about her exams scheduled for the next day to another volunteer when a ten-year-old girl put her hand on her shoulder and began talking with them. Janet was aware that her problems were nowhere near as serious as those of this child. Although the girl and her mother were not homeless, they were involved with the welfare system living in subsidized housing.

> In other words, she was this well behaved, very polite girl that obviously came from a home that was very loving but at the same time it's hard to imagine a child being that happy growing up in what she must be growing up in. . . . Driving through Boston in the van[,] . . . [w]e saw kids getting off the bus and crossing the road and walking into the projects in West Roxbury which is one of the most dangerous

neighborhoods in Boston. And just these little tiny children crossing the road and running into these dilapidated buildings. . . . The whole world is gray for them.

Janet's information here and later on was inaccurate. The project was in Roxbury, not West Roxbury, and West Roxbury was not known as one of the most dangerous neighborhoods in Boston. I heard Janet's projections about the girl's living environment (assumptions about the interior of her apartment from the exterior of the buildings) wrestle with her experience of the young girl as a person. While coming in contact with people whose class background and race were very different from her own (Janet was white and middle class) did create some disturbance in her worldview, Janet seemed to be maintaining that worldview by seeing this individual as an exception, like a standard deviation in a statistical norm. I noted an element of surprise in her realization that the girl came from "a loving home." Yet later in the conference, after discussing another individual, she widened her conclusion. "My whole placement there has been a contradiction to what I have assumed a battered women's shelter to be." (Of note here is a second factual error: the shelter, Rosie's Place, was not a *battered* women's shelter.) Janet's presumption of knowledge did not hold up. She appeared to believe that this example constituted another break in the stereotypes about homeless people and shelters, but I am not sure she really did agree. Or maybe what we have in her essay is another instance of what her teacher described, in reference to the conclusion of Janet's personal narrative, as "the paper fighting with itself." [Helena added, "This is the primary characteristic of a budding consciousness."]

Here are some excerpts from the final draft of the paper on the shelter. The tone was one of sentimental compassion, but the essay seemed to be laced with efforts to soften, if not completely erase, the profound problems in the lives of the women who used the shelter.

> In West Roxbury, there exists the faded beginnings of women and children forced to live day to day in apprehension and fear. In a world of American Dreamers, there exist partitions and stereotypes that prevent the women of the streets to begin again. . . . *Rosie's Place is the beginning of a new story and the end to the cruel cycles enforced by the stereotypes of lazy, alcoholic, or illiterate homeless women.*
>
> In America, one in five children are homeless or living in poverty. . . . These children are products of an unjust world that caters only to the working class and above. . . . These children will never succeed,

they are lost causes, regardless of how much help they are given, so why should we help? . . . Her anecdotes of fifth grade boys and the life trials of a ten year-old were not dissimilar to the stories of my own childhood. . . . One cannot help but admire a child that retains her innocence surrounded by depression and poverty. . . .

. . . [T]he homeless population of America [has] been grouped as underachievers and unmotivated leeches on society. Rosie's women nullify that stereotype. Somehow amidst the fear and the loneliness, these women succeed. They are wealthy in spirit and heart, enriched with the zeal of life. . . . [Emphasis mine]

I had a hard time with this rather rosy, if you will, depiction of the homeless shelter. In a discussion we had one night when we were both volunteering, I asked Janet why she saw Rosie's as a place of hope, as the "beginning of a new story." Had she heard it referred to in that way by any of the women? No, she had not, but she told me that she liked "to focus on the light in the darkness." Her notion of the hopeful beginning was derived entirely from the mission statement of the shelter: "The underlying philosophy of Rosie's Place is to provide a safe and nurturing environment to help poor and homeless women maintain their dignity, seek opportunity, and find security in their lives" *(Rosie's Place)*. [Helena pointed out to me that it was Janet's class background that enabled her to privilege this text and its authors over the homeless women.] Janet seemed unaware that there might have been two discrepancies: first, between what the agency intended and how its clients perceived the services they received; and second, between how *she* perceived the shelter and how the clients did.

In this conversation, I deferred to Janet's expertise about the shelter, acknowledging that she had been there far longer than I had. However, I told her that just that night I had spoken with a highly intelligent woman who had informed me that she had graduated from BC twenty years before and who circulated among all the city's shelters, staying at each one as long as she could. I did not feel as if I had learned all that much of her "life story," because the woman had extracted far more information from me than I had from her. It did not occur to me that this woman exemplified one of the "unmotivated leeches on society" but rather that she had a problem that was untreated. I guessed that it might be substance abuse or that she was supporting herself as a sex worker. I wrote in my field notebook the next day:

Talked with Valery, an attractive black woman with a bandana around her forehead. Her thick hair was pulled through it. . . . Says she doesn't bond with anyone in the shelters because of "dependency and codependency issues." Wants to go to school and work. May be a prostitute. Lost her house when "the feds" came and took back loans even though she "had done favors for the owners." A staff member came up to her [while we were talking] and said a man was outside waiting to see her. She said to tell him she wanted to eat her meal first but then she took off without eating it. Seemed really competent and together but something was off.

Janet and the founders of Rosie's Place spoke to the notion of community, but this woman had made a point of telling me that she did not bond. While the "starters" were impressive (all the fruits and vegetables I sliced had such labels as "Jacobs Farm, certified organic") and while the entrée provided by a suburban church group was quite tasty, I still could not see the services provided as an end to "the cruel cycles," as Janet put forth in her essay. Valery, for one, could not seem to break the cycle she was in.

I was curious to see how Helena would address what I perceived to be wishful middle-class thinking as it appeared in Janet's text. Excerpts from a conference that took place after Helena had read the second draft reveal that she did challenge Janet's perceptions.

The paper as a whole on one level is working to deflate certain stereotypes that we have of homeless people. There are a couple of places in the paper when you refer to "the savable" of the homeless as few. . . . Are you saying that you know there are a few to be extracted from the group as a whole?

Janet responded by offering something of a sermon on the potential of the human spirit, which could choose whether or not to be happy. Helena pointed out that she was talking about interior variables and wondered how much "actualizing one's potential has to do with resources." Janet wanted to see "Rosie's as a kind of oasis in the middle of this road. It's anything these women need it to be." Helena objected here, as she did not think Janet ought to have represented the shelter as a cure-all, but instead she should have written about what Rosie's could specifically have done for the women who went there.

Janet resisted.

I don't go to Rosie's and think, "Okay, women are coming for a meal and they're coming to get a handful of condoms and some shampoo and then they are going to leave." But Rosie's is a kind of forum for discussion among these women and it's kind of like a coupon swap, if you will. You know, they can swap ideas and they can sit and most of all they can gain a sense of community and a sense of belonging.

Helena acknowledged that there were two benefits at the shelter, one material and the other communal, and then concluded,

I would like to see more of that instead of this kind of statement, "Rosie's Place is the beginning of a new story and the end to the cruel cycle[s]." You know, what is Rosie's the way you see it, and what is Rosie's the way the women there see it too?

Janet did not address this critique but instead launched into a lengthy narrative about a resident she met and the value of the new resident having chores while staying there.

Helena was quite gentle in critiquing Janet's textual representation of the shelter, a representation that seemed idealized and not at all informed by the women's perceptions. They had a long dialogue before Helena actually said anything about Janet's glib assumption that the shelter was "the beginning of a new story and the end to the cruel cycles." Helena's message was simply that she would like to have read more about how the women there saw the shelter; she expressed her concerns as stylistic problems. Instead of making sweeping generalizations, such as that the shelter was a cure-all, Janet simply needed to transfer more of what actually happened there onto paper, "to get the daily-ness of their lives down." She told me, "I think it's more a matter of transferring it to the page rather than me getting her to re-think her position." Thus, at this point in the semester, Helena did not see many political differences between them. She did not address the strained comparison with a coupon swap or the way Janet actually minimized the women's need for material resources. The ideological differences between teacher and student were not accentuated by Helena's suggestions. Working within a framework of apparent agreement seemed to be part of the instructor's pedagogical style of building alliances with the student rather than accentuating difference.

In one of my interviews with Helena during the semester, she told me that she thought Janet was "very open-minded," "compassionate," and "sensitive," although she felt that Janet did have some problems in her writing. [After reading a manuscript draft of my book containing this sentence, Helena wrote, "I'd like to hear these comments in their original context some time. For this white middle class girl to step into a homeless shelter is a bigger step than you think. Some Boston College students won't ride the T (public transit system). I would say that my comment about her being open-minded is relative to the whole body of students I encounter there (unbelievably conservative)."]

The second problem Helena observed was Janet's tendency to make things cohere. ["That's really what we think of a paper as, and in doing that certain boundaries and distinctions get blurred because she's . . . making a tidy narrative."] Yet Helena defended Janet's accentuation of the positive because "one of [her] goals is to counter negative stereotypes of homeless women as lazy, or . . . welfare people as unmotivated." I found her assessment to be generous. I think ideological differences do underlie the rhetorical problems Helena cited. These differences would be revealed later in the semester.

Janet insisted on seeing happiness as internal, and she individualized what were primarily social problems. She wrote: "I see potential more within the human spirit . . . cause you can find happiness in the smallest thing." Her analysis reminds me of Lawrence Langer's critique of Viktor Frankl's theory of why some survived in the Nazi concentration camps and others did not:

> The fact that 60,000 survived Auschwitz is less a triumph of the will [as Frankl argues] than an accident of the body, combined with so many gratuitous and fortuitous circumstances that we will probably never be able to disentangle chance from choice, or relate effect to discernible cause. (28)

While some sort of inner strength may be important, a notion that is the basis of the new field of psychoneuroimmunology in medicine, the sheer brutality of the external factors could easily overcome the internal ones.[2] For Janet, it was as if inner drive or potential or the belief in the right to be happy was sufficient to overcome enormous deprivations. She tended to minimize the material needs of the women in order to postulate her theory that they came to the shelter for community, a notion that ignored any possible feelings of shame or defeat they might have felt in being seen there. To Janet, it was as if they arrived at Rosie's Place more for community than for a meal, condoms, soap, and shampoo, or for shelter.

The ideological differences I detected between Helena and her student did erupt in a class discussion on the homeless. In this discussion, Janet proved to be more conservative than several of her classmates who presented social causes of homelessness. She shared a confusing story about a panhandler; the details of this story may have been doctored to prove her point. It fed into certain stereotypes about the poor as being dishonest and playing on people's sympathies. In spite of the fact that those students arguing for the social causes of homelessness initially outnumbered Janet, her anecdote about the panhandler changed the prevailing attitude in the class from compassion to blame. After Janet had spoken, criticisms of the government were supplanted by skepticism about what panhandlers were using the money for, until finally one student recommended that people not give them any money at all.

However, Helena had a different perspective on this class. She did not see Janet as politically isolated as I did. ["It is not as if the others (in the class) were firmly rooted in the compassion model. I think they are all wrestling with issues like (poverty and homelessness). Many are conservative but fighting some because they feel they should, or because they are really beginning to see something."]

The reading for that day had been a report written by sociologists Peter Rossi and James Wright of a quantitative study of the homeless in Chicago. The study included street surveys conducted by teams of interviewers between midnight and 6:00 A.M. The authors concluded that homelessness had increased because of a combination of the decline in demand for low-skilled casual labor, cutbacks in social-welfare programs, reduction of "indoor support programs, such as mental hospitals," precipitous declines in the availability of low-cost housing, and changes in the number of disabled, mainly from alcoholism (168–69).

Janet's conference preceded the class. Helena immediately asked her if anything in the reading, such as the connection between mental and physical disabilities and homelessness, had surprised her. I am not sure Janet had read the essay. At any rate, she did not answer the question but instead responded with multiple and prolonged stories about homeless people she had met in her hometown, as well as in her work as the head of a United Way committee. She spoke for the better part of their thirty-minute conference, glibly using phrases like "the welfare cycle," "poor white trash," and "no work ethic." Helena occasionally questioned her, but Janet was clearly in charge. My own feelings were mixed. I wrote in my field notebook:

> Janet does seem to have compassion for the homeless. Going on and on. Why doesn't Helena cut her off or focus her or just tell her she just hasn't read her draft yet? . . . Now Janet is telling ANOTHER narrative. Says, "You have to take a grain of salt with the story." . . . A good story—man had a degree from Ethiopia and no job because he couldn't speak English. . . . Helena is infinitely patient with Janet. . . . Janet is so judgmental yet so compassionate. . . . I'm going crazy with the contradictions here. . . . Tape ends and I don't put a new one in. Helena concludes, "Anything you want to ask me? I feel like I got a lot more out of this session. You've worked really hard on your portfolio."

[In a draft of this chapter, next to the sentence "Janet does seem to have compassion for the homeless," Helena wrote, "This is interesting. While you might not have seen Janet as 'very open-minded,' your response to Janet was parallel to mine that you later critique. On my part, it makes me wonder what we were both seeing in the moment." By the sentence in the field notes that says "Janet is so judgmental yet so compassionate. . . . I'm going crazy with the contradictions here," Helena wrote another gloss: "These are the contradictions (that are) somewhat flattened in your critique. If you felt this, imagine how I felt *and* I had to *respond* without reflecting in a journal first!"]

While Janet held her own in conference, later in class there was an unusual flare-up between them as Helena briefly challenged Janet's opinions. [Or, as Helena put it in a gloss, there was an instance of her being "strategically confrontational."] In response to the sociologists' essay on the causes of homelessness, some students had been advocating more teaching of job skills in high school. Julie, a French student, pointed to problems in the economy as the source of homelessness. She dismissed the notion that increased job skills would reduce homelessness. "The unemployment rate is running so high now . . . [that] skilled people don't have jobs either," Julie said. Michelle then criticized a shelter at which she had volunteered in Chicago for not helping people find employment. Drawing on a book she had read in high school, *Travels with Lisbeth*, Katie described the difficulties of finding employment for people who did not have an address and were not clean. She explained how hard the government made it to get food stamps. To qualify, one needed to have an apartment with a full kitchen, which was more costly than renting a place with only a microwave. Helena spoke of the humiliations involved in applying for welfare and then concluded,

> It's not a wonder that the people opt to stand on a street corner and ask a stranger, you know, for money rather than go to their own government, which they should be able to do, I would say. So you've seen where my, you know [self-mocking laugh], opinions lie. I'm not trying to hide them.

Then Janet interjected a story that challenged the views of her fellow students and her instructor. I quote at some length from the transcript here both because the dialogue belies the representation of the "expressivist" classroom as not dealing with issues of social significance and because it captures the tension when student and teacher disagree publicly.

Janet: [Talking rapidly once she begins] I have a comment about that. . . . When my mother was living in Boston, . . . her neighbor in an apartment building she lived in used to pay his rent by panhandling as a homeless man. He dressed in rags in the street and *made like four hundred dollars a week*, CRAZY amounts of money. Since she's told me that I'm wary about giving anybody any money on the streets. But the other day I was at Cleveland Circle in front of CVS and there was a man saying—

Helena: [Also speaking rapidly] Okay, can I stop you for a minute?

Janet: Yes.

Helena: 'Cause I have a question.

Janet: Yes.

Helena: So he made four hundred dollars a week pan—

Janet: A month.

Helena: A month?

Janet: Yeah.

Helena: —panhandling and then you said, "So"—

Janet: To pay his rent.

Helena: "So I'm leery about giving anybody money on the street." What's the connection there? He shouldn't be making four hundred dollars a month?

Janet: No, no. He shouldn't be, no [inaudible] I, I don't have—

Helena: I'm not trying to shut you up.

Janet: I know what you're trying to do. [Class laughs] I don't have an issue with giving anybody money. . . . It just makes you wonder. Like

CONFRONTING BIAS IN STUDENT TEXTS

how many people out there aren't, how many people are using the money that you're giving them to buy food or something like that or are they using it to pay for their rent as this man did. Like he, he—

Helena: So he should be using it to pay for his rent?

Janet: No! He had a job. He was fine. He—

Helena: Oh, he had a job?!

Janet: Oh yeah, he just did that.

Helena: Oh! Oh I missed that.

Janet: Oh, yeah, he was perfectly fine. [Both talk]—

Helena: Now what was his job?

Janet: [Inaudible] I, I don't know. He was going to call a cab. Like he was fine—[both talk]

Helena: Oh, so he had a job.

Janet: [Inaudible]

Helena: Okay, I missed the point.

Janet: Yeah. No, this is just, this is just, this is so he could play with the money he made on his job.

Helena: Okay.

Janet: Like he was, he was an idiot. That's not fair.

Helena: Okay.

Janet: I mean he was, he was calling on people's sympathy to make money so that he didn't have to do anything but just like sit around all day and, and do whatever, you know. [Emphasis mine]

There was clear pedagogical tension in this interchange. For several minutes, each side stood its ground. Helena's statement that "[i]t's not a wonder that the people opt to stand on a street corner" rather than try to get welfare became Janet's "it just makes you wonder" what panhandlers are doing with the money. After Helena opened the discussion up to the class, what followed was a series of anecdotes critical, and self-righteously so, of how the homeless person uses money collected panhandling. Eventually Carrie advocated giving the money directly to a shelter as opposed to a person on the street who might be using it to buy alcohol. Helena said that her personal preference was to take a chance and give the person a dollar.

I think what became clear from Janet's anecdote was her strong and irrational judgment of the panhandler, a judgment that sounded strikingly like the myth of the social leech she was allegedly trying to root out in her paper. I say *judgmental* because she called him "an idiot" for panhandling when he had a job. I use the word *irrational* because someone who has a job and is panhandling enough to make four hundred dollars a week or a month (Janet waffled here) is not "just sit[ting] around all day." It is hard to know why Janet did not draw on her own information; on another occasion, she had described a woman who worked at Au Bon Pain and ate at Rosie's Place because her job only provided enough money to pay rent.

In the interchange, Helena seemed initially piqued by Janet's judgment but then backed off when she learned the panhandler had a job. When she asked what kind of job, Janet deflected her question with something about a cab. Some months later in an interview, I asked Helena why she had backed off when she had learned that the panhandler had a job. What difference did it make? She told me,

> I try not to push a certain thing down their throats. I don't expend my energy trying to change a mind that refuses to change at that moment. Some time in the semester a student might not be able to hear something but maybe they can later. You know how obstinate Janet is. I hope to God that if she does not get it from me, that she will from someone else.

When we get into these one-to-one debates with our students in class, it is often uncomfortable. Helena rarely had this type of prolonged interchange with a single student. In hindsight, I am surprised at how directly Janet challenged her teacher and wonder if she was this contentious with her white teachers.

Unfortunately, Janet's attitude toward the homeless affected the rest of the class discussion. What began as a criticism of a low-income worker panhandling to pay for his rent evoked suspicions toward all homeless people. [As Helena put it, "The class just wouldn't put themselves in the homeless person's shoes."] However, she did not see the impact of Janet's argument. ["These suspicions were already firmly rooted among the other students. Janet carved a space for them. I'm not defending Janet, but critiquing your earlier assessment of the group as more enlightened than she is. Many were not."]

Teachers can underestimate the power reiterated phrases, such as "the undeserving poor," have on people. If we expect that volunteering in a shelter, assigning progressive sociological essays, and writing about poverty will be sufficient to undermine condemnation of the poor, we are mistaken. The effect of the ideological apparatus on the citizenry has been to redirect class anger against the very wealthy, who may have far more leisure time than Janet's panhan-

79

dler. Instead of blaming the businesses that pay wages too low to support adequate housing and food, some people turn their anger against the victims of the wealthy.

Janet stayed with the topic of homelessness in her research paper, the final assignment for the course. Her untitled essay was based on information she had garnered studying the homeless in high school. As with her personal narrative, also originally written in high school, it was not clear to me how much she had changed the earlier paper. The draft for Helena's class described three homeless teenagers, Jen, Ronny, and Dan, whose stories, according to Janet, "attest to the emotional and psychological effects of cruelty in this world." The paper appeared to have been organized around their first-person accounts. However, since Janet did not tape her interviews and admitted to filling in gaps or "extracting" information from what she recalled and from the notes she took, I did not find her methodology particularly sound. The narratives were confusing, and the boundary between what a person actually said and what Janet added was unclear. However, Helena was impressed by the presence of "firsthand" information, and she gave Janet an A–.

Their final conference took place several hours before Helena would receive her award for teaching excellence, an event I described in the last chapter. She looked fine in a stylish black suit. In spite of being surprisingly generous about Janet's research methods and silent on the topic of this being a recycled high school paper, Helena was quite confident about her political differences with Janet. I experienced her as applying some of the power vested in her as a teacher and, at times, I wanted to applaud.

As I see it, the problem with Janet's study was that she was not aware of her own biases and the ways in which they prompted her to "fill in the gaps." Janet seems to have believed that she could use language to create a replica of reality that was only slightly imperfect. The only problem, as Janet saw it, was that she may have forgotten a few things. Helena asked her to get down "more of the details of the transfer" when I am not sure that Janet obtained those details in the first place. If Helena had required Janet to gather new data and insisted that she actually tape-record and transcribe interviews, it would have been easier to assess the validity of the information.[3] [After reading this section, Helena wrote, "Good suggestion. Why didn't you make it then? I could have used that advice, too. Sounds dumb, but I didn't think of it at the time."]

Despite overlooking the shortcomings in Janet's research methods, Helena was the firmest I had ever seen her regarding Janet's tendency to make generalizations about people based on reading material that disparages the working class. In her paper, quotations
from sociological readings marked the end of one story and the
beginning of the next. These quotations were, I felt, tacked on and
appeared to criticize either the subject or the subject's class and family. For example, Jen's poignant story began,

> When I was one year old, my parents abandoned me on a street cor-
> ner in Korea along with my twin sister. I was one and a half years
> old when I was adopted by an American couple. The adoption forced
> me to say good-bye to my twin sister and I continue to search for her
> today.

Janet concluded,

> "Although only a small minority of poor families abuse or neglect their
> children, empirical work generally shows that poor families are dis-
> proportionately identified in reported incidents of abuse and neglect"
> (Pelton 137).[4] The abuse of Jen, though inflicted years prior to our dis-
> cussion, is still evident in her haunted eyes and grim outlook on life.
> Her self-mutilation is a sign of post-traumatic stress disorder resulting
> from the apparent abuse of her childhood. Jen stated that her mother
> was alcoholic and that she beat her daughter regularly. *Due to the
> economic status of her family, it is probable that her father was abus-
> ing her mother* and that her mother's need for empowerment surfaced
> in the abuse of her daughter. [Emphasis mine]

Janet's research was not sound. It was based on a compilation
of her assumptions about Jen's history garnered from an interview
that appears to have revealed a scanty amount of information with
which Janet took great liberties. In this conference, Helena became
quite assertive about Janet's use of outside sources. Several times she
interrupted Janet before Janet could pick up the ball and run with
it as she had done so many times before. Nonetheless, throughout
the conference, Janet responded to criticism by inserting a multitude
of digressive anecdotes, attempting to use the authority of her experiences to deflect the problems in her writing.

> I don't think you can conclude with a certain FIRMNESS that you'd want
> to conclude in a research paper, that Jen's father abused the mother
> BECAUSE of economic status. I don't think that there's a necessary cause-
> and-effect relationship here. Now you, you say you've come across this

in your reading. I bet you have come across this in your reading, and this is what my question in the first draft was geared at. Of course you need to take into account, even though I am about to tell you what I think, you need to take into account my agenda and my biases because I have them too; but I think, I mean, what occurs to me is to ask, well, who writes those books?

So let me point out to you the sentence that I find a little bit troubling. "Due to the economic status of Jen's family, it is probable that her father was abusing her mother, and that her mother's need for empowerment surfaced in the abuse of her daughter." Now the latter part of this sentence I think, um, is a conclusion that you can make because of what Jen has told you, but the first part of the sentence, and when you say it is probable, although you've just said to me in conference that you don't want to make kind of a BLANKET assumption about what people in certain economic statuses would do or how they would behave, that kind of does.

In her ongoing concern with the student's comfort level, Helena later told Janet that she was only arguing with her because she knew she could take it. I do not think Janet was convinced by Helena's argument.

On the last day of class, Helena and I provided refreshments for the students. The males ate most of the food and took the rest home. Most of the females did not even approach the food table. As Helena and I were observing this phenomenon, Janet came up to me and we talked about why I had stopped volunteering at Rosie's Place. Here is my recollection of that final disturbing dialogue. [Helena pointed out here that, like Janet, I am reconstructing a conversation that was not taped.]

Karen: There are just some things I don't like about Rosie's Place—not about the management but about the insensitivity of the volunteers. . . . [I then gave her an example of how a BC student and a suburban volunteer sat down with Nancy, a woman who regularly ate her meals at the shelter, and began to talk to each other in front of her about low-fat diets and how they restrict food intake to certain times of the day to better burn calories.]

Janet: What should they do? Change their way of life for her?

Karen: Well, we're talking about someone who had to walk home in the blizzard [1 April 1997] on crutches with no gloves and no hat. The next day she was too swollen from the exposure to the cold to get out of bed and come to Rosie's Place, so she had nothing to eat that day.

Janet: Well, that's Nancy. She's always trying to get people's sympathy.

I was shocked by this last conversation as Janet simply dropped the persona of the well-meaning missionary. The only insight she seemed to have gained regarding her own subjectivities came as a result of a paper for her PULSE course. She informed me that there she admitted to being guilty of self-deception for overemphasizing her ability "to change the world."

When Researcher and Subject See Things Differently

I frequently felt irritated with Janet throughout the semester. In the beginning of this chapter, I revealed that this irritation was personal. Janet reminded me of my politically naive former self. In the light of this insight, I see now that I may be too harsh in my rendering of Janet. However, there was also my frustration with the amount of power Helena conceded to this student in their pedagogical relationship. At times, I felt that she was too passive in their conferences, allowing Janet to tick away the minutes, often encroaching upon another student's time, extemporizing on the homeless as a defense against the slightest criticism of her writing.

While I do not support a critical or confrontational pedagogy that silences student opinions, something I discuss in more detail in chapter 8 when I describe my visit to Patricia Bizzell's classroom, I think that Helena had more room to maneuver before she would actually have silenced Janet. She might have, for example, interrupted some of Janet's monologues sooner, cutting short her anecdotal reports, and used more of their time discussing specific points in the course readings on the social causes of poverty. Or Helena might have asked for evidence of substantive changes in the drafts of the papers Janet did in high school and turned in for her FWS assignments. Finally, Helena might have pointed out the contradiction in Janet's panhandler narrative (Did he earn four hundred dollars a week or four hundred dollars a month?) and defused the way she took over the class discussion. Helena chose to back off from continuing to challenge Janet's presentation of the story in class because she did not want to "push a certain thing down" the throat of someone whose views seemed intractable. Yet by making the decision to back off, Helena was denied the opportunity to have the class question the kind of dubious individual examples that are told to demean and essentialize groups of people.

I think Helena wanted to take Janet at her word, that Janet

wanted to deconstruct the negative representation of the poor. Had Helena helped Janet look more theoretically at her experiences with the homeless (as well as look at her racial and class subject positions) much earlier in the semester, there might have been some hope of Janet seeing the extent of her condescension, and she might have learned more from the course.[5] As it was, Janet appeared to be a poseur, a self-styled "liberal" hopping on the bandwagon of a popular issue to get good grades and to please authority figures. [Helena noted here, "I wonder to what extent we all fall into and out of this category as people who know privilege and reside in the academy."]

Of course, I also think that at times Helena did do a fine job of pointing Janet toward the contradictions and limitations of her argument, especially because it is difficult to think on one's feet. Moreover, had Helena intervened and challenged Janet earlier and more vigorously, I am not sure that she would have changed Janet's views. The fairly hardcore conservative aspects of Janet's worldview that were not represented in her papers emerged in the class discussion of the panhandler and in the conversation with me during the party when she made the pejorative remark about one of the shelter clients "always trying to get people's sympathy."

[Helena told me that we should focus on the long haul with our students: "Because you didn't see the product you wanted *at the end of our semester* does not mean that (Janet's intellectual growth was not fostered). Your interaction with Carol and Alan (the communist friends I mentioned at the beginning of this chapter)—despite your naïve statement that most certainly frustrated them—absolutely fostered your intellectual growth in the moment(s) when you 'got it' years later." Helena is telling me to be patient with the Janets.] Although I could not understand an anti-imperialist analysis of the war in Vietnam when it was first presented to me, eventually I could. Her work with Janet and the political activists' work with me represent only the beginning.

I agree with Paul Anderson that we need to consider the ethics of the person-based research we do in composition (63). I also agree with Newkirk that withholding "bad news" from one's informants until publication is unethical (see "Seduction" 3). Thus, throughout the semester, I frequently told Helena of my frustration with Janet. I wanted to know why she wasn't challenging Janet more. Perhaps some of our discussions prompted her to be a bit more direct with Janet than she might have been.

The bottom line is that Helena and I simply disagreed about the effectiveness of such challenges. As the reader can see from the comments I have inserted in this narrative, Helena viewed Janet as a "budding consciousness." Several times she excused Janet's views by telling me that she was "just a freshman." At other times she said, "I don't expend my energy trying to change a mind that refuses to change at that moment," and "Maybe it's my Catholicism." More recently Helena commented, "No matter how rude a statement is, I would rather have her get the statement out. As a person of color, I have a special condition. I have a long fuse. I have to. Of course, not all people of color do." [Helena commented on this quotation by saying, "This makes me seem resigned to take a beating as a person of color and I certainly am not."]

I believe that I would have interacted with Janet differently. Yet it would not have been easy or without repercussions. (Just this past semester I told a white student writing against affirmative action in government contracts that such sentences as "These people just want something for nothing" did not constitute academic arguments and were unacceptable. He went to the chair of the English Department where I was working and told him that I had called him a racist.) [Thus, as Helena put it, "We are two very different teachers. I disagree with the teaching style (very directive) you use, and you disagree with mine."]

Before concluding, I want to raise the issue of race. [Helena felt that I should not end this chapter by supplanting our pedagogical differences with the issue of race "as the possible all-answer to the problem. Race is a part."] Yet after hearing Helena's most recent defense of her approach to working with Janet (that she had a long fuse as a person of color), I began to give more consideration to the racial differences than I had before. At various times in my relationship with Helena, before and after this fieldwork interlude, I questioned why she did not respond to an irritating remark. She helped me to see that, if she had spoken up about everything, that if she had read every ambivalent comment or turn of events as racist, she would have been angry all the time. Maintaining such anger would have been draining and counterproductive and she chose not to do so.

The fact is, Helena is black; Janet is white; and I am white. Would I have been more ready to challenge Janet because I too am white? If Janet and her family protested such a challenge, would there have been more institutional backing for me as a white teacher than for Helena as a black teacher? I cannot say, and to try to imagine myself in the position of a young black teacher and scholar is difficult. I do know that the Jesuit administration of the college has awarded Helena for teaching excellence and has recognized her scholarship as a frequent presenter during Black History Month. Would she have been so favorably recognized if she were to have challenged her white middle-class students' biases more directly? Maybe not.

However, the point may be irrelevant; Helena did not want to be any more directive than she was. (I want to acknowledge again that at the end of the semester she did directly take on Janet's anti–working class biases.) Her goal was simply to develop the student's capacity for critical thinking regarding class and race in America; she was not interested in feigned compliance for external reward.

> I definitely think in dealing with a person like Janet, really strong directive tactics would have only got her to tell me what I wanted to hear for the grade—wouldn't have made a dent in the way she thinks. The way I did choose might not have done that either, but I think I had a better shot at it that way. (E-mail 3 May 1998)

I asked Helena if she would have handled Janet differently had she been black.

> No, if she had been black, I would have handled this particular situation the same way, I think. What we were dealing with was primarily a class barrier/prejudice, I think. She could be black and middle class and have those same prejudices; I would still have tried to orchestrate an "awakening" in the same way I did. The way I see it, I could strong-arm her for a short-term result (get her to say what I want her to say, but she might not really think it) or work on her and throw a few question marks in her mind that would, hopefully, stick and linger on her back burner. (E-mail 21 April 1998)

I think Helena was trying to help me understand why her interventions with Janet were so generous. I want to understand, but I still wish that Helena had been as comfortable asking more of Janet's essays on homelessness early in the process as she had been with her personal narrative. I remain uneasy that Janet was not encouraged to take on as much academic responsibility and accountability as she could have been.

Moreover, I am left wondering about other pedagogical situations in which teachers of color are working primarily with students from the dominant culture. It is fashionable these days to assign a certain number of multicultural essays in writing classes or to offer multicultural courses in English departments, but what happens when teachers of color stand firm in their antiracist beliefs? They are at risk of being denied tenure due to "bad" student evaluations (TuSmith, "Teaching"). In short, they are vulnerable.

5 ➤ "I'M JUST REALLY STRUGGLING IN THIS CLASS"
Facing Student Self-Doubt

In the preceding chapter, I demonstrated the highly politicized nature of Helena's classroom, especially at moments when there were differences between the teacher and her student Janet. The representation made it clear that this was not a classroom where controversial social topics were avoided.

Here I look at the classroom through another lens. Helena's work with her student Catherine was quite different from her work with Janet, as were the personalities of the two students. Catherine was interested in the topic of alcoholism, first as it affected her family and later as it affected her fellow college students. If this were the only student I focused on in the study, one might be tempted to conclude that the "expressivist" classroom highlights "a private and personal vision," as Berlin has described it (*Rhetoric and Reality* 74).

Even if Catherine's personal narrative on her alcoholic father had not eventually developed into a second paper on her broader social concerns regarding the effects of binge drinking in the college-age population, it would have been an important piece in its own right. Students come into our classrooms with personal problems that affect the kind of work they are able to do. In this case, Catherine was deeply affected by a family issue, and she understood that her father's illness had undermined her self-confidence. When asked why she chose to write about it, she told me that she felt compelled to do so. She selected her FWS as a place to get this problem off her chest and to shape it in such a way that it was accessible to an audience. Thus the task environment worked to utilize what could have been a distracting personal issue in the service of strengthening the student as a writer.

As in chapter 4, I insert Helena's glosses into my analysis. But because I am eventually more affirming of Helena's pedagogy in Catherine's case than in Janet's, Helena's comments frequently express reassurance that the student found her approach to be helpful. I also reproduce in my text the many places where Helena inscribed check marks (✓) to indicate agreement.

Responding to a Troubling First-Person Narrative

Imagine, for a moment, a student who is alert and insightful, engages actively in classroom discourse, and writes clear, well-organized, and compelling papers. The student invites you home to meet her family, perhaps for Sunday dinner or Friday night Shabbat dinner. It seems like a nice way to spend some time, so you accept. As soon as you arrive, you wonder if you haven't made some sort of mistake. It is a while before anyone opens the door, perhaps because the shouting is so loud that no one hears the doorbell. Your student, let's just call her Catherine, finally welcomes you. Her cheeks are stained with tears, and she seems nervous and embarrassed. There is no sign of dinner or even a set table. Catherine's mother comes in and curtly greets you. Her face is red, and she appears to be very angry. Catherine's father is yelling in the background, and then thudding can be heard as he chases someone up the steps. When he comes back down to meet you, he is still flustered; his eyes are red; and his gait is uneven. How would you feel?

This guided fantasy may not be the kind offered by a holistic healer, but it does simulate for me the experience of reading many of my students' personal narratives. I simply do not know how to behave when I am invited inside the textual representations of their families. Yet I know that, when asked to write about a first-person experience, many students offer this type of traumatic story as if seeking an audience for events that they may never have shared with an adult outside the home. How do we respond as composition teachers?

I asked the same question of my audience at the Research Network Forum at CCCC in Phoenix in the spring of 1997. One responder, Cezar Ornatowski, said that I was highlighting the very paradox of teaching writing. When dealing with personal narrative, we have the psychological moment and the textual moment. As teachers, we cannot assess the abusive childhood being described, but we can assess the textual construction. Of course, the line between the two is not as clear as the double yellow one that transportation departments paint on roads to instruct us not to pass. It is more like the broken line that lets us know that we may pass if it is safe.

In this chapter, I focus on how Helena worked in and around these lines as she helped Catherine develop and revise a personal narrative about her father's alcoholism, an analytic paper on college drinking, an argument paper on the death penalty, and a research paper on shyness. Unlike the apparently poised and confident Janet whose work was the subject of chapter 4, Catherine was a student who had trouble with self-confidence. Helena was much more consistently directive with Catherine than she had been with Janet. Many times during the semester Helena would begin a statement to her with "I don't know if I am overstepping a boundary here, crossing over into another discipline," as she struggled to find an appropriate way to deal with both the text and the student's feelings. In the end, the rhetorical discussions and Helena's use of her own personal experience worked so well together that the line crossings were no longer noticeable.

The problem with a pedagogy that invites personal essays is that the teacher may feel so much discomfort when textually transported to a student's home that he or she has difficulty performing the customary duties of a teacher. In this regard, it is interesting to look at a contradiction implicit in Peter Elbow's *Writing with Power.* He writes, "I think that writers win my trust when they are completely focused on the experience they want me to have. . . . I'm talking about the ability to get me to experience what they are talking about" (319). Yet Elbow later tells us that "renderings of smaller, less intense experiences" may be the most powerful.

> Writers often fail when they try to render deep, harrowing ones. They run into a double barrier. Not only is it harder for them as writers to put themselves wholeheartedly into such strong experiences; but even

if they do so, they are asking for an enormous expenditure on the part
of the reader. (330)

Apparently not even one of the pioneers of "expressivism" wants to
read what Bartholomae calls "sentimental realism" ("Writing" 67)
and risk having to put out "an enormous [emotional] expenditure."

Lorianne Schaub takes Elbow's argument one step further in her
essay on using the personal in academic papers. Schaub insists that,
when a writer makes a decision to disclose herself,

> such a decision, then, "victimizes" one's reader: the reader, like the
> wedding guest in Coleridge's "Rime of the Ancient Mariner," has little
> choice but to listen to a "personal" story she or he didn't ask to hear
> in an "academic" text. Thus the victimized writer in this relationship
> empowers herself rhetorically by metaphorically victimizing her reader,
> forcing her or him to become a passive witness to a story which they
> cannot control, prevent, avoid, or intercede on behalf of. (4–5)

Schaub does not distinguish between a voluntary reader, who can
choose to put down the irksome text, and a composition teacher,
who cannot do so without relinquishing responsibility.

Schaub's point could lead us to the extreme position of exorcis-
ing self-disclosure from all academic writing, potentially robbing
from this body of discourse an important goal in Aristotelian ethos,
convincing the audience of the speaker's moral character. From my
point of view, the question is, How do we as composition teachers
stay connected to the emotional life our students choose to write
about while remaining separate enough to support a strong revision
process? [✓✓✓] Teachers can respond to their students' autobiographical writings in a variety of ways along the spectrum of psychocognitive distance.

Borrowing some terms from family-therapy theorist Salvador
Minuchin and his colleagues helps to characterize some very different responses. In discussing the transactional rules for participation
among family members, they use the words *diffuse* or *enmeshed* in
opposition to *disengaged*. These words correspond roughly to a
broken but smeared yellow line and to the solid double line on a
highway. They write,

> All families can be conceived of as falling somewhere along a continu-
> um whose poles are the two extremes of diffuse boundaries, or enmesh-
> ment, and overly rigid boundaries, disengaged. The enmeshed family

is a system which has turned upon itself, developing its own micro-cosm. There is a high degree of communication and concern among family members, boundaries are blurred, and differentiation is diffused. . . . At the opposite extreme, the disengaged family has overly rigid boundaries. . . . Both extreme types of relating may cause problems when family adaptive mechanisms must be evoked. . . . The parents in an enmeshed family may become quite upset when a child does not eat dessert. The parents in a disengaged family may not respond to a child's delinquent behavior. (Minuchin et al. 56–57)

I think that writing faculty often replicate these transactional styles when students write personal narratives. We can be disengaged, en-meshed, or somewhere in between. Let me offer some examples I find in our literature.

When a student turns in an autobiographical essay and we ini-tially and primarily respond with criticisms of grammar and punc-tuation, we place ourselves at the disengaged end of the spectrum of psychocognitive distance. For example, in *Expressive Discourse,* Jeanette Harris points out, rightfully so, that assessment and evalu-ation are enormously difficult, if not impossible, with personal nar-ratives. [✓]

> It is . . . also difficult to determine the rhetorical effectiveness of writ-ing that discloses intimate personal feelings. Who among us feels com-fortable evaluating an essay in which a student tells of a personal trag-edy? Even if the essay is almost incoherent and riddled with errors, we are loath to denigrate the student's effort to write honestly and sin-cerely. (176)

Harris is arguing that it is difficult to "correct" a paper whose sub-ject is a personal tragedy. I have felt the discomfort she is describ-ing. However, while not the case in Harris's argument, others have noted a danger when the teacher becomes overly concerned about a text being "riddled with errors." James Berlin classifies the teacher with extreme concern in this area as a practitioner of "current-tra-ditional rhetoric." The emphasis is "on superficial correctness—on matters of form, grammar and usage" (*Rhetoric and Reality* 41)—as opposed to emphasis on invention and content.

Sometimes English teachers have an inappropriately harsh and perhaps self-righteous approach to what Janet Emig calls "accidents rather than the essences of discourse—that is, spelling, punctuation, penmanship, and length rather than thematic development, rhetorical and syntactic sophistication, and fulfillment of intent" (93). Susan Wall and Glenda Hull point out that correctness in writing is often regarded as a moral issue. "We are taken aback when we recognize the vigor with which readers denounce certain usages, certain errors or constructions" (261). Such vigorous critique disengages the reader from the theme of an essay, shifting the reader's focus onto its window treatments. A response that falls entirely within the realm of current-traditional rhetoric can be both pedagogically and emotionally unhelpful to the student writer.

At the other end of the transactional spectrum lies the kind of enmeshment that Susan Swartzlander and her colleagues warn us about in their essay, "The Ethics of Requiring Students to Write about Their Personal Lives." When responding to personal narratives, according to them, it is much too easy for writing faculty to cross the boundary into pseudotherapist with potentially damaging results.

> We know of a faculty member who acted as a therapist with students who revealed incest in their pasts; she held personal "sessions" after class to discuss incest. In a different case, one student complained of feeling uncomfortable with an instructor who revealed details of her own childhood with an alcoholic parent and details of her own psychotherapy. (B2)

They would probably find a case of impropriety in a 1992 essay called "Crossing Lines" by Carol Deletiner, who self-discloses and shares her personal feelings about her students' essays with them. "[M]y comrades are my students. We spend a lot of time reading, writing, and talking about pain" (809). Later she asks the reader, "If I moderated my self-exposure, kept my vulnerability a secret, would students respond to the class in the same way? Would they produce the kind of writing they do?" (814–15). She is referring here to the level of emotional intensity in her students' texts. Deletiner so elevates the importance of pathos that the line between teacher and student appears blurred. Her position is a troubling one, as it seems to place the composition teacher in another discipline. In fairness to this author, let me quote from an e-mail Deletiner wrote to me five years after the publication of her essay.

> [M]y teaching practice and the students I now teach are very different from the people I wrote about in that essay. That's not to say that stu-

dents don't write about painful events in their lives—they do—but I issue strong messages about safety and comfort levels and what one needs in order to take risks. Students also know, from the first day, that I will not be the only reader of their texts.

Helena's transactional style did not fall along either extreme of the spectrum. However, when I first began to observe her work with Catherine, it appeared that her pedagogy was disengaged and current-traditional in its focus on sentence-level error and word choice in early drafts. I came to see her approach as being more complicated than I had originally thought.

Evaluating the Writing When the Writer Is in Pain

For the assignment on the personal narrative, Catherine produced a powerful and well-written essay about the pain she felt from her father's alcoholism. Even though the man was then sober and the family, exclusive of Catherine and one of her siblings, was involved in therapy and support groups, Catherine refused to trust that this time he would not break his promises. Badly hurt by his blaming her for his drinking, she referred to him in the paper as "the corpse" and labeled her feelings toward him as "malice." Absent was the facile, forgiving, all-is-healed resolution that we saw in the first draft of Janet's personal narrative about the death of her grandmother.

Let me foreground my own subjectivities around the issue of alcoholic families. [Helena noted, "This is courageous; (it shows) much integrity."] Catherine's essay engaged me on a deeply emotional level, making me just the kind of evaluator who would appear to have the most trouble "determin[ing] its rhetorical effectiveness" (Harris 176). My mother died of alcoholism in October 1991. If Catherine had been my student, I might have done a limited amount of self-disclosure, such as telling her that I had personal experience with this disease in my own family, so I could relate to the narrator's pain. Then I would have moved on to discuss the essay as a rhetorical production. Catherine was not my student, and I eventually chose to reveal more than these details.

I was not able to attend Catherine's first conference. However, without telling me the topic, Helena suggested that I ask Catherine for a copy of her paper and attend the second conference. Helena was surprised when Catherine gave me permission to sit in, and we were both surprised when Catherine later chose to put the essay in the class magazine. I received a copy of the paper at the conference and read it while the tape recorder picked up their conversation. Here are some excerpts from the second draft of her paper titled "Untitled."

> My Father died just over a year ago. His memory still haunts me, though not as much as his identical corpse which still walks the earth. . . . Each August for two years my father relapsed and left our family. . . . He left that night with beer soaked breath, sputtering that I was the reason why he went back to the bottle. . . . I watched [my mom] break down on the phone when she discovered that our savings were held in a joint account, which could not be touched without my father's consent. . . . I watched her body spasm when she realized she would have to file for bankruptcy. . . . I will never be able to fully trust anyone because I live in aching fear of being hurt again. . . . Seventeen years was a long, excruciating process of withdrawing love and replacing it with a venomous hatred until I wanted him to die. . . . I wanted my father to die. . . . The corpse told me it was sorry. . . . My biggest fear is that I will go home one day and find the corpse sitting in my living room—part of my family. . . . Every emotion I feel stems from my father's alcoholism. . . . [T]he hatred has clogged each pore of my body. There is no room for love. . . . To forgive is to have strength, but I am weak. To forgive is to have courage, but I am afraid.
>
> I am terrified.

I found it difficult to sit through this conference because the written and oral discourses made equal demands on my attention. In my field notes I scribbled,

> I am so focused on the pain about her father's alcoholism that I am having trouble with Helena's [concern with] mechanics and errors. I just want to grab Catherine and tell her I had a parent who died of alcoholism. Helena is focused on diction and me on pain. (How can she? Yesterday [Helena] said she probably wouldn't have written about her parents' divorce for the personal narrative required in Lad[Tobin]'s course [on composition theory] because she wouldn't have wanted it to be "the subject of critique." But she is doing what she feared would happen.)

At the time, my own emotional reaction was so strong that it seemed to me that Helena was applying something of a "scorched earth" policy, marching problem by problem through the text.[1] However, I was reading the paper for the first time, and this was their second conference. Reviewing the transcript months later, what had originally struck me as a current-traditional emphasis on errors now seemed to me to be an emphasis laced with a profound pedagogical sensitivity toward the subject matter and a desire to ally with the student around a strong and clear presentation. [✓]

She told the student, "I feel very strongly about this paper. I want you to be clear that I am just trying to help you strengthen the presentation of it." Helena praised Catherine for the changes she had made from the first draft, such as clarifying the word *bipolar.* As Helena moved forward through the paper, her focus was on word choice. She questioned several phrases with a sympathetic critique that, for example, involved praising an adjective but calling for a smoother word order. Yet, in three instances, word choice was not a simple matter of style.

The first instance pertained to Catherine's use of the phrase *internally rupture* to describe the effect on the family of her father's abandonment. She wanted to avoid the cliché *heartbreak,* so as to sound "different." There was a great deal of emotion in what Catherine was describing, and neither she nor Helena came up with an expression that did not feel overused. In the next draft, Catherine eliminated the phrase and settled for a report of what happened. "In the weeks following my father's passing, I did not cry, but I remember watching my siblings do so when they learned we were to be evicted." It appeared that she had learned that sometimes detail works better at conveying information than an all-purpose expression. [Helena reported, "This (statement) really helps *me* to see things I couldn't see then."]

In the second instance, Helena, with some difficulty and hesitation, questioned the student's apparently inconsistent use of the phrase *the corpse,* pointing out that Catherine referred to him as "Father" when describing the time before he left her family and as the "corpse" in the present of the story. By naming him the "corpse," Helena felt that Catherine did a good job of conveying the distance she felt from the man. Apparently in the recent draft, she had changed the pattern, and Helena asked why. Catherine replied, "Where I'm referring to him as 'he,' I do that because it wasn't at the point when he was weak and he did this to us. He wasn't yet 'the corpse,' [pause] he was still my father." "I DO think that the pattern you set out in the first draft is very effective, BUT, umm, it wouldn't change, I don't think, dramatically, the effect of the paper, if you decided to change the pattern, but PICK a pattern." Helena noticed an inconsistency in the way Catherine referred to her father in this draft. Rather than come out and hit Catherine over the head with it, Helena slowly worked toward helping the student see the inconsistency. Given the slow pace of her remarks, it is apparent that she was highly aware that however Catherine referred to her father, it was a charged issue. [✓] Catherine was open about her difficulties in working on transferring this experience into text. She was not defensive about the rhetorical problem. Perhaps Helena's cautiousness is a factor here.

There was a third instance in the conference of an apparently simple matter of word choice having complex psychological ramifications. Helena pointed to Catherine's use of the word *malice* as an expression of her feelings toward her father. As she worked to accept Catherine's attitude, she found herself in uncharted disciplinary territory. I reproduce here some of the transcript material to try to communicate how Helena navigated her way.

Helena: Okay, this is hard. I don't want to pick on everything you've written [pause], umm, but, in treating it as a piece of writing, I just want you to make the most effective word choices that you can. . . . Here I definitely think [pause] a different word will work better there, although I'm not trying to water down, umm, the ANGER, the hatred that you're talking about. But MALICE implies that you want to bring HARM to [pause] and I don't think that's your meaning or [pause] or IS that? [Nervous laugh]

Catherine: No, I, I—

Helena: [Interrupting] I don't think "malice" is.

Catherine: I, I CAN replace the word, but, in all honesty—

Helena: [Interrupting] This is the one you want.

Catherine: Given the opportunity, I, I WOULD bring harm to him.

Helena: Then [quietly] this will be crossed out. [Nervous laugh] Okay I think I was, because of your use of the words "anger" and "hatred" [pause] before, I think that's the track I was on so that I [pause] imposed.

Catherine's declaration that she felt malice toward her father had to have been difficult for her composition teacher to hear. Yet Helena handled the junction of the rhetorical and the psychological quite well. She would rather not have had her student imply that she would bring harm to the man, but when Catherine said that was the way she felt, Helena dropped her inquiry, arguing about neither the word nor the feeling.

As the conference drew to a conclusion, it was clear that Helena was quite aware that she was walking a fine line as a composition teacher. She told Catherine that her piece was effective and that she had succeeded in conveying to the reader "the weight of the experience," and then Helena made a self-mocking joke about the number of her comments. "Like there could be any more, right? 'Your period's not quite dark enough in this one!' [Laughs] Umm, well, that's just me. What do you think?" Catherine immediately informed her,

> I feel very heavy. I don't know how to describe it. I guess I expected after writing it, to have kind of been DONE with it, and now I feel like, and this is GOOD, I want to go back and re-WORK it and re-DO it, but at the same time, I hate that [pause] so, I know, I KNOW, I'm gonna want to write about much lighter subjects in the future.

Helena immediately assured Catherine that she could write about whatever she wanted to write about and that she didn't have to "reveal [her] deepest things."

I was proud of Catherine for saying that she felt "heavy," even if she went on to assure her instructor that all was fine, that she was eager to revise. [✓] Feeling heavy myself at the end of the conference, I decided not to let Catherine simply walk away. [✓] We talked in a nearby hallway with bells signaling the elevator's arrival every few minutes. I told her that I thought she showed courage in writing the paper. She denied that it had been courage that had motivated her, saying only that it had been a "selfish" desire for "closure." When I asked her to describe the conference I had missed, she told me, "It wasn't very different from this one."

One point that came out early in our conversation was Catherine's lack of differentiation between revision and editing. [✓] I frequently see this blurring among freshmen; they expect that what constitutes a second draft is no more, perhaps, than a few word changes. Many are surprised when they realize that they may have to rethink their positions. Catherine told me that she felt somewhat "heavy" after her first conference but "not to this extent." She saw that she had to make "a couple of revisions," but after the second one she realized that she had some more thinking to do.

> I see where the problems lie, and I don't know if I [pause] really [pause] want to keep working with it. Now the revisions aren't definite. There are a lot of gray areas where I have to examine my feelings. For ex-

ample, in the case of the word "malice," um, I have to examine exactly how I feel, um, and, and that was what I felt I did the first time and that, THAT part I thought was done.

I was reminded of the concerns that have been raised by Swartzlander and others about the ethics of asking our students to write personal narratives, and I asked Catherine what it was like to write about such a heavy topic and then have it be the subject of "correction." She told me that it was "very, VERY DIFFICULT [✓], and this is something we DID discuss in the first conference, and I understand why the corrections need to be pointed out and grammar needs to be marked." Apparently Helena had told her that, because she was "focused on grammar," it did not mean that she was "missing the content." Catherine said to me,

> I'm not gonna lie. Any time corrections are made, you, you know it, it [pause] can kind of, um, feel like a mark on your writing style. [✓] In this case, um, I feel like I, this is something that's completely, um, every part of me, and it's, it's hard to write, it's hard to correct [✓], and it's definitely hard to have critiqued [pause] even though I'm very GLAD that I get the opportunity to have it critiqued.

I then asked Catherine how Helena demonstrated that she was attentive to the content. "She said she was only going to read the first paragraph initially, and when she read the first paragraph she decided to read the whole paper, so, automatically, I knew that she was reading it for the story, not for exactly how I'd written it." [Here Helena commented, "I am so happy to be able to read some of the dialogue that took place between you."]

Helena's initially appearing to read Catherine's essay for the story and not for "exactly how [she'd] written it" was important to Catherine perhaps because it helped her to see that her teacher was a human being and not just a correcting machine. [Later, in a gloss, Helena would confirm that this was a significant pedagogical moment.] Yet Catherine still felt "a mark on [her] writing style" as a result of the corrections. Given the personal, even lyrical, nature of the content of the paper, it struck me that she might have been inadvertently punning on the word *mark,* using it to mean both grade and brand.

In my interview with Catherine, I told her that many people in composition studies were backing away from teaching personal narratives because of just the kind of discomfort she and Helena had experienced. Curious about why Catherine had chosen the topic she did, I asked her about the process of invention subsequent to learning that she would be required to write some sort of personal narrative. She answered quickly and without her usual hesitation. "[My father's alcoholism] was the first thing I considered and I attempted to write about other things, but I could never get past this topic, and yet I decided it was something I had to get on paper." She had also considered writing about the importance of dancing or adjusting to college, topics that "would have been a lot easier to write about, but [she] couldn't."

Karen: You couldn't because?
Catherine: Because I need to [pause], *I needed to put this on paper.* [✓✓✓]
 I needed to, um, find some kind of outlet because I don't talk about this ordinarily. [Emphasis mine]

The rhetorical situation or task environment seems to have unearthed a psychological exigency. Once invited to select a personal topic, it was as if Catherine felt no choice but to write about her father's alcoholism.

The conversation continued with my talking more, telling her the difficulties I had in interacting with these types of texts because of my own relationship to alcoholism. I said that I had written an essay about my mother's death from the disease, and it was about to be published. I also let her know that I had been involved with a group of faculty who met with staff counselors to help us learn how to respond in appropriate ways to texts that troubled us on a personal level. Again she commented quickly, adamant that she did not write the paper to get counseling.

> I wrote it for me and I wrote it because I want my writing to get better, 'cause really I'm not happy with it, and I haven't been happy with it in the past. So I had EXPECTED the critique and that, for me, at least, I can't speak for other students, was the best way to handle it, but she did it tactfully, and I'm impressed even if it IS hard.

[Here Helena wrote: "I feel so good and relieved by this."] I let Catherine know that I felt that Helena was aware of the content, even during the times when she talked about mechanics.

Interviewing Catherine was part of my effort to triangulate the data I was gathering so that I could learn what she would say in the absence of her teacher. [✓ "A real opportunity, again, to see *your* dialogue."] I sought her out because I wanted to learn more about how Helena's pedagogy impacted both the student and the writing process. Catherine appears to have had three things to communicate to me: (1) she needed to write about her father's alcoholism; (2) she wanted her essay critiqued so that her writing would improve; and (3) it was difficult to experience the critique. In spite of the discomfort, she declared, "It would be silly to outlaw personal narrative. So as difficult as it is, there IS a benefit to it." [Helena interjected here, "Awesome."] Catherine's philosophy seems to be that, if a student chooses to write about a personal topic, the student must be resilient enough to tolerate the criticism. I found it striking that, given the open-ended possibilities for the assignment, it was as if she had no choice but to write about the effect of alcoholism on her family. Yet her boundaries were clear; the only kind of help she was interested in receiving was rhetorical. I think this case example shows the importance of creating space for autobiographical writing. It was almost as if Catherine could not move forward as a writer without having discharged this experience on paper and given it to a competent, caring teacher.

A few days later, I spoke with Helena about what, for her, the first conference with Catherine had been like. She affirmed my sense of her own cautiousness while defending her need to make corrections on any first draft. Helena had not seen Catherine's paper until the first conference, but she had gotten a sense that it was about something very personal, as Catherine had not shared it in peer group. She initially announced to Catherine that she would just read through the first paragraph; then she told Catherine that she was going to read through the whole thing. "And [Catherine] sort of smiled like, 'Yeah, you know, you need to.'"

> And [exhalation] at the end I just paused, I didn't say [pause] ANYTHING. My first response to her had to do with, you know, um, "This is going to be a bit tricky, dealing with this as a piece of writing and also, um, discussing the content of the essay. In other words, when I tell you that you need a comma HERE, I don't want you to think that I have missed the weight of the story. But me telling you, 'This is a fragment, don't write in a passive voice, um, insert an adjective HERE' is all to get you to make this into the strongest essay it can be because obviously this is a story you WANT told." Um, so that seemed to set a nice cushion for things I had to tell her, you know. It's really hard for me to make little technical critiques about a paper that has to deal, that deals with something this heavy, you know, so I tried to set that up, and I think that WORKED.

Helena was careful talking with Catherine about the paper because, "I knew what was at stake for HER. . . . [✓] I was actually SURPRISED that she was so open with you about the essay."

Thus, my initial judgment of Helena as disengaging from the student's feelings by focusing on error was incorrect. Although Helena did focus on sentence-level error, she was by no means disengaged from the pathos in the essay. She openly acknowledged to the student that she understood the weight of the content of the subject and that comments on technicalities were only in the service of making the paper better. Sometimes focusing on "technicalities" can protect the composition teacher from the emotional impact of the content. Yet Helena had managed to question Catherine's choice of words while retaining a grasp on "what was at stake" for her. Furthermore, she was completely upfront with the student regarding what she called the "trickiness" of the rhetorical situation. Balancing what must have been a dual consciousness is commendable. The slow pace of her speech and the frequent pauses in the second conference were now fully understandable.

Both student and teacher told the story of how what was supposed to be a look only at the first paragraph quickly turned into a reading of the whole essay. As I read the situation, it was that single spontaneous act that enabled teacher and student to form a relationship strong enough for one to offer and the other to receive textual critique. In short, Helena's interest in the subject and her sensitivity opened the door for the rhetorical work. In this case, sensitivity meant both an awareness of the student's emotional pain (what Catherine described as Helena's "tact") and a respect for disciplinary boundaries. Helena made no attempt to give her student what she did not want, namely, counseling. As Philip Morse puts it in his study of student-teacher conferences,

> Knowledge of helping agents' communication techniques does not in itself suggest that teachers are counselors or that they will even exercise a counselor's role in the classroom, but rather such skills are ones which are universally applicable in any interactive relationship where one person seeks the help of another, whether the helper be a minister, doctor, coach, family member, or teacher. (21)

Helena was able to function as the kind of helping agent she was paid to be.

Earlier I quoted from Jeanette Harris's book *Expressive Dis-*

course: "Who among us feels comfortable evaluating an essay in which a student tells of a personal tragedy? Even if the essay is almost incoherent and riddled with errors, we are loath to denigrate the student's effort to write honestly and sincerely" (176). Harris seems to create a false binary here. [✓] Either we correct the paper and denigrate the student's effort to write honestly and sincerely, or we do not correct the paper and leave it incoherent and riddled with errors. My observations of Helena demonstrate a third possibility, one that came to me as a result of interviewing both student and teacher. We can work with a student on issues like word choice, grammar, and punctuation *without* denigrating the student's efforts to write honestly and sincerely. Current-traditional pedagogy does not necessarily run counter to a humane one. [✓]

Nonetheless, the focus on sentence-level error in the first draft was troubling to me. Helena and I had several discussions about her approach; she maintained that she was preparing the student to make the corrections for a second draft, which would be graded. "If we, say, did three drafts of every paper, and the third draft is the one that was graded, then I would probably only react to the content of the first," she told me. Additionally, Helena believed that students wanted to know the grade, and she believed that the chance of the grade going up prompted them to make further revisions. (In the last chapter, I demonstrated that it was indeed this motivation that prompted Janet to revise one of her papers.) Helena also felt that an early emphasis on grammar was in the service of students who would come under the surveillance of other faculty in the college who were aggressively critical of these kinds of surface errors.

Helena and I continued to have these discussions. There were differences between us regarding writing-process pedagogy and the issue of when to deal with editing. Many teachers who do employ writing-process pedagogy do not grade essays until the end of the semester when they see them in the portfolio; and, by then, the essays have been revised three or four times, as well as edited. For example, when I view the first draft of an essay, I see it as something "in utero." It is not even born yet. I do not want to call attention to editing issues when I expect big chunks of the text to disappear and others to take their place. As Nancy Sommers puts it,

[T]leachers' comments [on first drafts] do not provide students with an inherent reason for revising the structure and meaning of their texts, since the comments suggest to the students that the meaning of the text is already there, finished, produced, and all that is necessary is a better word or phrase. ("Responding" 151)

In fact, Sommers argues that comments like "wordy," "spelling," "comma needed," and so on actually inhibit the process of revision from first to second drafts.

Helena chose to work on editing issues from the very beginning. In the first conference, she told Catherine that she was going to point out such things as fragments and the use of the passive voice. In the second conference, she focused on words and patterns that were highly cathected and vital to the pathos in the piece. Despite feeling the discomfort that Harris describes, Helena demonstrated that some of us can assess personal narratives. In fact, she appears to have been working toward what Kurt Spellmeyer, in his essay "After Theory," calls "a basic grammar of emotional life," a pedagogy in which we can be in touch with what our students "actually 'feel'" (911). Helena and Catherine's work together around her personal essay is a fine example of bringing together what is frequently split apart, school assignments and what matters most to students. As I indicated earlier, personal narratives in the writing classroom can unite the cognitive and the affective domains (Berthoff 27). [✓]

Before I move on to describe the other assignments during the semester, it is important to note that since Catherine had expressed interest in my own essay on family alcoholism, "My Mother and the Man Who Called the Ambulance," I gave her a copy at the end of the semester. (I waited until then because I did not want to risk any more intervention into her revision process.) Having had many more years than Catherine to "get help" with the impact of the disease, my attitude in the essay toward the alcoholic is neither anger nor forgiveness but rather a mixture of compassion, fear, and deep frustration at never having been able to get her into treatment. I am not sure if I would have shared the essay with Catherine had she been my student. After reading it, she sent me an e-mail message.

> I have just finished reading your essay, and I want you to know how much I appreciate your sharing it with me. I don't believe you need me to tell you it was moving, as I'm sure you've heard this repeatedly. This is something I think I will contemplate for a very long time. Thank You so much.

David Bleich cautions us not to practice a pedagogy of self-disclosure under compulsory conditions but rather to do so only where there is "a 'readiness' of context, which includes a certain level of trust of peers and authority figures." He adds, "[M]odes of self-disclosure are what many students have longed for since I have been in school but were taught to confine to ultra-private, often unsharable social locations apart from school" ("Collaboration" 48). Although my self-disclosure to Catherine was almost an accident of the research, her e-mail communicates to me that the exchange was meaningful. It brought the "unsharable" into the public domain. [✓]

Transitioning from Personal Narrative to Exposition

One of the critiques of "expressivist" pedagogy is that teaching experience-based personal narrative does not prepare students to write the information-based expository or persuasive prose that they will be required to write in other academic courses both within and outside of English departments. Freshman writing teachers are repeatedly asked to explain how one genre prepares for another and are frustrated by always being on the defensive. Before attempting to respond to this critique through the example of Helena's work, I want to turn the question around for a moment. As Elizabeth Chiseri-Strater asks in her ethnography on writing across the disciplines at the University of New Hampshire (UNH), "How are other disciplines creating contexts for such students to read, write, and talk *in creative, critical and personally engaging ways?*" (167, emphasis mine).

I join Chiseri-Strater and ask how *are* other faculty within and outside of English departments continuing the learning process begun in the FWS by helping their students write in personally engaging ways? Jackie, a Prose Writing student in Debby's class who went on to law school in Texas, thought that her other courses failed her in this regard. She took Prose Writing at BC in her senior year in an attempt to "find [her] own voice." "As a history major, I've written a lot of papers that don't come from me; they come from what I have been studying." [✓] According to Jackie, the cognitive effort required to write and revise her personal narratives was more than that required to read source material and recompose the information for course papers.

Yet precisely because the question regarding the transferability of skills from personal writing to other forms is asked so frequently, it deserves to be answered directly. Helena, for one, did teach other modes of discourse within her freshman writing classroom. In this regard, her freshman writing course was quite standard and was not, as some theorists would have it, particularly "self" oriented. However, despite Catherine's proclamation that she would be choosing lighter topics as she proceeded through the different modes, alcoholism remained the subject of her next assignment, an analytical paper. [✓] The transition between modes was not an easy one for her.

The class moved into its next phase with a reading from the course anthology entitled "Cause-and-Effect Analysis." It begins, "To make sense of the world, we try to understand why things happen and how events affect us. This is cause-and-effect analysis" ("Cause-and-Effect" 51). The guidelines for writing an analytic paper in Helena's course did not exclude personal topics. Since the purpose of cause-and-effect analysis is to "inform" or "share with the reader," the students "could explain the causes of [a] break-up with [a] best friend or the effects of [a] decision to change [one's] major" (51). In class, Helena encouraged her students to select a topic they cared about, and together they would shape it into an analytical paper.

To her next conference Catherine brought a draft of an essay about her roommate's drinking, a behavior that seemed to torture Catherine. The draft itself appeared to make her as uncomfortable as the drinking behavior, and she presented as a self-effacing student writer with no self-confidence. It would take much work for her to produce a text analyzing college drinking when she began with only her observations of one person.

The scene of the first conference on this paper felt utterly chaotic. There were six people meeting in the small office, which was divided with five-foot partitions. Helena sat at a long table with Catherine and I near the door. In back of us, sitting at their desks on each side of the partition, were one doctoral student working on a computer and another chatting with a friend. We were lucky that day; I had been in this space when three conferences were going on simultaneously. In spite of the lack of privacy, Catherine was not shy about her discouragement. This was how the first conference began on a paper she chose to revise nine times.

Helena: I have all sorts of amazing and wonderful suggestions for you. [Self-mocking laughter]

Catherine: Oh, God! You READ it already? I was going to try and convince
   you NOT to.
Helena: Of COURSE I read it! Oh STOP!
Catherine: I just want you to know I understand that it's not an analysis
   paper right now. I understand that it's HORRIBLE and I, I, I don't know.
   I, I apologize that you had to read it. I'm embarrassed that I wrote it.

Helena told her that she should not be so hard on herself but that
she did need to convert the format of the paper. It could still be first-
person writing, but she might consider something like interviewing
several students after a weekend of binge drinking. "There IS a place
for 'I' in the paper, but this is a fairly personal narrative about your
observation of ONE student."

Helena's handling of Catherine's self-abasement was astute. She
had already read the draft and discovered the problems. Instead of
possibly shaming Catherine with such a statement as, There are big
problems here, she began with a kind of self-mocking hope: "I have
all sorts of amazing and wonderful suggestions for you." Then,
rather than coddle the student and avoid the limitations of the draft,
Helena told Catherine not to be so hard on herself but also let her
know that the format needed to change. Here are some excerpts
from the first draft of Catherine's "analytic" paper. (I have preserved
the layout of the paper's text.)

> *She is sprawled on the floor, limbs limp, eyes half closed in
> drunken slits. As I come closer, I smell the alcohol and see the hickies
> which stain her neck. I look at the boy sitting next to her, his face
> wrought with guilt . . .*
>
> I met her in September and liked her instantly. She glowed with un-
> touched radiance few ever achieve and was filled with promise I envied.
> Though never confessed, I tried to pattern her vibrance, longing to clean
> my own blemishes and sparkle with passion as she did. I opened up little
> doors within me—cracked them just wide enough for her to see and let
> my own love escape . . . maybe too wide. I began to look at her as one
> of my closest friends, and trust her with my emotions. . . .
>
> For whatever reason, alcohol holds a place of contempt in my heart
> that reaches far beyond loathing—to the point of terror. I hate my
> abnormality, but I cannot help the disgust that I feel when I witness
> the transformation in my friends, sustained by alcohol but brought on
> for reasons I do not understand. . . .
>
> Finding her drunk had more of an effect than I have ever been able
> to say. It was more than a loss of trust and understanding, for it rep-
> resented a conflict within myself I had been unable to confront.

My reaction to this draft was surprise at the ease with which she revealed strong feelings of attraction to another woman, as well as the betrayal she later felt when her friend drank. Furthermore, I saw a commendable level of self-awareness; her friend was not the only one with the problem. Yet in the conference and in written remarks, Helena avoided responding on a subjective level. Instead of adding an end comment in one of what Summer Smith calls the "reader response genres" (the teacher's identification with the student or a description of the reading experience), Helena offered a positive evaluation of the topic and a series of explicit suggestions or directives for revision.

> Catherine, in the class response you wrote on 2/17, you say that you're interested in discussing the effects of college drinking. That's a fine topic for an analytic piece of writing. Any one or a combination of the following methods might help you delineate reasons why college kids drink and the effects of the behavior: speculate yourself why kids might drink; ask/interview people you know; skim an article or two on the subject (in the social work library: "College Students' Drinking Problems: A National Study, 1982–1991"). You might also want to include a set of your observations on how this behavior is destructive—you see people unable to remember where certain lumps & bruises came from, unsure of what they've done; affects performance as a student— late assignments, etc. There's a wide range of effects drinking to excess can have on a college student. You also need to convert the format of the essay a bit. You can start with a personal anecdote, but the paper should present the problem of college drinking in a more general/universal way. Maybe you could still keep [the italicized inserts about her friend that punctuate the paper].

In her end comment, I read Helena as having worked to find a place for the personal in the essay while she directed Catherine to generalize the problem. She even went so far as to do an on-line bibliography search to direct the student toward some academic sources. The student both needed and wanted to learn how to transform narrative and description into analysis. So insistent was Helena on giving Catherine a push in the right direction that the suggestion that the student include some of her observations about the effects of alcohol abuse among college students was followed by a list of Helena's own observations. In this case, she might have been less directive and asked for the student's own observations. After all,

Catherine was somewhat of an expert on what happens when people drink too much.

Catherine did not have an opportunity to read these end comments until after the conference, but her questions in the conference indicated that she wanted direct advice. While expressing firm commitment to her topic ("And I KNOW this is what I'm going to write about, and I'm not going to change it"), she knew she needed help in fulfilling the assignment. She told her instructor, "I don't know how to make it analytical." "Is there a good way to go about incorporating statistics? I've never done a T square. I do interviews and I'm not sure how to go about putting that in the paper." In the conference, Helena was as directive as her end notes would indicate, but she also encouraged Catherine to "trust her judgment." Instead of just writing that people drink "for whatever reason" or "for reasons I do not understand," Catherine needed to figure out those reasons; Helena told her that the figuring was "the work that this paper needs to do."

Yet Catherine was overwhelmed at the end of their meeting. "I've decided that I really don't like analysis papers. That's my conclusion. . . . It's impossible for me to write. I'm just not good at this." But Helena did not let her back out so easily. "I think you might be separating out some characteristics of analytic writing. They're floating on their own, and you, you need to have them grounded in something that's personally significant to YOU. See you CAN achieve both."

I think this conference is a remarkable example of combining pedagogical principles with emotional support and respect for the student. At the heart of the pedagogy is the belief that it is important for students to write about what matters to them. Rather than abandon that principle for the sake of teaching an author-evacuated mode of discourse, the kind of research paper Lester Faigley valorizes in *Fragments of Rationality,* Helena retained it in order to facilitate the learning process.

However, developing an exploratory essay from one observation is no easy rhetorical task. For the most part, Helena appeared to regard the student as what Anne DiPardo refers to as a "narrative knower," signifying that narrative is more than a mode of discourse; it is also a mode of thought (7). [Helena wrote here, "Nice."] Helena displayed her faith that Catherine can offer the reader some informed speculation about why college students drink.

Yet another problem emerged in the next conference. It became clear that Catherine's lack of self-confidence was interfering with her ability to provide evidence of her claims. In inquiring about why she thought college students binge drink, Helena discovered that Catherine had some ideas, but those ideas did not appear in the paper. "I think you have some ideas in your head but for some reason felt that they weren't, that you didn't have the authority to kind of surmise that, but you do."

Helena's intervention had the effect she intended: in a subsequent draft, Catherine did add reasons why college students drink to excess. She wrote, "You're kind of lost when you come to college." She speculated that students who were once ahead of everyone in their peer groups in academics or athletics were in college surrounded by many just like them. Yet even as Catherine moved forward through revisions of the paper, learning to theorize, she remained uncomfortable.

> I hated writing this paper. . . . I guess I don't like analysis papers. I didn't feel like it was mine. It's not my opinion, just what others have told me. The personal narrative came easier even though the paper was difficult to write. That paper was a part of me.

Catherine, like the students she was writing about in this assignment, experienced a loss. In her case, it was a loss of the intensity and the freedom to explore self and family that she had had in her first assignment. She did not feel that the paper was "hers." "It's not my opinion, just what others have told me." It is not clear whether these statements imply that she came to resent Helena's input into the paper, some of which she had requested. By the end of the second conference, she remained dissatisfied with the rhetorical compromise in which the personal and the general lay side by side. Helena was not satisfied either. "There are two things going on in this paper, and they can be brought together but they haven't been yet. That is, the relationship between this woman's story (right?) and problems with binge drinking in a larger context."

I think Catherine did bring the two stories together in her last draft, the fourth one handed in but the ninth one overall. In it she theorized about the problem of college drinking, as her instructor advised, while retaining the story of her friend. Her essay was an example of creative nonfiction, a hybrid discourse that can come out of the "expressive" writing classroom. Anne DiPardo writes that "the assumption is still commonly held (if tacitly, in many cases) that the narrative is something one grows out of as cognitive maturity allows abstract, reasoned, depersonalized exposition to emerge" (2). DiPardo argues for a narrative component in expository texts, for

> more spirited composing and *interactive comprehensions,* bringing the larger issues under discussion into one's personal purview by encouraging the reader or writer to weigh her own values, beliefs and background knowledge against the more public, depersonalized information under consideration. (14, emphasis mine) [✓ "Nice."]

Here are excerpts from Catherine's final draft, one in which she achieved "interactive comprehensions" between the personal and the public. (Again, I have preserved the form.)

> In a kind of possession that takes hold of so many college students, the monster intoxicates and humiliates, leaving not so fond memories but a vicious hangover and lasting regrets. The monster is alcohol; its quest . . . binge drinking. There is no doubt of its destructiveness; the question that must be asked is why students engage in its debilitating behavior.
>
> *She is sprawled on the floor, limbs limp, eyes half closed in drunken slits. As I come closer, I smell the alcohol and see the hickeys which stain her neck. I look at the boy sitting next to her, his face wrought with guilt . . .*
>
> The common sentiment among college students is that if you are not drunk, you are not having a good time. In a study done in 1994, 84% of college students admitted they drank during the school year. 44% were binge drinkers, and one-fifth of this percentage had engaged in binge drinking more than three times in the past two weeks (Beddingfield 52).[2] . . . It is the freedom, the escape, and the power and acceptance that comes along with booze. . . . [Then comes a paragraph on each of these explanations for excessive drinking in college.]
>
> Additionally, there is certainly a cause for concern when binge drinking becomes fatal. In the spring of 1996, an all-night graduation party at a fraternity house at the University of North Carolina–Chapel Hill, for example, turned into a nightmare when the house caught on fire and five students perished. Four of the victims who had not been able to escape were drunk. . . .
>
> *The next morning is set in Hell, and not because of her physical sickness. It is the blotches on her neck, purple and etched with blue veins. It is the eyes of her friends. It is her pain.*
>
> Though I may try to understand the reasons, I know I never truly will. She, like many who will continue to drink long after their last

binge, have motivations I cannot comprehend. She may drink again, but I hope she will be strong. I pray she will one day find herself and clasp it with welcoming arms, never letting go. But until I see this self-love within her I cannot help but shudder when every seven days the weekend creeps up behind her, taps her on the shoulder, and asks if she wants a drink. I wait for her reply. . . .

Catherine managed to set her personal example in the context of a public problem. Her text illustrates what James Kinneavy calls exploratory, or dialectic, discourse. Like scientific discourse, it is still reality based. However, because the narrator is present as an "inquiring mind" [Helena commented here, "Yes, this should always be the goal"], "there are 'character' intrusions into dialectic writing which are rarely seen in scientific writing" (187). Catherine's character was visible in the vexed representation of her friend, but the expression of her feelings changed from what Flower calls writer-based to reader-based prose. The reader did not feel as if he or she stumbled into someone's private diary. [Helena commented here, "Important for this assignment."] Instead, we read a paper that explored the causes of binge drinking in college, yet we knew why the writer wanted to engage us. Additionally, the revision process, during which she had been asked to figure out why college students binge drink, modified the attitude of the narrator. No longer harshly judgmental of the binge drinker, Catherine simply threw up her hands in incomprehension. Despite her investigation, she claimed not to know why college students drink. Her refusal to declare "objective" knowledge is unusual for freshmen writers, who are usually eager to claim access to "true facts." As I demonstrate below, the exploration seemed to give her more self-confidence in the larger academic arena.

A Woman's Problem with Writing the Traditional Argument Essay

A few weeks later, about two months into the course, Catherine entered the classroom discourse for the first time. Helena began the class by asking how the assignment went (the first draft of an argument paper). Marilyn, a heavyset black woman from an inner city, announced, "My paper is awful." Helena responded, "Well, I can't wait to read it. That's a good place to start!" Then she slapped the table. When the class was told that they would have to pair up and share the drafts, Catherine emoted, "This is so embarrassing." Helena promptly paired her up with Marilyn.

After the peer-response time, the class reconvened to discuss the assigned reading, Clara Spotted Elk's "Skeletons in the Attic." Reprinted from the *New York Times,* Spotted Elk's essay decries the sacrilegious and ignominious way that museums all over the country have desecrated graves and secreted the remains of Native Americans. It ends, "American Indians want only to reclaim and rebury their dead. Is this too much to ask?" (123). Catherine contributed to the lively discussion by introducing information about how the U.S. government gave the Indians blankets infected with smallpox in order to kill them off. [✓]

Something made Catherine forget her normal stance of letting others do the talking; I believe it was the way Helena had been working with her in conference, offering positive feedback and teaching her how to strengthen her writing. Later I praised Catherine for speaking in class; and in her next conference, she told Helena that she felt good about doing so. Nonetheless, she continued true to form. "I'm just really struggling in this class. I think I've ruled out English as a major. I'm kind of running out of opportunities here. This paper is ridiculous." Helena initially told her that she did not have to make a decision regarding her major for a while but eventually did some self-disclosure regarding her own educational background.

Helena: Physics kicks my butt at every turn. Umm, no matter how hard I
    work, you know, I could never get over like a B.
Catherine: Mm hmm.
Helena: In physics. That's just the best that I could do. Umm, but I loved
    physiology because we dissected SHEEP eyes and sheep brains, and I'm
    just very sorry you're eating.
Karen: I'm eating my lunch.
Catherine: [Laughs]
Helena: I'm sorry.
Karen: Well, there goes that.

The element of playfulness seemed to relax Catherine somewhat. Helena communicated to Catherine that we all struggle in some way in the academy.

For Catherine, the rhetorical dilemma raised by the task of producing an argument was one of making some kind of fixed decision.

[✓✓✓✓] As Helena told her, "It seemed to me that because you saw merit on at least two sides of the issues that you didn't have an argument." Catherine responded, "No, I think I had an argument. I just think it's hard for me to write a one-sided paper."

The issue that Catherine brought up is the same one raised in discussions of the subject by contemporary rhetoricians. Recently, feminist theorists have been promoting a revision of the traditional form that argument essays have taken, that is, where one side is right and the other wrong. Pamela Annas and Deborah Tenney state that female students have particular difficulty with this model. "We have learned from female students in this course that they sometimes feel dissociated from the positions they are taking" (128). Annas and Tenney propose a redefinition of argument "as a conversation with people who know how to listen and whose opinion we care about, on a subject we know something about and in which we have a passionate interest" (135). [Helena wrote, "Nice."] Similarly, Marjorie Ford and Jon Ford write, "[T]he dialogic argument acknowledges the importance of creating a bridge between opposing viewpoints that are often rigidly separated in traditional argument" (357).

Helena's approach to Catherine's difficulty with writing "a one-sided paper" was to suggest that Catherine allow the writing process itself to help her resolve her rhetorical dilemma. Helena did not press Catherine to obliterate an opposing point of view but instead to "use the body of the paper to work [her] way toward a decision." Helena repeated two of Catherine's arguments related to the death penalty. "Who are we to judge who lives and dies?" On the other hand, "It hasn't been MY mother, MY grandmother, MY son, who've been murdered by someone else. If it were, I'd probably feel differently."

Helena was suggesting that, by simply drafting the paper, by giving credence and space to different sides of an issue, Catherine would land in a place of cognitive comfort. Rather than help Catherine decide what she "really" thought, Helena essentially told Catherine to trust the process. The student resolved the dilemma by striking a rhetorical pose, constructing a self. In their next conference, Helena told Catherine that she did "a pretty mean job" on the draft. "I could hear your voice throughout; it's not a generic capital punishment paper." Catherine explained her process: "I eventually decided that I didn't have to fully agree with everything and just develop the things that I did agree with. I don't even know if I completely agree with everything I wrote, but for the sake of argument, I figured I could be a radical and do it too."

Their exchange is interesting precisely because it called attention to issues of "voice." Helena could hear Catherine's voice in the paper, but Catherine told Helena that she adopted a persona who took a position, essentially splitting off a side of her self. After writing her analysis paper on college drinking, Catherine expressed dismay over stating opinions that she did not necessarily embrace. Students in Annas's and Tenney's classes said that they felt that they were "engaging in an unethical act if they argue[d] for positions they [did] not believe in" (128). However, after drafting her argument paper, Catherine seemed pleased that she could take a position that might not fully be her own.

In this conference, Helena pushed Catherine to elaborate on alternatives to capital punishment. Since the student believed that people of "lower class . . . have to resort to crime," Helena encouraged Catherine to think of preventive measures and delineated some possibilities, just as she had listed common alcohol-related behaviors in the earlier conference on Catherine's analysis paper. "So other alternatives ARE making sure that everybody receives a fair level of education," Helena began. "That everybody has a chance to get a decent job, that when you work a forty-hour week at McDonald's, it's enough to take care of a family. So maybe raise the minimum wage."

The third draft that Catherine handed in (seventh overall) received an A− and an end comment that read, "Catherine, this piece is a strong, coherent, persuasive argument. You've done a great job here." The paper was clearly argued. Helena requested only word changes and some elaboration in different places.

In the paper, Catherine condemned the death penalty as barbaric ("[H]is lungs implode and his kidneys fail") and as promoting a double standard ("If this were justice, the executioner would then be put on trial and sentenced to death"). [In the margins of a draft of this chapter, Helena glossed, "Such a powerful thought; still striking in the way she articulates it here."] Catherine went on to argue that "the death penalty may actually *stimulate* violence within society." Moreover, "[R]arely are middle[-] or upper-class people sentenced to death." She stated that it was disproportionately applied to people living below the poverty level. Finally, "the death penalty has been recognized by the Supreme Court as being racially biased."

Her alternatives were weak and lacked explanation (e.g., "incarceration with rehabilitation"), but her analysis was strong. "Crime exists because society is unequal in structure, and measures must be taken to correct this." The voice of the narrator was by no means the uncertain one the author presented in her first conference on this assignment. [✓] She wrote, "I am disgusted with the knowledge that this country is saturated with crime, yet our focus is not on the source of the problem." The writer of this essay came a long way from the person who complained about "struggling in the class." ["Nice."]

I think this particular vignette offers an alternative view to the social constructionist critique of the "expressivist" classroom. Despite the fact that the case example shows the student and teacher involved in an extremely personal narrative about the writer and her family, seemingly the kind of solipsism with which Berlin found fault, the matter did not end there. The topic of alcoholism grew beyond Catherine's family to her college community. Eventually, this student, who had seemed to be interested in only one issue, went on to write some pretty strong statements about social and racial injustice. It is my opinion that because she had an opportunity to develop her voice in the arena where she was most comfortable she could then broach socially significant issues other than alcoholism with more confidence and authority. However, the problem was by no means resolved.

Self-Disclosure in Process Pedagogy

The final assignment for the semester was to produce a research paper. Catherine chose as her topic shyness because it was something she sought to change within herself. It was my least favorite of her papers. In spite of her having felt so personally connected to the topic, it was not particularly engaging. In her essay "Between the Drafts," Sommers describes what I experienced when I first read Catherine's essay. "When [students] write about their lives, they write with confidence. As soon as they begin to turn their attention toward outside sources, they too lose confidence, defer to the voice of the academy. They disguise themselves in the weighty, imponderable voice of acquired authority" (29). While this loss of confidence was not the case in the final draft of Catherine's essay on the death penalty, it was initially in her paper on shyness. In fact, in an end comment and in their first conference, Helena specifically requested more of Catherine's voice. For example, she wanted Catherine to critique what she was reading in the textbooks regarding shyness. Helena also thought the paper needed case-study material. Here are some excerpts from the paper, excerpts I selected to reflect the various voices Catherine did eventually assume.

> When the ego has been made "a seat of anxiety," someone is running away from himself and will not admit it. C. G. Jung

> Hell is not restricted to a mere dimension of the afterlife. For many, Hell is found in the threat of everyday conversation. Hell is the tense and knotted stomach, the free-flowing sweat, the unavoidable and embarrassingly scarlet cheeks. . . .
>
> The results of anxiety are both physical and emotional. Physically, changes occur in the autonomic nervous system, controlling involuntary responses with heart rate, respiration, and digestion. During social anxiety one may experience shortness of breath, accelerated heartbeat, sweating, dizziness, nausea, flushes or chills, change in voice, twitches or spasms, and stuttering (Berent [and Lemley] 22). . . .
>
> Excessive reticence does not enable a shy person to present themselves as they are, and may come off as being inhibited to the point of arrogance. . . . [S]hyness is a sociological condition, shaped by life experiences. . . . Parents who displayed nonacceptance in the forms of extreme punishment, severe criticism, and overprotectiveness had children that may be described as shy and self-conscious (Eastburg [and Johnson] 915). . . . A sense of inadequacy established in childhood will repeat over and over in a vicious cycle that continues into adulthood. . . . It goes without saying that shy people do not "display" their true selves. . . .
>
> Shyness is not permanent—It may be healed. . . . Yet unfortunately, shyness continues to pervade the lives of many. There are those who improve, and those who will never change.

This essay had some strengths. The lead paragraph was engaging. Catherine did a good job of integrating and paraphrasing source material without letting the authorities assume preponderance in her essay. The implied author was someone who knew the pain of "social anxiety." It occurs to me that my initial disappointment with the essay may have come not from what is in the text but from what is missing. I wish she had done some research on adult children of alcoholics. Perhaps then there would have been an informing awareness, if not an explicit comment, on her own shyness as stemming partly from a parent "who displayed nonacceptance," the parent who blamed her for his drinking. I am not sure that Catherine would agree with this notion. She might have told me, as Tobin's student did, "[My] paper is now not about that topic" (*Writing* 49). [✓✓✓✓✓ "You're a great writer—just the way you articulate and you phrase."]

Helena's approach to helping Catherine revise was quite personal; each shared feelings about being shy in a lengthy conference. (The transcript is eighteen double-spaced pages long.) By the end of the conference, Helena commented on what she saw as Catherine's diminishing shyness throughout the semester. At several points, just as the discussion seemed to be about to stray completely from the rhetorical, one or the other of them steered the conversation back to the text.

Helena liked the way Catherine integrated her sources, saying it was not "textbooky," but she also suggested that Catherine indicate that the topic meant something to her, but Catherine did not want to.

> I guess the only way that I felt like I could do that is by giving my own experience, and I wasn't sure how to do that . . . 'cause I don't want to take the same kind of . . . like, you know, with, with the one about binge drinking. [Clears her throat] I don't want to try that again.

Helena then suggested that the personal representation could be about another person, so that

> the reader could have an example of, How has this panned out in actual life? . . . Since you mentioned, you know, in some cases, people can reverse it and then some can't. Can you show me one of each? . . . We could look at the reasons why maybe this person was able to kind of reverse it and the other one couldn't.

Catherine's comments here show that she had learned something from the writing process; she had learned that bringing first-person experience into an academic text can create problems. She clearly wanted to avoid the kind of "case study" she did of the friend whose drinking bothered her. [✓] There seemed to be some embarrassment attached to the memory. Helena initially appeared not to have understood Catherine's concern about duplicating a past error, for she suggested that the personal representation be of another person, precisely the problem the student raised. Then Helena tied her suggestion back to the mention in the text of people who have had varying degrees of success with overcoming shyness. By focusing

Catherine on "the reasons" why one person could reverse the problem and another could not, Helena was providing Catherine with a different way of personalizing the paper. Helena was teaching her about the kind of personal experience that is more readily accepted in the academy, where clinically detached case studies have more authority than overly emotional reactions to friends with problems. Yet Catherine resisted.

Helena: If you thought about the people that you know who have changed, would you be able to say what you think they did?
Catherine: [Pause] No, because I think that if I knew what they did, I would be applying it to myself.
Helena: Okay, could you interview one or two of these people?
Catherine: That's the other thing. They're not people that I know. They are people who I've just seen.
Helena: Observed—
Catherine: Observed. I don't, I don't really know them and, you know, they were from my high school and so I don't, I don't talk to them.

Catherine's response invested the rhetorical task with the personal issue that was at stake here. If she had known what people did to overcome shyness, she would have done it herself. She identified the self who was writing the paper as someone who had the problem but did not have the solution. The suggestion Helena made, that she interview people, is right on target; but the problem may have been that Catherine was simply too shy to interview people about shyness. [✓]

About midway through the conference, Helena changed pedagogical tacks. Instead of offering Catherine some suggestions, she described some formerly shy people she knew, such as her mother, now "one of those people that anybody talks to. . . . She's like a people magnet." When she asked her mother how the change had come about, Helena was told that it related to entering the workforce as a payroll clerk when she was in her twenties.

> When something goes wrong with a person's paycheck and you know you've got to be calm, you've got to calm them. She was so busy taking care of other people, she didn't have time to think about her own insecurity. So it was almost as if problem solving kind of distracted her from the problem of her shyness.

Helena's example here was a good one. She was showing Catherine that she understood the problem of shyness and gave an example of someone close to her who changed and why. Yet Helena avoided the problems I raised earlier in reference to Swartzlander's concerns about inappropriate self-disclosure. Helena did not reveal anything about herself that might have made her student uncomfortable. Given that Catherine may have been too shy and too isolated to approach someone she did not know for an interview, the implied suggestion was that she find an informant she was closer to and ascertain that person's perspective, something Catherine did not do in her paper on college drinking.

Later in the conference, Catherine described her own difficulties making friends at college and the inner conflicts she experienced while talking with people. It was one of several moments in which the interpersonal problems of the student were brought into the conference to enrich the revision. Catherine revealed that she questioned whether she was fun to be around and that was precisely what she thought about when she talked to other people. "My thoughts are completely consumed by the idea. Do they even want to be talking with me right now?" A few moments later, Helena disclosed to the student that she felt the same way when she went to academic conferences, but she told herself, "'Well, this person is in EXACTLY the same position that I'm in.' You know they have as much to lose and gain by talking to me as I do to them, so I just kind of take a shot at it."

After this bit of self-revelation, Helena deftly directed the conversation back to the rhetorical task.

> The goal here isn't for us to come up with a cure-all and you know the goal is the research paper. You know it's an opportunity to just think the issue through, and who knows what will come out of that. There may be one teeny tiny [pause] kernel that you can use for yourself you know, umm, or that I can use for myself or [laugh] or some of my shy friends. Umm, the questions that we're asking are important, so back to the questions. You know, What are the techniques that the book lays out and why do you disagree with them? You know? And give a specific critique. That would be something that would add a needed personal dimension to the paper. Okay?

In this interlude in the conference, Catherine felt comfortable enough to describe her awkwardness in social situations, what she was actually thinking that contributed to her difficulty in connecting with people. She had her mind on how they were evaluating her.

Helena responded by sharing how she felt in one of her most trying social situations, meeting people at conferences, and she gave an example of how she talked her way through the anxiety. Helena would tell herself that the people she was meeting were in the same position. Helena was very clear, however, that the main purpose of the exchange in this conference was not to resolve Catherine's interpersonal conflicts but to write an engaging piece of expository prose that might help some people, including the two of them. Yet there was no rigid division between the personal and the rhetorical as the conversation itself might help the student deepen the analysis in her research paper on shyness.

Here is the concluding paragraph Catherine added to her final draft. She took on some authorities.

> I made the decision to research shyness because it is something that affects my life each day and in innumerable ways. I find it hard to believe that relaxation of the muscles and mind can cure internal wounds. How can deep breathing change self views when the road to self love is a process . . . a long and often excruciating one that does not occur overnight. What separates those who heal and those who continue to fear and evade life? I do not pretend to know the answer. I can only speculate that the solution will not be found within the pages of a book, or even in the office of a psychiatrist. Something must change within the shy person. A tiny spark of dignity, or perhaps a trickle of love, but never from an outside source. If a shy person is indeed running from himself, there must be a point when exhaustion halts his depreciating strides. There must be a day when he turns and slowly makes his way, stepping carefully in the other direction, towards and with revelation.

Helena gave the paper an A. In the end comment, she praised Catherine's papers as all reflecting her "voice and personal style." In this draft, Catherine did insert her own assessment of suggested treatments of shyness; she mocked them somewhat for not dealing with the underlying reason for shyness, lack of "self love." However, Helena had suggested that Catherine find some case examples of people who had overcome shyness, and there was no evidence that she had. According to Catherine, healing is something that happens within the individual and not with help from outside sources. I found Catherine's conclusion to be an instance of unsubstantiated wishful thinking and would have preferred a more substantial proposal for treating the core problem that she saw as a dearth of "self love." [✓] The ending seemed to me to have trivialized the topic of shyness.

Conclusion

During the course of the semester, Catherine showed signs of becoming a stronger and more confident writer. Yet each assignment provoked insecurities, many of which were worked through by drafting and revising. While her papers improved, she continued to express self-doubt about her writing abilities. Behind the voice of an increasingly self-assured narrator of the text was the voice of the actual author, problemizing the notion of "authentic voice." [✓] What the student learned would serve her well: she could take a rhetorical stance. [✓✓✓✓] Or, as she put it in relation to her essay on the death penalty, "[F]or the sake of argument, I figured I could be a radical." By thus splitting her actual self or selves from her assumed persona, she could write some effective prose. I suspect that she continued to struggle in her writing assignments for other courses. A writing course has its limits; it cannot heal a wounded ego. ["Yes."]

At the end of the semester, Helena came to my house for dinner. I wanted her to meet both my partner and one of my sons, Derek, who had just graduated from college. When Helena arrived, Derek was outside grilling a steak and smoking a stogie, a habit that has grown in popularity among male college students. Helena came inside and asked me, "What's up with the cigar?" I told her I was trying to "detach," as any reaction from me would probably guarantee a lifelong habit. There was much camaraderie that night, and afterward I wrote in my field notes, "Helena is such a warm and loving person. Have I conveyed this in my chapter? She is so easy to engage with. I hope I know her for the rest of my life." ["Thank you so much; this means a lot to me."]

After dinner, Helena and I talked privately. She described her final conference with Catherine: "I told her what a great person she was; you know, I gave her a string of adjectives. 'Don't be so hard on yourself; the world will be hard enough on you.' Her eyes filled up." Helena's pedagogical approach to Catherine had been very different from her approach to Janet, two women with very different personalities. [✓ "Yes, yes."] Janet came across as very self-assured and needed to learn to listen to received opinion that differed from her own; Catherine was lacking in self-confidence and needed to keep working on challenging received opinion. Helena tried to encourage Catherine to take more power. While the ending to her research paper seemed weak when taken out of the context of her development over the semester, she did create a persona that spoke up for itself and questioned the authorities. She claimed a stake for herself in the discourse about shyness. [Helena commented here, "A really important thing for Catherine."]

When I called Catherine during the summer to request the final draft of her research paper on shyness and to get her feedback on an earlier version of this chapter, I found out that she realized she could not work three jobs as planned. She had, however, signed up for an overload of six courses in the fall, a decision related to her selection of political science as a major. I wondered how much the overtly political content of the course with Helena had influenced that decision. Catherine, still driving and pushing herself to extremes, probably still shy in many social interactions as well, may have become a better person, student, and writer for having taken FWS with Helena. ["Thank you, again."]

Helena's pedagogy problemizes the social constructionist representation and critique of "expressivism." The assigned reading material was not "inconsequential"; it focused on the issues of race and class. She assigned personal narratives; but when she received one that revealed deep trauma, she did not abuse her institutional authority by crossing over the boundary into psychotherapist. Helena was able to be compassionate and still critique sentence-level error. The psychocognitive distance between Helena and her student was appropriate to their subject positions. She assigned more typically academic papers, as well, but she continued to invite Catherine's voice and opinions into the student's work. By building on the rapport established early on in her helping relationship, Helena was able to teach Catherine some notions of how to produce written texts in the modes of analysis, argumentation, and exposition, forms that are more likely to have been required in her other courses. Of course, it was incumbent upon Catherine to recreate as much of the process as possible by revising papers before turning them in. [Helena noted, "I've felt so good while reading this chapter. To some extent, I feel guilty for feeling so good because this is the chapter that praises me. I want to be clear on the fact that I got something out of the Janet chapter—maybe almost equal to the Catherine chapter *because* her case was such a struggle. I did, however, learn so much about what happened with Catherine in the course. I feel good about the chapter because, I think, it confirms one of the main positions I hold about teaching. I don't teach writing, for example, *primarily* out of a love for the subject, but a passion for being part of a student's growth—at least intellectually, and at most . . . the possibilities number more than I thought!"]

6 ❖ DEVELOPING VOICE, DEVELOPING AGENCY

In the last three chapters, I have positioned Helena—the first writing teacher I observed—in the context of the social constructionists' framing of composition. Helena was by no means an inner-directed theorist. Based on the socially significant topics her students chose to write about, the course readings, and the classroom discussions, it would be tough to argue that Helena's teaching is an example of anything like the critical representations of "expressivism." However, the pedagogy of the second teacher I observed—Debby— might at first blush appear to lend itself to such criticisms as "lack[s] . . . social significance" and overemphasizes "the private vision." Debby's course packet had no unifying theme, and only a few handouts were of an explicitly political nature. In one instance, it appeared that she was guiding a student essay away from discussing the political and educational ramifications of racial discrimination and toward an emphasis on a purely personal reaction. In fact, in one class discussion in which some left-wing ideas were aired, Debby seemed uncomfortable and tried to redirect the emphasis. Yet despite these initial appearances, I show that, in the context of developing personalized writing relationships with her students, Debby created an atmosphere in which they could examine the rhetorical effectiveness of their writing and that of their classmates in both an autobiographical and a wider social sense.

A Teaching Philosophy

The second teacher I observed in the spring of 1997 at BC was Debby, a white Jewish faculty member in her mid fifties. She was at the time a thin woman of medium height with light brown hair. Before returning to graduate school, Debby ran a career-counseling center for women. In 1980, she completed her master's degree in English at BC, was offered a position as an adjunct lecturer, and had been teaching in the English department ever since.

Her graduate studies involved only traditional literature courses. At the time, there were no writing classes, and she received no formal training in teaching writing. At first she taught a course called Critical Reading and Writing; students wrote only analytical papers. At the time of my visit, she had been teaching the Prose Writing course for over ten years. For her, this course always involved personal writing, and the approach had the support of the program director. Debby had recently begun to sense that there had been a shift in the program toward what she called "Lexus-nexus," or research writing.[1]

Debby was quite comfortable with autobiographical writing in the academy; she believed that it was an asset to personal growth for her students and strengthened their writing abilities. However, the writing also had to have a purpose for a larger audience. "It isn't just about their own soccer game victory when they were ten," she told me.

> [T]he end result is for them to feel more confident and strengthen who they are. I see it as a personal journey for them. It seems to me that when you read catalogs about what a liberal arts education is supposed to do, it's supposed to create a greater understanding for students of who they are. Very often I wonder if some of the courses they take do integrate the person into the material. Certainly if you look at . . . the courses they take in the English department [at BC], I think there is very little room for them to understand who they are, especially with all those analytical papers. And I am just as guilty of that in my literature course because those are the types of papers I assign, too. But I think there needs to be a place where they can do some self-examining, not just diary writing, because this is a writing course and writing involves an audience, and I think they have to get beyond the personal angst kind of thing. But I really stress them trying to find a voice, their own voice, and I think just in them thinking about themselves in

those terms, there is a transference to who they are as people. I felt that with Tanya; her empowering herself through writing would help her to feel better about herself as a person. (Interview 10 February 1999 ["Tanya" was the only student of color in her class, and their work together is the focus of chapter 7.])

When I asked Debby about possible ethical problems with assigning personal writing, she said that she does not worry about these problems because her students make their own choices in what they write about. She did not require them to write personal narratives.

> In fact it always amazes me, like this last semester[,] the first paper a student wrote was about being physically abused by a past boyfriend. She was very willing to read it in class, and the class was really blown away. It gave permission to a couple of students to write about some other uncomfortable situations that they've been in. I didn't ask her to write that paper.

Debby was as relaxed in her classroom as she was about her students' topics. In Helena's class, I only contributed to the discourse toward the end of the semester; but I found myself talking right away in Debby's, even before checking with her about it. Later she would call on me as if I were just another student. At the end of the semester, I asked Tanya if my taping her conferences and reading her work had had any effect on her. She said that, since I was there from day one, it felt like I was part of the class. "Actually it was good, you know, having you there and giving your side . . . instead of one point of view."[2]

Apparently Helena and Debby talked about how they felt about my studying their classes; Debby told Helena that she expected to be nervous but said that she did not even feel observed after the first few minutes. I do not mean to argue that my research was "objective" and that my observations had no effect. I simply want to point out that there was a relatively high degree of ease regarding my presence, and I attribute this comfort level to the welcoming nature of Debby's classroom. In fact, a friendship developed between us in the course of the research. I was in the midst of negotiating a hostile and combative divorce, and it was helpful to talk privately with Debby and to hear descriptions of her own divorce and its aftermath over the prior fifteen years.

The First Day

I observed Debby teaching a section of what was then called Prose Writing. This course was limited to fifteen students, from sophomores to seniors. In her section, there were ten females and five males. Class time was spent discussing the week's reading and workshopping students' essays. Debby would often present a mini-lecture on some writing-related topic. Although the program director discouraged teaching the formal modes of discourse in this course, Debby felt the need for some structure. She reached a compromise by assigning some reading on the modes, lecturing on them, and inviting, without requiring, the students to try their hands at, for example, process analysis or argument papers. In fact, she never gave any specific writing assignments other than to pass in an essay each week. Most of the student texts I saw were personal narratives, essays that involved experiences from childhood or about such topics as volunteer work in Appalachia. "Mark" was the only student to write a third-person expository essay, and the subject was Albert Einstein.

The readings for the class were initially engaging: Lois Lowry's *The Giver* and Tobias Wolff's *This Boy's Life: A Memoir*. Lowry's young adult novel is set in a futuristic would-be utopian society that has found a way to sanitize itself by suppressing human emotional responses. Clearly Debby did not want class members to imitate this invented society in their writing. In fact, throughout the semester, I heard her comment on student papers in conference, "I'm not sure how you are feeling here."

In the class on the Lowry novel, Debby asked her students to make a list of childhood memories and told them that no one else would see the list. Then they were to freewrite on one particular episode. "I want to encourage you to tap into your memories." She wanted them to search for what Virginia Woolf calls "moments of being," epiphanous moments in their lives. The memory exercise was a vehicle for invention. Yet she did not want her students to see the exercise as a mandate to produce autobiographical essays. "Just because it's a memory, doesn't mean it has to be a personal narrative. It could become exposition."

She asked the students to consider issues of representation in narrative. "How do you write about something that happened when you were ten now? How do you write about it from the perspective of a ten-year-old? Don't you impose your twenty-year-old self on the ten-year-old?" Like Georges Gusdorf, Debby complicated the autobiographical persona who was not a simple reproduction of the self being described. Gusdorf writes, "The man who remembers his past has not been for a long time the same being . . . who lived that past" (38). Or, as Robert Graham puts it, "The protagonist cannot know what the narrator knows, namely, his own future" (23). So rather than perpetuate notions of a unified self, as "expressivists" are accused of doing by social constructionists, Debby immediately made her students aware that the writer self is not the same as the subject self.

Furthermore, in a discussion about the difference between creative writing and nonfiction, she asked the class to consider what is truth. "Have you ever heard a sibling tell a different version of something that happened? Perhaps psychological truth is more important than whether or not all the characters were in the room at the same time." Psychological truth apparently varies according to perspective. By way of example she gave the class two descriptions of a murderer, one from the *New York Times* and the other from the *Daily News*. While I saw the comparable pieces as exercises in psychological perspective, Debby explained to me that she actually introduced them "to show how you write differently for a different audience."

Subsequent reading came from a variety of handouts and an anthology she assembled. While Helena's course packet, the McGraw-Hill Primis reader, had a clear antiracist focus, Debby's did not, although there were some overtly political pieces. Unlike her literature classes, which had a strong multicultural emphasis, her Prose Writing classes never had a particular theme. The handouts were offered only as strong writing samples. Gay Talese's "New York" is filled with odd bits of information, such as the number of stray cats in the city. Patricia Smith's column from the *Boston Globe,* "Label It What It Is: Racism," deals with a black couple falsely accused of shoplifting in an expensive clothing boutique. Jo Goodwin Parker's "What is Poverty?" gives the reader a detailed description of what it is like to be poor from the perspective of someone who is living in poverty.

In the first class, Debby went over the course syllabus. Under "purpose and organization," she wrote,

Prose Writing is a unique course that focuses on your own writing and is designed to help sharpen your writing skills, especially in the areas of: finding a subject, establishing a purpose, providing specific information, addressing an audience, choosing the most effective form, developing a voice and style, and editing to achieve greater clarity and focus.

Since the course was based on weekly fifteen-minute conferences with each student, Debby asked them to think about their work beforehand.

Where have you achieved what you set out to achieve? Where does your paper still need work? What are its strengths and weaknesses? Is the subject too small or too large? Is there a clearly defined audience for the paper? What is the relationship between your form and your purpose? Which paragraphs, sentences, and words need revision?

In the first class, Debby also read from a separate document called "Course Overview and Philosophy," which consisted of excerpts from Donald Murray's *Learning by Teaching.*

The layman believes, and most often writes badly himself because of it, that the writer has a complete thought or vision he merely copies down, acting as a stenographer for the muse. . . . For most writers the act of putting words on paper is not the recording of a discovery, but the very act of exploration itself.

Writing, then, is thinking.

One exercise the first day included asking the students to write and then talk about their reasons for signing up for the class and what they hoped to accomplish. Many students made a similar point: they were tired of the kind of writing they had been doing at BC, writing that they felt merely asked them to regurgitate already published information. They wanted to find their own voices. Here are some excerpts from their comments.

Ann Marie (communication/English major; journalist for a campus newspaper): I want to write for a living. I want to develop my distinct voice. Writing helps you develop who you are.
Tanya (elementary education major): Writing is my weakness because of grammatical errors.
Lisa (psychology major): 90% of writing in college is really research papers.
Rachel (English major): I miss the Freshman Writing Seminar. I am kind

of tired of always having to have a thesis or always writing research papers.[3]

Jackie (history major; was to enter law school the following semester): I don't know if I like to write. I've written a lot of papers but they don't come from me; they come from what I have been studying. I want to find my voice.

Pete (philosophy major; exempted from freshman writing): I haven't done any creative writing since third grade. I need the freedom to experiment, the tools for effective writing, and the discipline to do it.

Mark (philosophy major): I love ideas and want to learn how to communicate them.

Emily (English major; wrote for campus newspaper; exempted from freshman writing): I felt lucky to avoid the portfolio that everyone [in freshman writing] was flipping out over last year. I like creative writing and haven't been doing any in college. I have only been writing critical essays.

My impression from these comments is that Prose Writing had a reputation on campus as being a place where one could experiment with style and voice without worrying about satisfying the rigorous demands usually placed on them in courses that required more text-based research. Tanya, the only African American student in the class, was also the only one to express a more traditional goal: to improve her grammar. The story behind that concern would unfold during the semester.

Mark: From *The Swiss Family Robinson* to Albert Einstein

Mark, a philosophy major, told the class that he loved ideas and wanted "to learn how to express them." He produced a range of papers, from a trenchant essay on a former neighbor to a traditional piece of expository prose on Einstein, and workshopped both essays in class.[4] Mark described the first paper to me as having "a rich emotional, philosophical theme." In "Salvaging Ten," the narrator reported how he and his friends created their own version of *The Swiss Family Robinson* by foraging for essentials on property belonging to a man named Marvin. Mark offered his audience two views of Marvin, one called "Ten" and the other "Twenty." In "Ten," the narrator described how "the family" (his group of ten-year-old friends) would borrow items they "needed" with Marvin's permission, but eventually a "covert operation" developed. The text read,

"His dwindling sanity provided opportunities for us; when Marvin wasn't around, we might take a few extra bricks." Marvin joined the game, pretending to chase them. "[S]omehow he never caught us, but let the suspense build and provided the excitement that our invisible 'Enemy' did not."

In the section called "Twenty," the narrator offered a different portrayal of the character of Marvin.

> This past winter, when I was home for Christmas, I heard Marvin's story for the first time. While I was at college, our neighbor Matt found Marvin freezing and starving amidst the stacks of newspapers he filled his house with. It was from Matt that I heard how, late one quiet night some thirty years before, Marvin's wife had woken up and left with their kids. Matt said the dishwasher had not been unloaded since the last night Marvin had seen his family.

Playing on the image of Marvin as the collector of neighborhood trash, Mark concluded his essay,

> At ten I was fascinated with broken shovels and sneaking around the bushes, just as Marvin [a bank employee] had been absorbed in numbers. At twenty I know the taste of regret and the thirst to salvage my mistakes, what Marvin learned the morning he woke up in an abandoned house.

The paper also informed us that Marvin's son returned home after a thirty-year estrangement and placed Marvin in a nursing home close enough to where his son lived to allow frequent visits.

After Mark read the first draft, Debby asked the class, "What are some of the problems in this paper?"; and later, "Is it about [the narrator] or about Marvin?" One student felt the paper jumped too abruptly between the two perspectives; another student said, "It lacks a personal touch." After Mark read the second draft, Ann Marie commented, "It is a paper about what is salvageable," yard debris and human relationships. The comments felt very distant, and in my field notes I wrote, "There is a real focus on the writing in this class. . . . [There are] no comments on the fact that this is a very sad story."

Mark informed the class that he had had a dream the night before the workshop. He related it to the fact that Debby had repeatedly asked him what the paper was about. "I didn't know what to say because I wasn't sure so I had this dream that I told my father I was writing this paper about Marvin and he asked me, 'Who is it about?'" Debby laughed and declared, "So now I am a father figure!" When I interviewed Mark about two weeks later, he reported that in an actual telephone conversation, he had told his father that he was writing about Marvin. When his father had asked him what the essay was about *in the dream,* Mark told him that the paper was about him, his father.

Feeling too awkward to "share a deep, personal feeling with [his] father over the phone," he mailed the essay to his family.

> My sister called me when she finally read it. She said she thought it was wonderful, and my mom thought it was great. Umm, I don't remember my dad commenting on anything specifically. . . . [Laughs] But, you know, it's not like he would say, "That was the most wonderful thing in the world. Give me a hug." . . . But, I mean, I know he's very proud of me.

When I last saw Mark, near the end of the semester, he was writing an essay on his father that was inspired by a classmate's essay on her grandfather.

The scenario reminds me of Janet's showing her mother the paper on the rift in their family. The writing task inadvertently served to connect home and school cultures, in effect bringing the family system to college. Mark's link to his family over the Marvin narrative was a natural consequence of a course in which he was free to choose his own writing topics. Debby had not asked him to write about Marvin or to tell his family about the essay, just as Helena had not asked Janet to write the paper about the feud with her grandmother or to show it to her mother. The students made these choices, and the important connections they made with their families of origin as a result seemed to be beneficial. In this small way, these students not only avoided the distance that often occurs between a child and his or her family when the former matriculates, but the parties also came together around an issue that had been submerged in the annals of family life.

Incidentally, when a student is the first in the family to go to college, that student's enrollment can initiate a process where class differences arise and academia serves to split the student off from his or her working-class roots. Family-based narratives can work against these kinds of class antagonisms within the family, although in these two cases there were no specific class issues that I am aware of.

Debby believed that some courses in the academy should "integrate the person with the material," and that was what happened in her Prose Writing Seminar. In the first class of the semester, Debby had talked about how "truth" might change if we were to write about something when we were ten and then again when we were twenty. Based on recent reports on a neighbor, Mark came up with an essay from those two different age perspectives. His family knew the subject, Marvin. Through writing about Marvin and sharing the essay with his teacher, his classmates, and ultimately his family, Mark integrated his academic work with his personal life. He felt his family's support for him in their affirmations. After all, he was writing about a subject they knew well, and they could see how carefully he had treated it. How often is it that our students' families can really evaluate the kind of work their children are doing in schools for which they are paying a great deal of money? Here at least, Debby created a forum to integrate the person and his family into the course material.

Later in the semester, Mark workshopped an expository essay entitled "The Unread Einstein." The author's intention was to bring to light Einstein's thought and writings outside of science. Drawing on Einstein's books *The World As I See It* and *Out of My Later Years,* Mark argued that Einstein wanted scientists to think about the impact of their work on society. Einstein's "thought was pervaded by the notion that increases in freedom constitute progress." In the essay, Mark never defined the word *freedom*. Furthermore, Mark was absent from his text and there were no specific examples. In short, I found it to be a promising essay that ultimately failed to sustain my interest.

Mark immediately told his classmates, "I didn't write this for you guys." He had written the paper to apply for an internship and had already turned it in. The class seemed to feel somewhat cheated by not having had a chance to offer input earlier. As Jackie put it, "This is a workshop!" Nonetheless, the class engaged with the content of the essay and brought a fair amount of knowledge to the table.

Debby began the discussion by asking Mark to name the audience and learned that it was the Union of Concerned Scientists. Debby told him, "Well, that's important because we are going to evaluate it from that perspective." Yet Mark seemed uncomfortable, aware that his essay was different from those of his classmates. In fact, they had already workshopped two more personal papers that day, one by Jackie on a private school she had attended in Texas and a humorous piece by Tanya on observing her sister give birth. Mark apologized, "It's not a personal narrative like the other two." Debby told him that was okay, but he continued, "So it's not immediately interesting." The class laughed at this point, but Mark added, "Einstein's thought I find very exciting personally."

Once the discussion of the essay began, Jackie immediately challenged Mark's thesis that Einstein was highly moral. "Wasn't he one of the people who instigated the research for the atomic bomb?" "Ned" confirmed her statement, saying that Einstein had written a letter to Franklin Delano Roosevelt. Jackie announced that she had seen the letter and that it said something like "other people might start developing this, and we need to develop it to protect ourselves." Debby then pointed out that when the atomic bomb was used, Einstein "was almost sorry that he had been involved in the development of it."

While Mark had anticipated that his classmates would not find the essay interesting, they actually examined it quite closely. Brian asked about whether the first letter of a discipline (such as physics or economics) ought to be capitalized, and the class observed Mark's inconsistency here. Other students asked about his thesis. Mark told them, "I am writing it more from the angle of just kind of an analytic or an expository paper on Einstein's thought." Debby countered, "But even his thoughts in your paper should have a thesis." The thesis, according to Mark, was that Einstein "claims that science must intelligently and responsibly engage with its social world." Kathy then pointed out that her calculus teacher at BC had taught them that "the scientific world kind of pushed Einstein out because they started believing in quantum physics." Students asked questions about the goals of the Union of Concerned Scientists and suggested ways to connect these goals with some of what Mark was highlighting in Einstein's work. They were explicitly thinking of how to persuade his particular audience. As the discussion came to a close, Mark asked for a bit more help.

Mark: Are there specific parts that are unclear or vague or you think—
Debby: I suppose if there were places where we were really lost, we would have noticed that. I think generally for a difficult subject you did a really good job of clarifying it. . . . I'm impressed with the class that you can go from the variety here from Jackie's to Tanya's to Mark's, that we can really deal with this wide range of different subjects. . . .

135

Karen: I think that more quotes from Einstein, umm, shorter, sharper quotes
would liven it up . . . to really convince me that Einstein is the kind of
guy you say he is. I'm not completely convinced.

Mark: That's a good point. . . .

Debby: Okay. Good job, everybody.

Despite the fact that many of his classmates had commented
energetically about the essay, I wondered if Mark had continued to
feel somewhat "less than" by being the only student to workshop
an expository essay. The opposite seemed to be the case. In an interview with me a few weeks later, he described his paper as being
"formal" and "dense." With laughter, he declared, "I boast and say
[it was] a seminal paper, and most of the papers were personal narratives or light, casual reflections." Mark, rather than having felt
less than for not presenting a personal narrative, reported that he
had worried that he might have seemed "flashy" or as if he had been
"showing off." "And I did feel a little uncomfortable. Some people
didn't comment as much as they might have, as they had on other
papers. But some people felt right at home and told me what they
thought." He recalled that Jackie and three male students (Pete,
Brian, and Ned) had the most to say.

Apparently Pete, another philosophy major, had come up to him
some time after the class and said, "Oh, boy, I was excited to finally
have a paper about ideas I could argue with. But it was pretty tight
so I couldn't really [argue.]" Since Mark expected people to be "put
off by the essay rather than intrigued by it," he was especially surprised when he ran into Tanya on campus later that day and she told
him how interesting she found his essay. "'I didn't understand all
of it, but I didn't even know [Einstein] wrote about that other kind
of thing or thought about that stuff.'"

I asked Mark in this same interview what the relationship was
between the kind of writing he was doing in Debby's class and the
kind of writing he was doing in other classes.

> You know I'm a philosophy major, and I like to think of myself as a
> major philosopher sometimes. [Laughs]. I love thinking about funda-
> mental things and the meaning and value of the universe, et cetera. In
> my philosophy classes often those kinds of ideas are sparked. How-
> ever, I have to usually write papers talking about text and what Marx
> said or what Plato said or what Einstein said. I much prefer to do my
> own thinking. . . . [S]o I kind of want to write about the important
> ideas that changed the way you live and think about things.

Mark went on to say that it was easier for him to do "his" kind of philosophy in a public-speaking class he was taking that semester than in Prose Writing. In the public-speaking course, the audience was "clear" and he knew when he was to give an evocative, informative, or persuasive speech and how to "tailor the wording to them." He noted that there was less structure and direction in his writing class and that it was not clear who the audience was. Furthermore, he always needed to be asking himself what he wanted to write about. This lack of direction in terms of assignments seemed to make him uneasy, but later in our conversation, he declared,

> I think this class is great because there's more freedom for you to explore than there is in most classes. . . . In the public-speaking class . . . the goal was to get you to convey things clearly. And what most people conveyed was stuff they heard on the news. There's nothing really interesting. But this [writing] class has a very artistic and personal developmental goal.

Mark's essays took on a variety of forms. He first wrote a narrative about Marvin, then an argument paper in the form of a letter to the editor, then the expository Einstein paper, and, at the time of our interview, he was writing a personal essay about his father. Mark was taking the class as pass/fail and confessed in the interview, "I mean, I didn't put my all into this class. It wasn't a real center. I do feel that I just touched upon developing my writing." Despite this feeling of not having put much into it, there was an ineffable achievement.

> I feel more competent as a writer just from doing it. The sentences flow more easily. . . . You know, writing something like that Marvin paper is great because I think it's philosophy, but it makes it accessible to everyone and personalizes it. Writing that kind of thing I'd like to do again.

I wondered where his feeling of confidence came from, so I asked him.

Karen: Is [the confidence] the result of writing a paper and having close one-on-one attention revising it . . . having it displayed in the classroom?

Mark: The public thing I think is a big part of it. Even just the stuff I had published in the *Observer* [a conservative campus newspaper] I feel good about that. Part of it is my own evaluation. I read it and I say, "Boy, that's good." . . . When you see yourself write something that's clear and flows and is somewhat snappy and it holds together, that feels good.

Mark also credited the public reading for his enhanced confidence. He was looking to see how the audience would take his work. "When you see the public opinion of the class, of four or five people saying the same thing. . . . If they say something good, that's affirming."

In a self-evaluation turned in to Debby with his portfolio, Mark wrote that he wanted to develop "a sharpness of wit" in his writing that paralleled Gilbert Keith Chesterton's. His final statement praised the class.

> This has been one of my best classes at BC; it has involved me and all that I have learned here more personally than any other class I have taken. The freedom of creativity and direction this class allowed is closer to the goals of college than most of the other classes I have taken. I found this freedom daunting, at times, since it does not provide easy steps for one to mechanically follow. This was a very good thing, and the professor and the structure of the class provided a degree of guidance, which was very helpful. Thank you.

In her *Sourcebook for Teachers of Writing,* Patricia Roberts argues that "because [students] are most familiar with the narrative structure a personal essay often involves, students have an easy time organizing their expressive papers" (158). Mark apparently did not find writing narratives to be easy. In fact, he found it to be more challenging than writing papers about the thinking of famous philosophers. So did his classmate Jackie, the woman who was upset that he brought his Einstein paper to class after turning it in for an internship application. She told me, "I feel much more comfortable in writing analysis papers because there is almost more of a formula to them and there's a security in that formula that I think personal narratives don't have." While what they perceived as "freedom," seemed daunting at first, both students felt pleased and empowered by their efforts. Debby had never told her students that her goal was for them to find their rhetorical voices as a way to achieve personal agency. Nor had she ever told them that she wanted a course that integrated the person into the material, but this was precisely what happened for Mark, Jackie, and the subject of my next chapter, Tanya.

7 ➤ "AFRICAN AMERICANS HAVE THIS SLANG"
Grammar, Dialect, and Racism

As a result of the civil rights movement in the 1960s, many predominantly white colleges and universities began to increase the number of students of color on campus. White students who had never lived near or attended school with students of color were now doing so. Black students who had grown up almost entirely among other black people were now living and attending classes with white students. While efforts to integrate remain admirable, one result has been that students of color are often in the minority. In the English Department at BC, it was not uncommon to have only one black student in the required core literature class of thirty-six. When a faculty member would describe some issue related to these demographics, the initial response was often "Welcome to BC."[1]

In the context of describing my qualitative study, which challenges the social constructionist textual representation of "expressivist" pedagogy as naive, modernist, self-centered, apolitical, and asocial, I have selected Tanya, the only student of color in Debby's class, as a way of highlighting what can happen given imbalanced racial demographics. One effect is that among the many personal essays that Tanya and her classmates produced that semester was an important one on the issue of race. Because of the close working relationship she developed with her white teacher, Tanya was able to write an essay about a troubling experience, her student teaching practicum in a wealthy white suburb where criticism of her language usage was a metonym for racism. As I trace the progression of Tanya's writing over the semester, I revisit the problem of teaching grammar in the process-writing classroom. In addition, I discuss white teachers' overt and covert biases against the use of Black English. My conclusion emphasizes the importance of working through humiliating educational experiences in the professional formation of young teachers. Debby and I disagreed about some things along the way, but we agreed on the outcome: the Prose Writing Seminar provided a positive educational experience for Tanya. With the exception of the limited work done with grammar, Tanya agreed. (I incorporate Debby's oral and e-mail responses to an early draft of this chapter throughout my text.)

The First Hurricane

Tanya, a husky and dark-skinned African American senior who grew up in an inner city in Connecticut, could be either very subdued or rather excitable. Her attire was typical of many college women at the time: she often wore a baseball cap; she also donned a bright yellow and black jacket, which said "Ignacio Volunteers," a reference to a Jesuit missionary program sponsored by the school. When talking about a painful subject, one of Tanya's cheeks would twitch slightly. She was raised by her grandmother, who died when she was a senior in high school.

Tanya's first essay described Hurricane Gloria from the perspective of her ten-year-old self. The memory occurred as a flashback as an older self was locking up a house preparing to move. She watched the storm warnings on television while her grandmother and an aunt, with whom she was living, were at work. Another aunt dismissed her worries. After her grandmother returned, the narrator began to implement the advice she had seen on television to make the house secure: checking food supplies, filling the bathtub with water, and taping the windows so they would not break under the force of the 150-mile-an-hour winds. At the end, the narrator returned to the present, as the family was about to move. "Now the security from the storm has disappeared. I turned to the car leaving behind the tiny windows of the sun porch. I felt the fear surging inside once I entered the car."

Debby did most of the talking during their first conference. She pushed Tanya for explicitness around what she was feeling at the time of the hurricane. "I need to be a little bit more in touch with how YOU feel," such as when her aunt told her to relax about the hurricane and when it seemed like such a long wait for her grandmother to come home. "As each thing happens, I want to know your feelings because that's what this paper's about, right?" Tanya did not question these requests.

Whereas I thought Tanya's feelings were clearly communicated through actions, such as hurriedly taping windows, Debby wanted Tanya to name the emotions. At one point in the conference, Debby told Tanya that she might want to write "My grandmother made me feel better, but not THIS time." Moreover, Debby took the first draft at face value, that the hurricane was about a time when Tanya felt insecure, a time when she acted to try to make herself feel safe, just as she wanted to feel safe again when they moved. She did not probe any deeper into Tanya's history or ask if the reader needed to know why she was living with her grandmother. I wondered if the insecurity she felt about the storm was related to the absence of her mother. At the end of the semester, I would learn that the insecurity around moving *was* metonymic for insecurity around another experience, but not the one I imagined.[2]

Months later, I asked Debby about why she did not explore the narrator's living circumstances. She responded:

It felt important to me to get her to write a paper that she felt good about. Clarity and focus seemed like important issues to deal with in her writing. I didn't want to open up new possibilities in this paper that might muddy up the waters or might bring up new issues that I thought she might have trouble incorporating into this paper. I was thinking of [the] Langston Hughes story "Salvation," in which he mentions he lives with his aunt, but never goes into any explanation of that because that's not the purpose of his story. Of course, you might say his losing faith could be connected to his living situation, just as you could say (did, in fact) that Tanya's feeling of insecurity might be related to living with her grandmother. I just thought it was too heavy for her to get into in this paper, and I wanted her to have a success. In addition, she was just not adjusting well to class yet and since I was trying to build up a comfortable relationship with her, I didn't want to ask her about her grandmother at this time. *I didn't want her to have to explain to another white teacher why she was different from the other kids in the class.* (E-mail 3 October 1997, emphasis mine)

Tanya actually began to adjust to the class in her conferences with Debby by speaking up. Instead of continuing to assent to whatever Debby suggested regarding her hurricane paper, she complimented herself. "All right. I really liked my point. I don't know. I guess the point where you catch the reader. I really liked that part of my paper. I don't know." Although Tanya's self-praise was broken up twice by statements reflecting self-doubt ("I don't know"), she had stepped out of the role of subservient student listening carefully to what her teacher wanted changed.

The final draft of Tanya's paper showed some changes along the lines Debby had urged, that is, naming feelings. Tanya added words like *nervous* and *panic,* as well as more description about her grandmother's return home.

> I finally heard the clicking of the lock; it was my grandmother. I ran and gave her a hug as if it had been years since I had seen her. I was so happy and anxious that I tried to tell her about the storm all in one breath. She nodded her head vigorously, giving me a clue that she knew and that was why she was home early. Screaming and waving my arms about, I told her I was watching the news and we had to prepare our home for the storm.

Tanya chose to focus the narrative time on an event experienced by her ten-year-old self. She deliberately left out anything about how she came to live with her grandmother even though her mother was alive. She also did not anticipate the future death of her grandmother in the essay. However, Tanya did add more descriptive details in her final draft, and she revised the conclusion. She was looking back at the house, remembering the storm, as they prepared to move to a new one.

> I was so proud of myself for protecting the house. Now that we are leaving the house forever, the only security I have are the memories. I turned away from the house and felt unprotected because of the long journey ahead to our new home.

Tanya affirmed her younger self in the essay ("I was so proud of myself") in the same way that she had done in the conference when she said, "I really liked my point." I saw these assertions as a good sign, coming as they did from someone who had not yet spoken up in class. I would soon learn how much her self-confidence had recently been eroded in an academic setting.

The METCO Program: Dialect and Racism

Tanya's next paper dealt with a student teaching experience in a wealthy white suburb. In it we learned that she was the only black teacher in the school. There were eleven black students voluntarily bused in each day from the inner city in a program called METCO (Metropolitan Council for Educational Opportunity). A few of these students were in Tanya's classes. The racial dynamics at this school exactly replicated her situation at BC at large, where students of color constituted a minority, and replicated her situation in the microcosm of the Prose Writing classroom, where she was the only student of color. Just drafting the paper seemed to have had an impact on her classroom demeanor.

After she had written the paper, but before her conference with Debby, Tanya arrived in class with a new hairstyle sans baseball cap. Someone had worked from 5:00 P.M. until dawn the next day putting her hair in cornrows. She spoke up early in a discussion about O. J. Simpson: "Compare O. J.'s car chase to that of an ordinary citizen." Debby and the class laughed a bit, but her point was not pursued. When Tanya spoke again, Ned, a critical and competitive white male student, interrupted her, not letting her finish. A few minutes later, Debby corroborated Ned's point. I was disturbed and wrote in my field notebook, "If Debby wants a quiet student like Tanya to speak up, she has to provide her field support, give her space, and hold Ned back." On the other hand, Tanya was active in peer group later in class. I noted, "Tanya presents for her group. Yes! She was not silenced."

Tanya's paper on her teaching practicum began as a personal narrative but moved into a critique of the METCO program. Here are some unedited excerpts from the first draft, which was discussed later that afternoon:

> Have you ever felt misplaced or misunderstood? Or felt as if no one cared or could relate to your feelings? Well I can honestly answer yes to both of these questions. This past semester I had the opportunity to face these challenges in my placement at the Nixon School.
> During my teaching experience at the General Nixon School, I have

143

contemplated being an African-American in a predominantly all white institution. I found it extremely hard because this was not my goal nor was it the reason I decided to do my practicum at this school. . . .

The students did not call me Miss Evans because during the introduction the guidance counselor referred to me as Tanya Evans. The students felt it was okay to use my first name. This did not bother me until I realized that many of the [METCO] students thought of me as an older sister and not a teacher! . . .

I tried my hardest to think and be positive about Nixon. However, I kept thinking about the students who are part of the METCO program. . . . Who does the student turn to when they have issues that a teacher can not answer? . . . Are these students having the same feelings I am? Are they feeling lonely, alienated, unconnected to the school socially? . . .

[Several paragraphs followed about the history of METCO in the community, information she acquired by going to speak with the school principal. She wanted to know why there were so few METCO students in the school.]

Even though there are many issues that students have to face, I believe that the classroom teacher plays a major role in their life. They can either empower students or disable them. I am not too familiar with all the METCO students but in my classroom we make it our business to respect other cultures and be are [sic] of stereotypes and racial misconceptions of a certain race. I think that all future teachers should be aware of cultural and socially [sic] differences.

I thought this first draft was an interesting mix of the personal and the political, a weaving together of her subjective responses, the difficulties experienced by the METCO students, and a critique of the program as it then existed. The writer, however, did not seem to be aware of a contradiction in her feelings. On the one hand, she wanted to be respected as a teacher and not as "an older sister." On the other hand, she closely identified with the predicament of being a black student in a white environment. She asked, "Are these students having the same feelings I am?"

Debby's initial questions about the paper had to do with focus. I perceived Debby as wanting the paper to either be a personal-experience essay or be a critique of the METCO program. Tanya disagreed. My field notes, written after the conference, read, "Debby plays it close to the vest regarding her feelings about METCO. . . . Tanya more animated than I've ever seen her. She interrupts Debby a lot. This is her turf. . . . When she talks about the difficulties of being at BC, her face twitches."

The two interlocutors positioned themselves fairly quickly in a conference that took place in the basement cafeteria of the building where the class was held. The room, as usual, was noisy. Debby told her, "And then I lose you completely. Then you're describing the METCO program. So then it becomes like an expository paper all about this information about METCO, and I don't know where you're fitting in." Tanya responded that that dual focus was her intention. "That's what I wanted it to mean. Like me telling the story about the program, but yet at the same time like I felt part of the program, you know, feelings like misplaced and having some of the same feelings like some of the kids that they had there." Then Debby repeated her point: "You are spending so much time explaining the program that I lose where you're connected to it. And then at the end you end up with almost like an argument paper, 'I think our future teachers should be aware of cultural and social differences.'"

Debby came across to me here as having traditional notions about the discreteness of rhetorical forms and being troubled by more hybrid discourse. Because she was attempting to narrow the student's focus to Tanya's experience and feelings, I initially saw Debby as limiting the implications of that experience, as well as the scope of the paper. Why should a personal lead not take us forward into a public critique of a long-standing education program? Isn't one of the recommended exordiums, or introductions, of the Aristotelian Edward P. J. Corbett the anecdotal lead, the introduction narrative, which "rouse[s] interest in our subject by adopting the anecdotal lead-in . . . one of the oldest and most effective gambits for seizing the attention of the reader" (286)?

Debby responded to my assessment on two different occasions. In an e-mail, she wrote,

> I thought the paper would be much more interesting if it came out of her own feelings, rather than a critique of METCO that anyone could write. What happened to her gave her ideas about METCO more credibility and I thought they would appear more powerful to the reader. I also sensed that she wanted to tell the story of what happened to her at Nixon, and so I thought it was important to find a way to incorporate her own experiences and use them as evidence for why the program doesn't work so well.

Then, after Debby had read the first draft of this chapter, she wanted to let me know that she was not being "slavish" to the rhetorical forms.

> I couldn't tell from that paper whether she wanted to write a paper purely criticizing METCO or whether she wanted to talk about her own experience. And it's true very often they blend, but they've got to connect in some way. Her first draft was not connecting. There was this HUGE section in the middle that was totally expository, whereas the beginning was so personal. Didn't she start off with questions? "Do you ever feel like?" But then she never carried through with that. (Interview 24 December 1997)

Debby also believed that Tanya was not using the personal narrative as simply a rhetorical device to introduce the paper and capture the reader's attention.

> That beginning was VERY troubled. . . . She raised a lot of emotional issues that she never really followed through with, and it was almost, it seemed to me, as if she started with those other things and either got so caught up in them or emotionally charged by them and then had to back off and kind of HIDE her feelings by dealing with the sort of expository aspect as a way to feel more comfortable with it. Maybe she was a little NERVOUS [that] she had gone too far.

Thus Debby argued that she was not opposed to blending the forms, but she felt that Tanya's first draft did not succeed in connecting the personal material with the expository critique of the program.

While our perceptions differed on the first draft, we both agreed that Tanya's final draft did successfully blend the dual rhetorical purposes in the paper. Their conference on the METCO essay, which was lengthy, went way beyond their differences over the paper's focus. Eventually Tanya discussed why she had chosen to attend BC, placing herself in a minority position not unlike the METCO students she was writing about. She also described an interaction at her practicum that had humiliated her. Before these revelations, Debby had asked Tanya a number of questions about how METCO operated in the school. The conversational pattern took the form of Debby asking a question and Tanya giving a brief response. Sometimes Debby would make statements regarding her student's feelings and wait for a confirmation. When Debby told Tanya that she did not want to "put words in her mouth," it did at times appear that Debby was doing just that, but her words emerged largely from the essay itself. However, the question and monosyllabic response pattern broke down as Tanya began to describe more things than she had revealed in the paper. As she revealed more, she became less compliant.

I think the change came about as a result of Debby showing that she was compassionate toward Tanya's position as a person of color who was outnumbered by white people in this elementary school. Initially Debby had presented herself as so impartial toward METCO that she could have been taking testimony from a witness. However, when Tanya blurted out that she was the only black teacher at the school, Debby's empathy revealed itself in a metaphor she introduced. "You are in this kind of sea of white teachers or nonblack teachers, and there are these eleven kids . . . in that same experience." It was just after the use of this image of a sea of white teachers that Tanya began to do more than passively respond to Debby's direct questions. Tanya introduced incidents into the conversation that were not reported in the text. As she did so, both participants in the conference became agitated, their speech rapid, and they often cut each other off. I found their conversation hard to follow and am still not sure of several passages, even after listening to the tape a number of times. I could not always distinguish Tanya's point from Debby's restatement of it. When Tanya became excited, two things happened. First, she did not completely describe situations so that her audience (Debby and I) could understand them, using what Linda Flower might call writer-based speech. There were frequent elisions and an absence of causality. Conclusions were left unsaid. I suspected that she also wanted to avoid labeling situations racist to her white audience. Debby, perhaps attempting clarification, often interrupted Tanya before I could tell if she might have explained situations more fully. Debby commented here,

> I think [the interrupting] had to do with my often not understanding what she was getting at. And also time constraints. There was a conference after her. Right? I was trying to get her to the point. . . . She doesn't always tell the story, as you know, in a way. . . . You don't hear the pieces. (Interview 24 December 1997)

Here is an excerpt of the transcript of this difficult conversation:

Tanya: Umm, but what I was going to say, like, there were different like incidents like I was involved in [with?] METCO students. Like, one day it was lice check and—

Debby: Who told you to do that?

Tanya: I didn't. No, they were doing lice checks in the whole entire school.

Debby: Oh.

Tanya: They pulled the braids out of this [black] girl's hair.

Debby: Yes.

Tanya: And yet she was in tears, and they wanted to know what to do so they were like, "Tanya, can you help?" and you know, "Can you help her out?" And what's that? You know I respond with her because she was like, she wore the same hairstyle that I put in her hair. Like, you know, I was put in a teacher's role and then taken out, so, you know—

Debby: Right, so that's what I wanted to ask you. How did you feel about them having you do METCO duty at the end of the day?

Tanya: I mean, that was, they were doing that too, but me being the student teacher, you know, they were like, "Okay here's some responsibility."

Debby: So you think it was, you think it was only because you were a student teacher, not because you were black?

Tanya: Right. That, that, but the lice—

Debby: You do?

Tanya: Yeah, but the lice thing—

Debby: But the lice thing was because you were?

Tanya: Right. Yeah.

Debby: So you must have had mixed feelings about that. On the one hand feeling put upon, but on the other hand being able to help her?

Tanya: Yeah, yeah.

Debby: I mean, I don't know.

Tanya: Yeah, that's how I felt and, uh, and, then there was this other situation. There was like this one kid who, his name was Kalu, and he wouldn't speak to anyone but with his mom and his family and stuff like that.

Tanya used a kind of agitated speech, rushing from one episode to another, neither of which had been in the first draft of her essay. It was initially hard for me to understand what Tanya thought the problem was because "the lice thing" could have meant either her checking for lice or her being sought out to rebraid the girl's hair after the lice check. It was the latter. Other teachers were also involved in the lice check, but no other teacher was asked to rebraid the hair of a black girl.

From a pedagogical point of view, we can see the importance of the one-to-one conference: it created the opportunity for inquiries and for the teacher's display of empathy. Without these factors, the fuller narrative regarding the practicum might not have emerged.

Tanya did include the story about Kalu in a subsequent draft, and it would become the subject of much discussion when she work-shopped the paper in class. After listening to Tanya's description of a number of incidents that had taken place at the school, Debby made a clarifying statement in their conference. "From listening to you, I'm getting the feeling that this was a pretty monumental experience for you, and you haven't sorted it all out." Tanya replied, "When I was writing I was just like, 'Okay there's a lot here,' and I guess I just wanted to talk about the METCO program and maybe I can just do that and just, you know, talk about my feelings and, you know, see METCO in a lot of situations."

Tanya continued to affirm her desire to unite her subjectivity with a critique of the program. At this juncture, Debby suggested that Tanya take another tack.

> So I think you've got a lot of things to sort out. I think maybe you've got a couple of papers here. . . . You know, you may even want to, you might want to deal with it as a personal narrative about being mis-placed and understood. . . . The other possibilities are to sort of come to some other conclusion about how you feel about the METCO stu-dents and then give some examples.

Debby seems to have been suggesting with the second possibility that Tanya remove how she personally felt as a student teacher. I think Tanya was proposing something more rhetorically complex.

As their conversation proceeded, Tanya spoke about METCO in the Nixon School, speculating that the problems she observed were the result of two factors: that both the school and the program were new and that the METCO students coming to the town were spread out into too many schools. Tanya also speculated that, if more time had passed, they would eventually have hired a person of color. Debby responded quickly to this point, "Now, but that's valid. That's what the, that's what makes this interesting. And it's your opinions I want to find out about rather than all the details of the METCO."

Subsequently in the conference, Tanya mentioned her own goals as a teacher, saying that she had initially expected to learn some things from this wealthy school system with all its resources that she could take back to the inner city. "I want to do a lot of empower-ing. And you know a lot of inner-city kids never got to college and stuff like that." After what would amount to nineteen pages of tran-script between them, I interrupted. "Well, I have a question. Is it somewhat like, I mean I can't help but ask, does [your practicum] replicate your experience here at BC?" I participated in the ensuing conversation that would comprise fourteen more pages of transcript.

Tanya began to reveal her discomfort in the Prose Writing class itself; the discomfort was related to racial and class differences. Referring particularly to a classmate's paper about dating or "going on a manhunt," she said, "I don't feel like I should say anything." Debby thanked her for bringing up her feelings. "And I certainly don't want to single you out if you're feeling uncomfortable, but on the other hand, I'm sure you must have a lot to offer." Tanya reported that she experienced things differently from the other students. She felt intimidated because this was the first English class she had been in since her FWS. "And, um, and the way English is, the way you analyze things, I never, you know, really done that."

I then asked her what she might have said if she had contributed to the workshop of the "manhunt" paper. "Okay, I don't know . . . the perfect man? I was like okay, there's some ideas that I'll flow with, but I don't know if he was there 'tanning' and 'the ivory skin' and all that." Tanya was laughing as she let us know that her image of the perfect man is not a white man. She then mentioned Emily's paper on a family cabin in the backwoods of Georgia, a paper that had also been workshopped in class that day. "Like, that [paper]'s really good. Like, I felt like that's how I want to write, like that. I don't feel like I write that way." Debby informed Tanya that what Emily had read aloud was her fourth draft.

After Debby invited Tanya to workshop her student teaching paper in class, because it could "broaden people's perspectives and raise their consciousness about other lives," it became clearer how much Tanya feared being "misplaced and misunderstood." "I don't like to touch on the issue of race because I don't want people to be like, 'Oh, there's another story about race.'" I suggested that she was bringing up issues related to class, as well as race, and she emphatically agreed. "Like I don't relate to certain people because, you know, economically we're not coming from the same place." Debby asked her why she had chosen to attend BC. It was both because of financial reasons ("They gave me the most money") and because she was convinced by the school's promotional pitch regarding support services for students of color. (Many of these students were surprised at how much of a minority they actually were once they arrived.) Debby then allied herself with Tanya's discomfort.

Tanya: And it, I mean BC is a good school—

Debby: Yeah, we know that. It is a good school, but I often wonder if I were a minority person, I mean, I'm Jewish, and I would never recommend a Jewish kid to come to this school.

Tanya: Right.

Karen: You wouldn't?

Debby: No.

Karen: Why?

Debby: Because it's—

Tanya: Catholics.

Debby: —so overwhelmingly Catholic.

Tanya: Yeah.

Debby: You have to feel like an outsider.

Tanya: Yup, yup.

Debby: I mean, okay, it's not as obvious a situation as with you, but in five seconds it is.

I think this exchange between them was particularly important. Debby implied that she felt like a religious outsider, and Tanya quickly responded to Debby's disclosure creating a bond between them of the "misplaced and misunderstood." Even though I too am Jewish, it was Tanya who quickly understood what Debby was saying, interjecting the word *Catholics* before Debby even had a chance to respond to my question. I think the interchange had the same kind of impact on their relationship as Helena's initial reading of Catherine's essay on her father's alcoholism did on their student-teacher relationship. Instead of just reading the first paragraph and stopping, as she had said she would do, Helena read right through it, showing Catherine that the content was engaging. This reading created a bond that would carry them through the constructive criticism that followed. Debby's indication that she felt like a religious outsider at BC enabled Tanya to experience Debby as empathetic and Tanya, in turn, would open up more.

Tanya proceeded to describe how she felt going from a nearly all-black inner-city school to a largely middle-class white campus. Her voice rose nervously, and her face twitched as she revealed that she had felt inadequately prepared to be at BC.

> I have to present myself like I didn't get in here affirmative action and I have good grades, but then again my grades are not as good as yours, and this is what I have a hard time with now, just, like, I'm not ready for college. Like, you know, maybe I should have went to a preparatory school for a semester.

That Tanya did not feel entirely comfortable showing her insecurity to us was indicated by her suddenly switching to the second-person plural, fusing the two of us with the white students she was hypothetically speaking to. ("My schooling was not as good as yours"; "my grades are not as good as yours.")

I asked Tanya why, in the first class, she had said that she needed help with grammar because I hadn't seen any special problems in her papers. (Debby later explained to me that I often saw drafts of papers that Tanya had edited in response to Debby's corrections. Tanya, in a later interview, cited this approach to her grammar problems as not being helpful.)

What came out at this point, after about thirty minutes of conference dialogue, was a description of the most painful incident that she experienced in her practicum, the event driving her feeling "misplaced and misunderstood." Behind her concern about grammar lay the issue of black dialect; she had been required to repeat her practicum for using Black English. Tanya's supervisor and her teachers told her that she needed to spend "more time in the classroom. 'Your grammar needs to come out more' and things like that. Like I dropped the 'e-d's' when I'm talking."

Debby: I don't notice that.

Tanya: And I have this slang.

Karen: That's disgusting. So they were criticizing you for not using Standard English. Is that—

Tanya: Yeah, exactly. That's what it was, and I was just like, okay, and that's why I'm doing this extended—

Debby: No wonder you don't like to talk in class. You think everybody's going to be—

Tanya: No, I'm just like, oh God no. [Voice rises, inaudible] changes on me.

Debby: Oh.

Tanya: Maybe that, maybe that's it. I mean I, I, I see myself as a very outspoken person and, umm, when that happened to me I was in tears. I was—

Debby: I don't blame you.

Tanya: I was just really upset. And they told me like a week left before it ended. Like my practicum ended. I was going to be all done. There was a week left. They were like, "You need to do an extended practicum. You need to work on the verbal communication to your students."

Karen: [Laughs]

Tanya: [Laughs]

Debby: What's wrong with them?

Tanya: And I think that, that, that's why I was like, okay, let me focus on my grammar. Like, let me have resources, you know, so I can work on the, that's the way I am.

The experience of being chastised for her oral speech had made a big impact on Tanya. She would take their advice to heart by doing a second practicum in another school and by naming her focus in Prose Writing as grammar, even though, at the time, the criticism she received did not seem to me to have anything to do with written expression. The extent to which she internalized the criticism was illustrated by her switch from first to third person. "I needed more time in the classroom. 'Your grammar needs to come out more.'" Suddenly she was the voice of authority addressing herself. Tanya did not explicitly tell us that she thought their criticism was racist, and I think she had mixed feelings here: both that she did, in fact, have poor grammar and that she was being discriminated against for using black dialect.

Debby and I were upset about the story and immediately sympathetic toward Tanya, but I wonder now about my laughter. As I replay the tapes of her conferences and struggle to transfer oral into written discourse, I find a part of myself wanting her to be clearer, more precise. I think of a discussion about taping and transcribing in *Writing Ethnographic Fieldnotes* (Emerson et al.) that argues that a transcript is never verbatim reproduction. The authors write,

> [A] transcript is the product of a transcriber's ongoing interpretive and analytic decisions about a variety of problematic matters: how to transform naturally occurring speech into specific words (in the face of natural speech elisions); how to determine when to punctuate to indicate a completed sentence (given common lack of clear-cut endings in ordinary speech); deciding whether or not to try to represent such matters as spaces and silences, overlapped speech and sounds, pace stresses and volume, and inaudible or incomprehensible sounds or words. In sum, even those means of recording that researchers claim come the closest to realizing an "objective mirroring" necessarily make reductions in the lived complexity of social life similar in principle to those made in writing fieldnotes. (9–10)

In many parts of the tape recording of Debby and Tanya, I am frustrated by "incomprehensible sounds or words," as well as my own inability to communicate changes in pitch that indicate anxiety. I have come to see an opposite frustration: that at times I could hear what she was saying all too well. I had a strong desire to present Tanya at her "best" so that my invoked white reader would sympathize with her. When I examine what I mean by her "best," I realize that I am no different from her supervisor and the teachers at her practicum. I wanted her to use Standard English, and she did not. I felt myself flinch when I typed her statement "I should have went to preparatory school" and fought off the urge to edit. In making this admission, I become conscious of a warning issued to me by one of my readers, Dr. Bonnie TuSmith, prior to beginning my data gathering: "Be aware of your visible whiteness as you undertake this multicultural project."

I now recognize my own racism in wanting Tanya to be less guilty of "natural speech elisions" than a white student, and I am not sure I was the only one who felt this way. When Debby and I discussed the conference the following week, Debby revealed deep compassion, as well as a fear of being disappointed by Tanya's revision. Debby was surprised at how open Tanya was. "Here's this person who never says a word in class, [and] all of a sudden she's so open. . . . I've never really had that kind of an open conversation with anybody." I told her that I had felt a great deal of pain for Tanya over the weekend.

Debby: Like upset about her language, which was infuriating.
Karen: I know. It's like—
Debby: I mean, she, she speaks—
Karen: Right.
Debby: —perfectly.
Karen: I know. It's just like—
Debby: And even if she didn't [speak perfectly], to say it?
Karen: Did you read the paper [Tanya's second draft] yet?
Debby: No. [Laughs] I was a little bit, I haven't had the chance anyway, but I was a little bit—
Karen: Umm, I was—
Debby: —reluctant to read it because I was so hopeful.
Karen: Right.
Debby: Knowing I'd be disappointed in some way.
Karen: All right.

I think both of us struggled with unacknowledged racial bias here. Debby asserted that Tanya spoke perfectly and then undermined her assertion with a hint that the real problem might have been that her supervisors were inappropriately direct with her about her lack of "perfect" English. "And even if she didn't [speak perfectly], to say it?" At the end, Debby expressed her reluctance to read Tanya's revision "knowing [she'd] be disappointed in some way," as if she suspected that Tanya would somehow fail. My own failure to question Debby on these points indicated a passive complicity with her doubts about Tanya's oral speech and her ability to revise. Actually, the revision could have disappointed Debby in many ways, as they really had not come to agreement on how to negotiate the personal experience and the critique of METCO.

After learning that Tanya had to do another practicum, Debby had an insight about the METCO paper. We had been talking about Tanya's reticence in class being the consequence of the comments made to her by her practicum supervisor, and Debby attributed what she perceived to be the problem with Tanya's paper to the same source. "That paper last week, I, it starts out being [about] her for about a paragraph . . . and then it's about the kids and the METCO program and whatever, and I want to read about her. This is her experience." Debby's perception was interesting; Tanya may have dropped herself as the focus of the text because she either did not want to recall or did not want to make public the shaming she had felt at her practicum.

In their next conference, Debby conceded that Tanya had two goals in her student teaching paper: to reveal that she had felt like an outsider at the school and to argue for changes that needed to take place in the METCO program. Debby offered a compromise: "So I think, I think we can get from your own experience to your own understanding of the METCO program because of what you went through."

Three weeks after their conferences, Tanya workshopped the paper in the Prose Writing Seminar. In the draft she presented to the class, there were tighter connections between her own feelings as a person of color in a majority white institution, the problems the METCO students faced, and her call for changes. What follows are sections from the third draft.

> Have you ever been so frustrated about something you could not control? . . . Well, I have felt this need to change a program in a school that I was working in. This program is METCO. . . .
> My own experience at the Nixon helped me to focus on the issues of the METCO program. Like those students I found it very difficult

being there. I had feelings of misplacement and a lack of recognition. . . .

[A few paragraphs describe the METCO program and the activities students miss because of their long commute.]

The cultural differences are tremendous. . . . All of the teachers at Nixon are white. . . . There are no foundations set in place to help the METCO students emotionally nor socially. . . . I bet the teachers overlook these students' concerns because they do not affect the class as a whole. . . .

[Two paragraphs describe Kalu, the Nigerian student who had not spoken to anyone in the school for the two years he had been there. Tanya formed a relationship with him and he became verbal.] I felt that Kalu was overlooked because he was not seen as a problem child. He never talked and as long as he was not disturbing anyone then it was okay. . . .

Through this experience I discovered the need for change in the METCO program. I think that if METCO wants to integrate students, there should be support systems for the students in the school. There should be teachers who are the same race as METCO students, and there should be seminars to help teachers become more culturally aware of their students' environment. Through supportive services established within school systems that have METCO students, the METCO program can change the lives of many young people in a positive way, instead of making them feel as alone and isolated as I felt.

I think Tanya's achievement here was impressive. Instead of pulling the reader in two directions, Tanya fulfilled her rhetorical mission: to share how she felt and to critique the program. While there were links between the two from the beginning to the end of the paper, the main transition was accomplished through the sentence "My own experience at the Nixon helped me to focus on the issues of the METCO program."

I am reminded of Aristotle's chapter on narration in the *Rhetorica*. He calls for intermittent narration in oratory, using it to depict character and demonstrate moral purpose. The orator should first argue by enthymeme, but enthymeme should be avoided "when you are trying to arouse feeling; for it will either kill the feeling or will itself fall flat" (1446). When pathos is the goal, providing narrative examples is in order. Tanya skillfully blended narrative elements within her argument about the program. The examples she offered made her argument more compelling.

I found the class in which she workshopped this paper to be

thrilling. Part of the energy came from the tension of not knowing how her white classmates would respond, and the other part came from how they did respond. The class was the most highly politicized one I observed. A discussion on a *Boston Globe* column distributed by Debby and written by Patricia Smith, a black journalist, followed the discussion of Tanya's paper; the column pertains to the frequency with which people of color are falsely accused of shoplifting. This discussion prompted talk about two episodes of racism on campus. One involved a black student who worked in the audiovisual department who was handcuffed and arrested by campus police while he waited for a class to finish so he could pick up a slide projector. The other was about a black student denied admission to a basketball game when some white students had been allowed in.

During the workshop of Tanya's paper, Debby seemed to want to protect Tanya from criticism, as she ran interference between Tanya and any student who made a comment. This pattern was so extensive that students began simply to direct their comments to Debby and speak of Tanya in the third person.

Tanya read her paper to the class in a very soft voice. I was quite conscious at the time that she was describing an experience of being the only black teacher in a school in a classroom that duplicated it. The copy she read had her teacher's corrections on it, and when she couldn't read a notation, Tanya would ask Debby about it and then read it the corrected way. When she was finished, Debby started the class discussion with the comment, "So what she's doing is using her own personal experience and the areas and successes of that to come to understand and to make some recommendations about changes that need to be made. What do you think about this approach?" The first responder was Brian, and I felt myself tense up shortly after he began because it initially appeared that he was going to directly challenge Tanya. "Yes, the person, like, should use personal experience, I think, in order to get your point across, and maybe it's just because I can relate to it. Umm, I mean I'm on the other side. You know, being a white male."

At this point I cringed, but Brian had his own there-are-problems-with-METCO story to tell. The school in which he was a student teacher was 99 percent Caucasian, and the teacher to whom he had been assigned complained about having to do "diversity stuff" and then offered no assistance whatsoever to a non–English speaking student from Ecuador, saying that eventually she would catch on. "What I found really amazing was that we were working in the groups one day, and [the student from Ecuador] was in the group and there were two METCO students in the group, and they were actually helping her trying to translate."

When Brian began with the self-description as "a white male" being "on the other side," it seemed as though he was going to define himself in opposition to Tanya but, in fact, the opposite was true. He affirmed her assessment with his own observations. His commentary added to the level of intensity in the room, intensity that had already been created when Tanya read her paper. It is very powerful when a white person can step out of whatever antiblack ideological "cookies," to borrow a term from computer technology, have been implanted in him and develop a different worldview. Marxist theorist Lucien Goldmann believes that only seldom can an individual step outside the mental structures, feelings, and habits of thought intact in his or her social group. In fact, he writes that such an individual can only "transpose [his or her worldview] on a plane of imaginary creation, conceptual thought, etc." (129). Yet Brian's experience afforded him more than an imaginary change in point of view. His second comment, the last student remark in the workshop, reflected something more concrete.

> Umm, I think the effective method that she wrote this paper is really good because it's sort of a viewpoint that a lot of people who aren't educated thoroughly enough about the METCO program will think, "Hey, it's a great program. You know, here are all these people donating this money so underprivileged kids can get a great education and all this stuff." But the way, I mean, all of us in this class now see it is just, it just makes it more skeptical of the program, that the program could use changes.

It was not uncommon in this class for one of three different female students to make supportive comments to an author about an experience described in a paper, but this was the first time a male student played such a role. It was also the first time anyone had shared an experience of what Tanya deliberately did not want to name, racism.

Brian's view was indirectly challenged soon after he spoke for the first time. Ned, a highly critical student, questioned Tanya directly: "Why did you choose to *tell* so much of what was said, just giving us these stories?" Tanya told him that she wanted to make sure people understood METCO. From the discussion, it was not clear to me what his complaint was, other than that her narrative was too expository and not literary enough, that she was "telling" rather than "showing." In his self-evaluation turned in at the end of the course, Ned wrote,

> I apologize if I have been too critical in class discussions. It was frustrating at times, when a student read an essay on the school system, and all of the comments around the room were on the policies of the school, and not the essay itself. I think she had a great point to make, but the way she constructed her paper and the focus she gave to some issues took away from its power. I really wanted to see that point be made. I know that class discussions are informal, and you let us talk freely, but it seemed like her writing was being ignored because the students wanted to voice their opinions on black children in white schools.

Ned began what was supposed to be self-reflection by apologizing for being too critical and then by again becoming critical and justifying it. His statement was fairly strong and I think off base considering that Brian was the only student who spoke about the problem of black students in a predominantly white school apart from the essay as a rhetorical work. Even so, in his second comment, Brian did speak of the effective method Tanya used to write the paper.

In class, all of the other student comments were related to the narrative as a text not as an experience. After Ned's challenge to Tanya, Jackie, who had already been accepted to law school in her home state of Texas, supported Tanya's approach of "really making us see the program through [one] child" rather than "just making broad generalizations." She added, "I thought this was really effective because a lot of times I think, especially with policy, people don't really . . . I guess you don't care as much until you get personal with it, you know." Allison, as if to demonstrate Jackie's point about persuasive papers needing to be personal for an outsider to care, wanted Tanya to make the entire paper about one student, introducing him from the beginning because "that's where you get the reader's backing." Later Ann Marie compared Tanya's strategy to Jonathan Kozol's in *Rachel and Her Children,* where he invokes the reader's support by giving examples of people prior to offering numerous generalizations.

Kathy questioned whether or not the neglect of Kalu, the silent student, was peculiar to METCO or whether it wasn't something that could happen in any school. She suggested that Tanya incorporate some information she had provided in the class discussion—that Kalu was not eligible to have an aide, as a local student would have been, because the Nixon School would not offer any services not paid for by METCO. Debby asked Kathy why she wanted Tanya to put this information in the essay: "Because that feels more discriminatory?" "Not, yeah, sort of more discriminatory. More like about what she's writing about the program."

In the workshop, it seemed to me that most of the students who spoke wanted Tanya to focus on the treatment of Kalu, but they appeared to feel some discomfort when she made "broader generalizations" about METCO at the Nixon School. Aside from Brian, and exclusive of Ned, they were supportive of her perceptions, to a degree. The discussion of Tanya's paper ended with a comment by Debby who, for the first time, revealed her own experience with METCO.

> METCO's been around for quite a long time, and those things are still not changed because I remember when my kids were growing up when the METCO program first came to the town we lived in, that was one of the things that was so glaringly absent is that there were no support services. And, you know, how could you take these kids, bus these kids in and just plunk them there and expect them to thrive just because you were providing them with good information and good resources? And, you know that was a long time ago. My children are way past grade school age, and obviously there haven't been very many changes if this situation is still happening.

Debby then suggested that Tanya could make her paper even stronger by interviewing other people, like Brian and people from the School of Education, so that she could offer a wider range of experiences with METCO.

Susan Miller has critiqued composition classes for producing essays on topics that are "inconsequential" outside of the classroom. I think that all aspects of the textual production of Tanya's paper, including the conferences and the class workshop, indicate that classrooms open to personal writing can produce essays that have significance outside that classroom. Both Tanya and Brian, future teachers, had an opportunity to discuss some troubling events in their student teaching experience. Their classmates had an opportunity to hear an antiracist critique of an educational system, exposing them to experiences outside their awareness. In spite of some students' desire to have Tanya reduce her paper to just one person's experience, limiting the generalizability of her observations, it was an experience that they had to contend with nonetheless. The class had been highly involved in the workshop; and even after it ended, the intensity level remained strong.

After Tanya's paper had been discussed, Debby then asked the students to brainstorm proposals for an argument paper. When it was Emily's turn to describe her possible topic, she began to share what she was learning in another course about the negative impact of U.S. involvement in Third World countries. She told the class about sweatshop zones in Nicaragua that were guarded by the military. Women worked fifteen-hour days to make clothes for Eddie Bauer and the GAP. Because the labels are not sewn on until the garments reach the United States, the workers do not know what companies they are employed by, making it more difficult to sue. Emily also informed us that twenty-three Americans and one hundred thousand Iraqis died in the Gulf War. She gave a frightening example: "We killed Kuwaiti [Iraqi?] conscripts, fourteen-year-old boys, by dumping sand on them in the night." After she spoke for a while, Debby told her that she needed to narrow the focus of what she would write about and asked her if she was calling for a change in U.S. policy.

Debby's role in this highly politicized class was to alternately stimulate the discussion and redirect it by prompting students to focus on more traditional notions of argument. I had the feeling that she eventually became uncomfortable with the left liberal and antiracist discussion that had been unleashed. Later she would use the word *heavy-handed* with Tanya to describe her concern that the class was getting too focused on one theme.

In their conference after class, Debby asked Tanya how she felt about the workshop. Tanya responded, "I just felt like there was some uneasiness there." Neither Debby nor I asked her what she meant, thus corroborating some uneasiness of our own regarding race; instead, we commented on Ned's negative contribution. Then I mentioned that Tanya's essay had led to other topics.

Karen: You know your critique of METCO and what's really going on there, you know racism in stores and then, you know Nicaragua and Iraq. You know, things just kept, I mean—

Tanya: [Very animated] —kept going and, you know, I felt that too. And when that *[Globe]* article [on the false shoplifting charge at Cache] came out, I was just like [laughs], oh boy, 'cause I know Copley [Place]. I've been stopped so many times. And I just, like some places are just like never, you will never see me spend my money. Even if I had the money.

Debby: Right.

Karen: Well, and then you felt free to bring up your personal example about that.

Tanya: Yeah.

Debby: Right, right.

Tanya: But the *[Globe],* I don't know. I guess my paper, then the article, I was just like, "Oh, wow." [Laughs]

Debby: Yeah, well I worried about that a little bit.

Tanya: Yeah.

Debby: It was just, you know, *it was a heavy-handed thing.*

Tanya: Um hmm.

Debby: But I don't know. Did you think—

Tanya: *I thought it was great.* [Emphasis mine]

Here is a clear contrast. Debby felt that perhaps the accumulation of antiracist essays and discussion was in some way overwhelming for the white majority or too focused on one theme. For Tanya, however, the experience of the reality black people face was affirmed.

Initially Tanya had expressed her sense of "uneasiness" in the class. As the conference proceeded, Debby shared the discomfort *she* once felt when a former student, the only black person in a large literature class, complained in his course evaluation about Debby using the word *nigger* when she was quoting directly from Toni Morrison's *Beloved*.[3] Tanya then asked if there were many Black English majors at BC and spoke of the white freshmen having to get used to her presence on the hall her first year. She told us,

> If I was there [in Prose Writing] my freshman year, I would have had to drop out of the class. I don't know, 'cause you, there's a lot of interaction in that class, and you have to be able to talk, and I don't think I would have been able to do it because I'm coming from an all-, all-, all-black neighborhood coming to BC . . . but when I came to BC I was like, "Whoa."

Tanya demonstrated that she was aware of the difficulties of racial integration from two perspectives, that of the white students who reacted to her presence and that of the black students, like herself, who had grown up primarily in black communities. During the conference as a whole, Tanya interacted with both of us with ease and assertiveness, even interrupting Debby to make her point. It is my sense that the experience of sharing some of what life is like for black people to her white classmates and of having them listen with a combination of identification, respect, and discomfort enhanced her self-confidence.

Debby and I had several conversations about why she redirected the political discussion in the class after Tanya had workshopped her paper. In one such conversation the semester after my study, in December 1997, she said that, whereas racism was often a clear theme in her literature classes, she did not like her Prose Writing Seminar to have any prevailing theme: "[T]he topics ought to come from the students." I pointed out that racism had come from Tanya and that Tanya was, in fact, the only student who would have brought up this topic. Furthermore, Debby herself had introduced the piece on false shoplifting charges against blacks. Debby responded that her focus in both Tanya's essay and the *Boston Globe* article was not meant to be the political issue of racism but rather the rhetorical issue of moving from personal experience to a broader focus.

Debby: Okay, [you wrote that] I was not comfortable with the left liberal, antiracist discussion that had been unleashed. Why did you have that feeling?

Karen: Emily was just effervescing about the horrors of U.S. imperialism . . . and I thought you were just a little dismissive of her, the point she was trying to make. Here was this student that came from a background where, you know, "America is the best country in the world." . . . When they have that kind of educational, spiritual, or whatever awakening, I would validate it, you know?

Debby: Yeah, I think, I think you might be right. . . . I guess I get more concerned about making sure that we manage to hear everybody's arguments and I get them on track so then the next week when they go to write a paper, they'll at least be focused. (Interview 24 December 1997)

Debby also told me that during the subsequent semester, the fall of 1997, she had a student who wrote a paper about a school in Georgia where the United States trains South American militant murderers, "to kill the Jesuits, to do all these horrible things that had been going on in Central and South America. . . . Students in the class were SHOCKED. WE, AMERICANS, DO THIS?" One of the students in the class had turned to Debby, asking her if she had known about this school. Debby told the class,

> Well I don't know that I knew about this particular school or the numbers of revolutionaries that had been trained there but certainly I know that we've messed up in Central and South America for YEARS, that we'd been so uptight about keeping Communism out that we've supported anybody no matter what kind of a murderer he was.

Debby shared this teaching story with me to point out that in this instance she thought the political discussion was relevant to the discussion of the paper and the validity of its argument. "But I think you may be right about [the instance after Tanya's workshop]. That I do become more sort of institutional at times."

Debby went on to contrast this "institutional" tendency with her goals for a multicultural literature course.

> When I read their final exams, and I see what these students say about the horrors of slavery and how it's impacted African Americans to this DAY because it was so devastating, I say, "Thank God they got it." . . . I want it to touch who they are as people, but somehow maybe I do shy away from it in this class.

By the time Tanya workshopped her next paper, a humorous narrative of her participation in her sister's labor and delivery, she, for all practical purposes, had become one of the gang. The class laughed boisterously when she elaborated on the experience as her expectations, grounded in cinematic images of childbirth, were continually defied by the reality. "And I was pushing when she was. I don't want to tell everyone this part. When the doctor said, 'Push,' I was pushing. And I'm thinking, 'What am *I* pushing for?'"

The atmosphere in this workshop was animated with people talking over each other. There was a big contrast to the "uneasiness" in the discussion of her METCO paper. The students praised or critiqued parts of the essay without hesitation, probably somewhat relieved not to be talking about racism.

Tanya: And when I saw the head, I started crying. I was like, "Oh my God, the baby's blue."
Class: [Laughs]
Tanya: Not thinking that all babies are blue, I was just like crying.

Yes, newborns tend to be bluish from oxygen deprivation, and Tanya's white classmates seemed delighted to share a universal experience with her. In my exit interview, I checked with Tanya about the change in her demeanor after the METCO workshop when she went from being quiet to rather chatty. She quickly referred to her classmates' response to the childbirth paper. "Everyone enjoyed it, so I was like really happy."

I was not able to attend the final conference between Debby and Tanya, but Debby telephoned me to talk about it. In the conference, Tanya said that at the beginning of the semester she had wanted to drop out of the class, but she had really appreciated the way Debby had reached out to her. After workshopping the labor and delivery paper, Tanya's classmates began to approach her on campus and talk with her. Debby said that she felt so moved by their last conference that at one point she just reached out and touched Tanya's arm and, as she put it, "I nearly started to cry in the conference." She then told Tanya that she could use this experience in her own teaching, that she could reach out to a student who feels marginalized.

Tanya wrote two more papers for the class. The first was a detailed piece on getting hair extensions, as she wanted to see if she could write "process analysis." The final assignment, to be included with the portfolio, was a three-page assessment of work in the class. The assignment directed students to critique their papers; describe the problems and achievements in each one; discuss their writing progress over the semester; refer back to goals stated in the first class and discuss whether they accomplished them; list the strengths and weakness of their writing in general, as well as the elements of the course that were most helpful to their development as writers.

When I compare Tanya's self-reflexive piece with some comments she made to me in our exit interview, I can see that this story does not have an unambiguous happy ending. An emotional palimpsest of inadequacy regarding what she loosely called grammar lay partly visible along with a new layer of self-confidence. What she referred to as grammar problems harked back to what her practicum supervisor and teachers were actually criticizing, her use of Black English.

Moreover, Debby and I learned in Tanya's self-evaluation that the feelings of insecurity she had described in her hurricane paper had not pertained to some disruption in her family relationships, as I had conjectured, but to her feelings about the Prose Writing Seminar itself. Here are some excerpts from her written self-assessment passed in to Debby.

I entered this class thinking that I had a serious problem with writing and I was scared to show my work to anyone. I thought that this class would be a way for me to improve my grammar. However, the purpose of the class was not grammar, it was writing. . . . At first I was going to drop this class because I did [not] think I would get anything out of it. I was wrong. This class has been a big help with my other classes and with my student teaching. . . . I felt that the professor did a great job in class and during conferences to make me feel a part of the group, even though I felt out of place. . . . The first paper I wrote [on the hurricane] was my hardest paper and I feel it was my least successful one. I think the reason for this is because I was too focused on my grammar and not ideas. . . . I had been trying to suppress the past. This story brought back feelings of unhappiness and in many ways was emotional for me. I was trying to create a story that reminded me of a happier time in my past. This house was one of the better times and I wanted my story to convey that, but it shifted from happy to secure [insecure?].

I also believe that my first paper shows my uncertainties that I had about the class. I did not give it my all and I was afraid of my writing. . . . I just wanted to write stories as clearly and perfect as [my class-mates'] stories.

After the first paper I felt more confident, so I created a story about a controversial issue. I did not have any idea that I was going to read it to the class, but when I did I received very positive feedback. *The feedback that I received was so constructive that I felt, for the first time, proud of my writing. . . . I think that I taught the students something.* . . . I feel that my confidence grew every time that I wrote a paper. It was a great feeling and I know that I can use writing to inspire my students to love writing. . . . I know that grammar is important, but I feel that if I concentrate and develop a good paper then I can go back and correct my mistakes. . . . This semester I think the most important thing I learned is that writing can be very fun. . . . I also learned that I need to have confidence in my writing because if I am not confident you can hear it in the tone of my paper. . . . I know that grammar is very important, especially important to educators. In the future I hope that I can help students to enjoy writing as this class has helped me. [Emphasis mine]

Writing teachers at BC often have their students include this kind of self-evaluation in their final portfolio. Whatever one thinks about the possibility of "authentic voice," it is difficult for a teacher to determine when the student is writing these affirmations for a grade. As Lynn Bloom reminds us, grades can undermine good teaching practice that includes dialogic discussions in which the student has an equal right to speak up. "But grades automatically signal who is more equal than all the rest put together" (364). With multiple revisions and plenty of teacher corrections on each draft, "at some point [the teacher will] be grading her own writing rather than the student's, anyway" (365). With these final self-reflective types of assignments, I think it is unlikely that a student would write an "honest" criticism of a course because it might negatively impact that student's grade.

Tanya's self-evaluation, however, was not a uniform or monolithic statement; instead, there were parallel threads. The accumulation of positive comments, her praise for the class, her developing self-confidence, her inspiration to pass on the pleasure that can accompany the writing process to future students, was intersected by a subplot, the lingering self-doubt about her grammar. She tried to minimize this concern: "I know that grammar is important, but I feel that if I concentrate and develop a good paper then I can go back and correct my mistakes." Yet the fact that she used the word *grammar* six times demonstrated her existing concern. Her feelings before she workshopped what she called her most successful paper, the one on childbirth, were revealing: "At first, I was scared because of my grammar errors, but I knew that everything was going to be okay when I heard them laughing." She seemed to be saying that, even if there were grammar errors, the humor of the piece blocked their significance.

In our one-to-one exit interview, Tanya fleshed out some more of her student teaching narrative, revealing why she felt that there were serious grammar problems in her writing. She also expressed some criticism of her Prose Writing instructor for not being more helpful in this area.

Tanya: The reason why I have a BIG worry about my grammar was doing, um, last semester in Sudbury, and you know how the language, like how language in your environment y', you talk the way you speak because of other people [*sic*] influences— . . . And African Americans have this slang. . . . Um, so when I was in Sudbury and I guess the "e-d's," I kept dropping the "e-d's."

Karen: But that was in your oral speech.

Tanya: Right. So, so, um, and then in my journals, but that's my journals and I didn't take time to look at it and stuff like that, um—

Karen: They went over your journals there?

Tanya: Ye—no, my prof, my supervisor did and she said that I also could use to correct, correct, correct that too, you know, correct, but that's just because my journals were my journals and I wrote fast and— [both talk]

Karen: Yeah that seems really unfair. Journals are, they're supposed to be freewriting. Th', that doesn't seem like a fair criticism—

Tanya: Yeah.

Karen: —if you ask me.

Tanya: Well a lot of people felt that way too, and um, that's, I just said you know "Whatever." Whatever I do, like picking the Prose Writing class will just help me; it will improve my writing. . . .

As I said to Tanya later in the conversation, it was almost as if the teachers at her practicum had put a kind of hex on her so that she would always have some doubt or shame about her linguistic endeavors. While her response to the criticism, taking another writing course and doing a second practicum, was propitious for her and her future as an educator, the feelings of inferiority for using Black English seemed to have stuck with her. However, she also faulted Debby for not helping her more with grammar.

> She did a lot of corrections but I wished she did them with me so I could see and make understanding of it. And I didn't ask her during our conferences 'cause I was concerned about what the paper was about. I could see my mistakes but I wish I was there so I could understand it.

I asked Tanya if she thought she might not be able to do it correctly the next time. "I, I would make the same mistakes but maybe by reading it over again and focusing more on it I probably could correct it myself."

Tanya waffled in the discussion of grammar. She faulted Debby for just making corrections and not going over them with her. Then Tanya explained that she herself didn't want to use conference time to discuss the mistakes because she "was concerned about what the paper was about." She felt that she would probably continue to repeat her errors but concluded that in proofreading she would be able to catch them.

I think Tanya raised a problem that implicitly critiqued the writing process. We say that we wait until later drafts to work on grammar, but I find that even regular fifteen-minute weekly conferences with my students do not provide enough time to discuss editing issues. The focus is often the paper's content. Debby had her own method of working with grammar and syntax, and she explained it to Tanya at the end of their initial conference.

Debby: I did notice one thing about your writing, which was you could be more concise. You sort of spread an idea out into two maybe three sentences; maybe combine it into one. So that's something you might want specifically to work on.

Tanya: Mm hmm.

Debby: Umm, but *I think if you look at the way I changed the sentences, you'll start to get the idea of that.*

Tanya: Mm hmm.

Debby: But, umm, look it over carefully and then come back to me next time with specific questions about why I, you know, made these kind of suggestions, and WHY it was the way that you did it, not as good. And I think that's how you will learn. Just use specifics rather than my saying to you, you know, this rule and that rule. [Emphasis mine]

So right at the beginning of the semester, Debby had put the onus on Tanya to go to Debby with questions about her corrections. Tanya seemed to recall that suggestion as she said to me in the exit interview that she didn't want to take up conference time with asking Debby those kinds of questions. Clearly this method did not work for Tanya, and I think both of them were accountable here. Tanya could have told Debby that she had questions about the corrections but wanted to talk about content in their time together. And Debby could have noticed that Tanya was not asking questions, even though Tanya had explicitly stated that improvement in grammar was one of her goals for the class. I did learn from Debby that she had given Tanya a grammar handbook at the beginning of the semester. Perhaps she could have also told her about the Academic Development Center and referred her there.

Like Helena, Debby also raised objections to Nancy Sommers's suggestion that writing teachers not mark errors in the first draft ("Responding"). Debby's argument is that, if we do not correct mistakes, students re-create them in the next draft. "It's probably even worse for a minority student because if they are unsure and you don't correct it, then they might start to internalize, 'Well maybe this is right.'" Of course, the act of "correcting mistakes" has not been demonstrated as an effective way of teaching grammar.

It occurs to me that a pedagogy that combined Debby's attention to content, purpose, and organization and Helena's attention to word choice and sentence-level error might have been most helpful to Tanya. Unfortunately, fifteen-minute weekly conferences would not suffice for such a comprehensive pedagogy.

Thinking and Writing in College, by Barbara Walvoord and Lucille Parkinson McCarthy, is the account of a seven-year ethnographic study of writing across the curriculum. A collaborative chapter written with business teacher A. Kimbrough Sherman concludes with a statement that indicates that the process stimulated pedagogical growth in the primary researcher. "In her composition classes, Walvoord has tried, *since our study,* to suggest to students what features to look for, what questions to ask, and what common pitfalls to avoid, as they enter classes in other disciplines" (95, emphasis mine). At the end of my study of the Prose Writing class, Debby asked me if I had become more sensitive to students of color who want more help with grammar in early drafts. I told her that I would probably do more mini-lessons for the whole class regarding such issues as comma usage. It has come to pass; as a result of my work with both Debby and Helena (and their work with Tanya and Catherine), I do find myself spending more class time on punctuation and grammar than I had in the past. I ask for student volunteers ("human sacrifices") to put sentences on the board that I have marked with, say, a *p* for punctuation error, and then as a class we work on copyediting.

I have focused on Debby's work with Tanya in the Prose Writing Seminar because it highlights many of the issues that set the context for teaching writing on college campuses today: helping a student flesh out a personal narrative without being psychologically invasive; writing a blend of personal narrative and argument; discussing the content of essays without pushing grammar out of the picture; white teachers working with black students in predominantly white institutions; black students receiving an education in environments that they experience as hostile or indifferent; white educators needing to examine their own hidden preferences for Standard English; and, finally, small writing classes and regular one-to-one conferences effectively establishing what Lad Tobin calls "writing relationships." Tanya's course evaluation showed ambivalence; she felt that she did not learn rules of grammar, but she also said that she could now do a better job of correcting her own mistakes. Because of the strength of her relationship with Debby, Tanya was able to share a very damaging experience in an educational environment that exactly duplicated the demographics of the site of that experience. Tanya took a big risk here, as both her teacher and her classmates could have reenacted the same pedagogical trauma and faulted her for using conventions of Black English. That did not happen. In fact, with the exception of one student, Ned, everyone was either supportive or constructively critical of her work. I doubt that the Prose Writing Seminar erased the memory of her practicum, but it is my sense that it did go a long way in helping her to value herself as a writer. Perhaps in her later education she will eventually come to view herself as someone who can revise and eventually produce well-written essays, able to employ Standard English for certain audiences. While learning the language of the dominant classes, she may also come to believe that, as Lisa Delpit puts it, "Each cultural group should have the right to maintain its own language style" (292).

At some time during our education, each of us has had a vexing or shaming experience. I think Tanya's example shows us the importance of working through these experiences in a supportive environment. Without such help, we are at risk of passing along the abuse to some of our own students. New students in academic institutions are often given by their classmates short lists of faculty to avoid. They are told that such faculty might be mean, unpredictable, irascible, punitive, or simply that they are not "good teachers." [My mentor, Bonnie TuSmith, wrote on an early draft of this chapter that, while this type of underground student support system is mostly valid, occasionally distortions can occur due to racism, anti-Semitism, or homophobia among the student body.] I often wonder how many of these difficult faculty members were trained in academic environments by teachers who themselves had had trying experiences. Educational improprieties then become multigenerational.

For those of us who have had such humiliating experiences, I think it is important that we break the silence in ways that do not threaten our careers. I frequently ask friends of mine, now tenured or in tenure-track academic positions, about their graduate training and professional self-development. Many times I have been told that they do not want to talk about their academic pasts simply because they are too painful. "Jane," now a tenured professor, shared one event with me through e-mail.

When we took our written qualifier, at the beginning of the second year, the graduate director told us all not to worry if it was hard, that the department had decided to make a more difficult exam that year! It was! One person got about a 70, there were 5 in the 50's, and one was in the 30's (he was already writing his thesis!!!). I got the highest score in the 50's. This twerp [the graduate director] got up at the faculty meeting and announced that they hadn't given a hard enough exam because I did as well as the other obviously better qualified students.

Jane's story is a troubling one, and I do not know what impact it has had on her own teaching. I am sure that many of us now working in academia have our own stories to tell. The fact that Jane could share the story suggests that the professor's view of her is no longer her own. That Tanya could share her experience with Debby and with me demonstrated that she did not completely embrace her evaluators' view of her. There is a real danger of passing on what is pedagogically unsound and what still controls our professional self-image. As Tanya put it in the first draft of her METCO paper, "Even though there are many issues that students have to face, I believe that the classroom teacher plays a major role in their life. *They can either empower students or disable them*" (emphasis mine). Given her experience in the Prose Writing Seminar, I would say that Tanya's prognosis as a teacher is good.

Before ending this chapter, I would like to acknowledge how difficult it is for subjects to agree to participate in ethnographic work and then read and discuss critical observations. When Debby and I met to discuss an earlier draft of this chapter, she told me, "I asked myself, 'What did I set myself up for?'" In fact, I myself commented to Debby in an e-mail: "I was thinking after our meeting yesterday that if someone asked me to be an informant in their ethnography, I would say, 'NO way!'" Debby then e-mailed (25 December 1997):

[I]f I knew I was going to be an "informant," I might not have agreed either. What a peculiar word. It sounds like I'm a spy. But don't feel bad about my involvement. It really was a fine experience. After I got over the initial defensiveness, examining my motives helped me define my reasons for what I do. The thought process has helped me to see areas in which I might want to rethink some things. I would especially like to see your revised draft with a discussion of our different approaches. I think that would also make your paper more interesting. . . . By the way, I never told you how clearly and well written I think the chapter is. . . . If you don't think Helena would mind, I'd like to see the chapter you wrote about her.

8 ➤ THE PERSONAL IN SOCIAL CONSTRUCTIONIST PEDAGOGY
A Visit to the Classroom of Patricia Bizzell

Is Social Constructionist Pedagogy Necessarily Confrontational?

Throughout this book, my aim has been to unravel a taxonomy of composition created by Berlin and perpetuated by Faigley and others that posits a binary between pedagogies that valorize the expression of the personal and those that emphasize the social. I have shown the social, political, and cultural aspects of the classrooms of two teachers in what would be called an "expressivist" program. In this chapter, I reflect on my visit to the classroom of social constructionist Patricia Bizzell to determine whether "the personal" is excluded in favor of a cultural studies approach.

In much composition literature, "expressivist" pedagogy is often contrasted to other approaches, such as "critical pedagogy" or "critical teaching." The expressed goal of these left-wing pedagogies is to create what Paulo Freire calls "critical consciousness." As Cy Knoblauch and Lil Brannon put it, critical pedagogy depends upon

> teachers unwilling to deny or ignore the sociopolitical contexts of their
> disciplinary practices, their school lives, or their lives as American citi-

zens; teachers accepting the responsibility to pose problems for students' critical attention; . . . teachers attentive to the dynamics of gender, race, and class in the forming of their classrooms and their schoolwork; *students challenged to think, not told how or what to think*; students offered many opportunities to critique but no imperatives of "political correctness"; . . . [and] the necessity of *self*-critique . . . (55, emphasis mine)

While there is nothing compulsory in this list, sometimes critical pedagogy becomes what has been called *liberatory,* or *confrontational, pedagogy* in which students are harshly and quickly stripped of the ideological illusions they come to class with and they *are* "told how [and] what to think." For example, in her essay "Power, Authority, and Critical Pedagogy" (1991), Bizzell expresses discomfort with "classroom situations in which persuasion becomes inadequate to the task of moving students in the direction of [a teacher's] own left-oriented political goals" (57). I expressed this same frustration in relation to Janet and her condescension toward the homeless. Yet when I read the Bizzell essay I am disconcerted by an apparent apology for bell hooks's statement on critical pedagogy in hooks's *Talking Back* (1989). Bizzell quotes hooks: "'I began to see that courses that work to shift paradigms, to change consciousness, cannot necessarily be experienced immediately as fun or positive or safe and this was not a worthwhile criteria to use in evaluation'" (qtd. in Bizzell, "Power" 65). Bizzell then hypothesizes,

I suspect that hooks is able to persuade her students partly because she initially links her interests to theirs through open avowal of her own moral agenda. . . . [H]ence, reimposing an oppressive hierarchy in her own classroom would damage her interests by hurting her sense of her own self-worth. (65)

When I read this excerpt from hooks in Bizzell's essay, I want Bizzell to be critical of hooks. I frankly do not see how "open avowal of [one's] own moral agenda" links a teacher's interests to her students'. In fact, revealing a left agenda may prompt conservative students to dig in their heels. Bizzell might like to think away the possibility of an oppressive hierarchy in hooks's classroom, but the quote from *Talking Back* speaks otherwise. Bizzell represents hooks as being quite clear when she says that courses that work to change consciousness are not fun, positive, or safe and that these criteria are not worthwhile in course evaluation.[1]

For several years after reading Bizzell's essay, my image of hooks was based on Bizzell's citation and commentary on *Talking Back*. In short, I thought of hooks as someone who utilized a confrontational pedagogy. However, when I read hooks's subsequent book, *Teaching to Transgress* (1994), I formed another opinion. She writes about an engaged pedagogy, an exciting classroom atmosphere, the active participation of all students (14), and opposition to domination by professors (18). Hooks uses the word *safe* in a different context. "[M]any students, especially students of color, may not feel at all 'safe' in what appears to be a neutral setting. It is the absence of a feeling of safety that often promotes prolonged silence or lack of student engagement" (39). The hooks of *Teaching to Transgress* wants to, in accord with Freire's teaching, "create a climate of openness and intellectual rigor" (40). In her classes, there is much "feedback because students do feel free to talk—and talk back" (42). While her engaged pedagogy does not mean shoving left-wing ideas down the throats of her students, it does mean that students can be uncomfortable. "To some extent, we all know that whenever we address in the classroom subjects that students are passionate about there is always the possibility of confrontation, forceful expression of ideas, or even conflict" (39). Yet I do not read hooks as wanting to silence dissent.

It seems to me that what Bizzell is doing in her 1991 essay is conflating a confrontational, top-down pedagogy with a dialogical pedagogy in the manner of Paulo Freire, Ira Shor, Henry Giroux, or Thia Wolf. In fact, Bizzell's more current work on creating contact zones in the classroom, where views from many areas of the political spectrum are extant, is a far cry from what she represents hooks as arguing. Frankly, I see little evidence of how a confrontational pedagogy would change the way people think and plenty of evidence of it being just another form of banking pedagogy, one in which students are intimidated into responding noncritically. Or, as Sherrie Gradin puts it,

> The potential for misuse is present for teachers who honor social-constructivist and Marxist theories for writing instruction. . . . [T]he social-epistemic agenda, if not carefully applied, can shut down students rather than empower them. Of course, force-feeding students an ideology, whether it is one we would consider desirable or not, will not necessarily create politically aware students. (111–12)

Yet Gradin demonstrates a bias when she conflates the "social-epistemic agenda" with "force-feeding," and it is a bias that I have recently realized I share. Critical pedagogy, as defined by Knoblauch and Brannon, is explicitly opposed to "force-feeding students an ideology." They write, "[S]tudents [are] challenged to think, not told how or what to think; students [are] offered many opportunities to critique, but [are given] no imperatives of 'political correctness'" (55). Furthermore, the Marxist Giroux is self-critical about his tendency to be "politically enlightened in [his] theorizing and pedagogically wrong in [his] organization of concrete class relations" (11). He developed "border writing," which allows students to "acknowledge their own emotional and affective investments in issues regarding race, colonialism, and the politics of representation" as opposed to just having them "articulate the meaning of other people's theories" (11). Border writing is not stimulated by "force-feeding."

Another representation of a nonconfrontational critical pedagogy is offered by Thia Wolf's teacher research, "Conflict as Opportunity in Collaborative Praxis." She believes that she "must accustom [her students] to their right to say 'no' if [she] expects them to begin using it independent of [her] wishes" (105). For example, she may direct a peer group to carry out certain activities, including deciding which of them they refuse to do and why (103–4).

In short, I was wrong to think that Marxist, or social constructionist, pedagogy is necessarily confrontational. I have my own story to tell here. While writing the first chapter of this book and critiquing the social construction of "expressivism," I experienced a great deal of relief from the frustration I felt reading the work of certain left theorists in graduate school. Prior to writing my doctoral dissertation, one social constructionist professor told me that I was much "too emotional" about my objections. (The charge of being "too emotional" may indicate anti-Semitism. Melanie Kaye/Kantrowitz writes, "As Jewish women, we are often blamed for our strength." Kaye/Kantrowitz tells us, referring to her experiences in a women's collective, "They found me 'loud' [of course] and 'emotional.' Interestingly, I got along fine with all the women of color in the group" [83].) Both my emotional intensity on the subject and my inappropriate conflation of social constructionism with confrontational pedagogy have a source. Before taking a look at the larger issue I explore in this chapter, the quest for a place for the personal in the social constructionist classroom, let me engage in what David Bleich calls the "pedagogy of disclosure."

> The need for disclosure arises because our historical and social place-ments and memberships are material: they exist and have an effect on all parts of our present experience. To articulate these memberships is what I mean by disclosure. Distinct from expression, confession, and revelation, disclosure is a different value in the teaching of writing. (xvi)

Although I carried no card, from 1967 to 1975 I was a com-munist, a member of a pro-Maoist, sectarian Marxist party. While involved with the Progressive Labor Party (PLP) and later, after it split in two, with the Party for Workers Power (PWP), I participated in antiwar and antiracist political organizing on an army base, on two college campuses, in two factory jobs, and in a working-class community. I ran for the Boston School Committee as the PLP candidate during the "desegregation crisis" in the early seventies. For these activities, I was repeatedly arrested and spent a day in jail when I was seven months pregnant with my first child. The FBI and CIA have detailed files on my political organizing. (I obtained these files under the Freedom of Information Act. It was most disconcert-ing to see whole sections whited out, the excuse being the need to protect the identities of the agents. Apparently quite a few of my "friends" and "political allies" were working for the government.)

However, after eight years of involvement with PLP/PWP, it became clear to me that the relationship between the leaders and the members was abusive, characterized by monologue as opposed to dialogue. "The party line" would change overnight, and it was un-comfortable if you were the member caught still operating on the old one. Because it was not safe to express disagreements, and it was a violation of "democratic centralism" to criticize the leader-ship, I believe the PLP/PWP simply reenacted the class dynamics of the very system it opposed. I can still recall being telephoned by the party leader in the middle of the night and told to organize a pro-test against Congressman Wilbur Mills that morning at what was then Boston State College. I was too sleepy and too intimidated to reveal the obvious: I knew nothing about Wilbur Mills.

If this was the way we communicated with each other within the PLP/PWP, I did not see much hope for anything different in a socialist society. I turned away from authoritarian Marxism to human services and eventually became a family therapist. It seemed to me that, unless individuals gained some emotional health, by looking, for example, at how they were affected by a family system, a site of social construction decidedly overlooked by the left, they would reenact problematic behavior in collectives that would only reproduce the social relations of capitalism.

Memories of this political oppression returned in graduate school twenty years later when I took the required course the Graduate Study of Literature. Two team teachers attempted to "shift our paradigms." Most of the students were too afraid of the teachers to question their politics. One day we were "discussing" an essay by Louis Althusser and one of the professors told a student who had questioned Althusser's perspective, "What you have just offered was a hostile reading. What we want in this class is a generous reading." Needless to say, most of the students subsequently suppressed their critical impulses and became "generous." (Later in the semester, I did shift my position on the Israeli Occupation of Palestine, no small transformation for a Jew, as a result of the professors' "confrontational pedagogy," but I did not like feeling intellectually battered or having my observations regarding anti-Semitism in the work of Edward Said silenced.)

Having had these experiences, I wondered if there was room for a more humane pedagogy in the social constructionist classroom. I attempted to answer my question by visiting Patricia Bizzell's classroom at the College of the Holy Cross in Worcester, Massachusetts. As I mentioned, I was troubled by an essay she published in 1991, "Power, Authority, and Critical Pedagogy," which seemed to affirm confrontational pedagogy. On the other hand, I felt drawn to the persona in her introduction to *Academic Discourse and Critical Consciousness* (1992) and wondered if it manifested itself in her classroom. I also wanted to see what she was doing to achieve her ongoing goal of "foster[ing] social justice, defined in some left-liberal way, in [her] teaching" (*Academic* 29). Finally, I was curious about whether she was employing the harsh confrontational methods I had associated with critical or liberatory pedagogies.

I suspected that Bizzell minimized personal writing in favor of writing that focused on issues of class or race or gender. My suspicion was grounded, in part, in a description she offers of a 1985 CCCC session in which she and Bruce Herzberg debated another well-known "composition couple," Knoblauch and Brannon, whose work I cited at the beginning of this chapter. Bizzell tells us that they disagreed about how best to teach academic discourse. In 1985, Knoblauch and Brannon had argued "that allowing students to frame personally relevant meanings through writing would eventually lead students to academic habits of thought" (Bizzell, *Academic* 23). On the other hand, Bizzell and Herzberg

> thought that students could be taught to argue, support assertions, and evaluate evidence in ways that would lead more directly to academic thinking than would writing in which they presented personal experience the authenticity of which few could question, which would require little "support." (Bizzell, *Academic* 23)

In view of her 1985 stance, I was especially drawn to the 1992 narrative of her professional life and the development of her ideas in the introduction to *Academic Discourse*. I admired the way she weaves her personal life into the story of the ideological shifts. She tells us, for example, "I now see my crisis of confidence and theoretical revisionism as related somehow to Bruce's and my adoption of two little girls in 1984" (24). It felt new to read of this kind of connection. Certainly Lester Faigley, whose work was the subject of critique earlier, never juxtaposes his intellectual development and his personal life in *Fragments of Rationality*.

As it turned out, the class I visited lent itself to both turns of thought. I experienced the first part of the class as a highly politicized discussion of the course reading and the second as a quite personal discussion about teaching. While I found Bizzell's pedagogy to be primarily dialogic, there were key moments when apparent consensus elided underlying disagreements between some students and the teacher.

Bizzell gave me permission to observe and tape an undergraduate class she was teaching at the College of the Holy Cross in the spring of 1994. Later on, in the fall of 1994, I had an opportunity to attend a presentation Bizzell made to a graduate composition class at BC. Additionally, Bizzell agreed to be interviewed, to read many drafts of my representation of her class, and to allow me to incorporate her responses back into my text. (These glosses are indicated in this chapter by brackets.) I am pleased to have at least some of the debate go on within the text itself because I am not comfortable with the journal format of statement–counterstatement as a way of negotiating difference, a format that contributes to the theory cleansing I see in the field. As John Schilb puts it, "Because we often communicate with one another through articles and books, our interpretations of one another will never smoothly coincide" (156). I seek to be part of a nonhostile discourse community.

Pat Bizzell Live

After reading Bizzell's work and identifying with her goals of teaching social justice, I now attempt to assess her praxis first in a presentation to a graduate class at BC and then in an undergraduate course taught at the College of the Holy Cross. In doing so, I am reversing the chronology of events so that I may keep connected the two more overtly political aspects of her work.

Paul Doherty invited Bizzell to address his graduate composition seminar at BC on 7 November 1994. Bizzell spoke about teaching in the "contact zone," a term she explicitly borrows from Mary Louise Pratt, in which teachers try to stimulate a diversity of opinion around major texts. Bizzell distributed an annotated table of contents from a then forthcoming book coauthored with Bruce Herzberg, *Negotiating Difference*. It is a collection of primary documents (treaties, laws, deeds) and articles that speak from varying political perspectives on six different units: contending English and Native American accounts of New England from 1620 to 1720; the debate around slavery; defining the "women's sphere" in American society from 1830 to 1870; class conflict in America from 1865 to 1900; Japanese American internment in World War II; and the Vietnam War. Although critics might point out that these are all areas in which one side has clearly won out, I see the project as a model for encouraging wide-ranging debates around texts in our composition and literature classes. As Bizzell told the graduate seminar, "In a contact zone, you have to communicate with your interlocutors." To me, the right to express disagreement in the contact zone brings the infrequently realized ideals of democracy into the classroom.

In the question-and-answer period, I spoke of a student of mine who was writing a paper critical of affirmative action in college admissions, directly blaming it for his rejection from Harvard. I commented on the ambivalence I feel while in the contact zone. In short, it is very difficult for me not to respond with some form of pedagogical petulance to such a student. When I expressed the dis-ease I feel in the classroom, Bizzell responded by saying that her own goals are modest. "There is only so much we can do in one semester." She does not want her students to feel that they are "taking a class in guilt and victimage." Her intent is to persuade her students, not to manipulate or indoctrinate them.

Subsequently a BC faculty member, Ellen Castle, picked up on my remark and was somewhat critical of contact zones. Referring to reproduced speeches in the forthcoming *Negotiating Difference,* she said, "I cannot imagine teaching Spiro Agnew in my classroom. Furthermore, I am afraid of further empowering the student who argues for the dominant ideology." Her point was, I believe, that the expression of such a perspective within the classroom would be more than simply part of a process in which everyone's culture is put out in the open for critical inquiry but would become the predominant voice. I felt supported when Castle spoke, not because I could not teach Spiro Agnew, but because I think Bizzell was a bit reticent on the subject of how irritating it can feel to create space for and then listen to right-wing ideas. The contact zone brings back many memories from the sixties.

I believe that many of us sixties radicals feel a great deal of frustration and self-doubt in our teaching. Theory and practice once interanimated each other because of the mass movements three decades ago. As students, we sought to politicize our classes and protested our universities' complicity with the war in Vietnam. We sometimes had the power to shut down the institution. As Harvard graduate Richard L. Baker put it at his twenty-fifth reunion, "'You had the feeling we could do anything, that we could change anything'" (Flint 16). Those were heady times. We may have been young, exuberant, and grandiose, but we were willing to take personal risks to end a war that many of us linked with the needs of U.S. imperialism to expand markets and gain access to cheap raw materials and labor.

The frenzy of involvement rushes back as I read Richard Ohmann's *English in America,* published in 1976 and "collectively misplaced" (Trimbur 389) for a period of time.

> By November, 1966, there was no day when I did not feel rage, anguish, and frustration over our government's actions. . . . If humanistic culture really is a civilizing force, why wouldn't the college I worked for and the profession I worked in TAKE A STAND? So I pressed for motions in faculty meetings, for days to be set aside to discuss the war, for resolutions in MLA and NCTE, and for crash programs of all kinds

to translate our moral views into political acts. And if I were giving a scholarly talk on language and literature, I would find a way to link it to Vietnam. (21)

Students and many teachers like Ohmann were alive with the possibility of making change. I often try to describe to my students the collective intimacy many of us experienced during the antiwar days, a loss that nothing has filled. When they respond unsympathetically to narratives by people who are marginalized, I feel quite distant from my students and from a time when we did speak up for the pain of oppressed people. Yet, when I set aside the idealized memory of the politicized academy of the sixties, I too recall the darker moments in the contact zone, the unmediated anger and hostility in discussions with people across the political spectrum. I did not make many allies by inviting strangers to buy "a communist newspaper," even though "it only cost[s] ten cents."

One Class Visit

On 21 April 1994, some months before Bizzell's presentation at BC, I was invited to observe one session of her undergraduate class, Composition Theory and Pedagogy. While I felt I was in a contact zone, in the sense of a space for diverse opinions, there were some gaps in the dialogic process. Let me preface my remarks by stating the obvious: one classroom visit does not an ethnography make.

Bizzell has written of pedagogy in a way that affirms a dialogic model.

> [I] would encourage my students to imitate my exercise of rhetorical authority. . . . They should be allowed to try to persuade me (a move I think academics seldom make with students whose views are radically different from their own) and other members of the class. ("Politics" 6)

Shor describes a classroom experience that seems to demonstrate Bizzell's argument.

> At my college the students are not pushovers. They are smart, articulate, and committed to ideologies they bring to class. I argued for my point of view, but in that verbal battleground I had to fight my way in and out of the debate while some of them tried to convince me and other students I was wrong—which is the way it should be in democratic education. (*Empowering* 64–65)

Thus both Bizzell and Shor are calling for greater communication with one's student interlocutors. I think that such classrooms are exceptional and, while I seek to imitate them, I often drive home from school feeling, to recall my sons' wrestling days, as if I have been pinned. That was not my experience of Bizzell's class.

The twenty-eight students, mostly sophomores and mostly white, in Bizzell's class were part of a peer-tutoring program designed by Bizzell. They applied to be in the class and submitted a writing sample and faculty references. In evaluating their work, Bizzell said that she looked

> for signs of mastery, signs of accomplished writing. At Holy Cross that usually means students who are writing conventional Standard English and conventional academic discourse although not always. Sadiqa [a black woman] doesn't write that way but I think she may be one of the most talented writers in the class.

Students who passed the course became eligible to work as paid tutors in the Writer's Workshop.

The syllabus was divided into three parts: "Composing Processes"; "Tutoring Processes," which coincided with the beginning of practice tutoring; and "Educational Processes." Students read from work that invoked "the competing theories of process" (Faigley, "Competing" 527) in Composition Studies: works by Patricia Bizzell, Janet Emig, Linda Flower, John Hayes, Nancy Sommers, Mina Shaughnessy, Elaine Maimon, David Bartholomae, Kenneth Bruffee, Anthony Petrosky, Anne DiPardo, and E. D. Hirsch Jr. Notably absent were more left critics in the field, namely, James Berlin, Richard Ohmann, Ira Shor, and James Sledd.

In the first part of the class, students discussed Mike Rose's *Lives on the Boundary* in relationship to prior readings from Patricia Williams's essay "Crimes without Passion" from *The Alchemy of Race and Rights: Diary of a Law Professor,* and Victor Villanueva's *Bootstraps: From an American Academic of Color.* In this part, I could observe the efforts of a social constructionist to create a discourse community. Having agreed to participate in class, I was introduced by Bizzell as a graduate student interested in some of the same things they were. After announcing that I wanted to tape the class, she asked, "That's no problem for anybody, is it?" Bizzell's question here could be viewed as a rhetorical one. I was happy to be allowed to use my tape recorder, but I am also aware that she was not offering the students a real choice.

Some students joked about wanting to be anonymous, but if anyone had been silenced by my presence, the unobserved class must have been pandemonium. There was frequent and widespread student participation, including active commentary on the part of Jackie and Sadiqa, two black women. During the sixty minutes of the class that I taped, there were fifty-eight student comments and forty-three comments by Bizzell, indicating a predominant but not total pattern of back-and-forth dialogue between student and teacher. In spite of the structure of the classroom, with all chairs facing forward toward the teacher, students often picked up on each other's comments. [Bizzell, in the margin of a draft of this chapter, noted: "This is a problem. We tried to get moved into a larger room where we could turn the desks more easily to face each other but the Registrar couldn't find one for us."] The longest Bizzell spoke involved thirty lines of transcript; the longest student expression involved fifteen lines. Bizzell was the most active contributor to the class, but I found the level of involvement among the students to be reflective of both strong motivation and comfort. Shor would most likely find her style dialogic, "the democratic negation, or opposite, of teacher talk" which "silences students" (*Empowering* 95). While Bizzell definitely maintained control of the discussion, there was no evidence of confrontational pedagogy.

Bizzell announced that they would be discussing Rose, as well as picking up on Williams and Villanueva. "This actually ties in, I don't know if you all remember what Sadiqa was saying at the end of the last hour. Do you want to repeat it, Sadiqa, or should I kind of summarize it?" I did not see in what way Sadiqa responded, but Bizzell went on to say,

> The issue we've been talking about [is], [D]oes everybody have to learn traditional academic discourse and what does it cost to learn traditional academic discourse? My memory is that Sadiqa was talking about how difficult it was to have to be translating all the time, like another language, translating yourself and your thoughts. . . . Maybe a good way of starting this is to compare these guys in terms of what they are doing to be nontraditional and academic at the same time. . . . What does Williams do that is nontraditional?

Sadiqa's notion of the difficulty of translating back and forth between two discourses was not pursued in this class.

Instead, Bizzell posed questions in relation to all three authors. Students generated a total of twenty-three responses, which Bizzell wrote on the blackboard either as stated or as revised. Often she pushed for more awareness of social context. The first student said that Williams told stories, and Bizzell asked, "What kinds of stories? What happens in these stories? Does she tell what she got for her birthday? They tend to be stories of discrimination." After seven student comments, as well as six more comments of her own, Bizzell summed it up based on a point Sarah made about the connection between personal and social issues.

Sarah: I just think there's a connection between all the stories that she tells, a lot of them have . . . the issues she's proposing, how those issues came about as part of her development. So there's a personal aspect of why she's so engaged in these issues.

Bizzell: I think this is a really important point, that she relates her personal story and the issues; and Sarah's quite right that one way of doing that is by developing it over time, showing that it's something that has been an issue for her since she was young. So the stories that she tells about herself are not just personal stories, they are representative . . . and I think that's very important.

When Sarah seemed to make the perfect social constructionist point, that the self is constructed in a social context, Bizzell framed it. After actively soliciting, receiving, and acknowledging student commentary, she emphasized one remark, possibly because it coincided with what she was looking for. [Bizzell noted here: "Yeah, sure! Why not?"] During the interchange, Bizzell wrote on the board "stories of discrimination." While Bizzell emphasized the "representative" nature of the stories, one could argue that Sarah's focus was on the personal. In fact, Sarah concluded her comment with "So there's a personal aspect of why she's so engaged in these issues." As a social constructionist, Bizzell clearly emphasized the critical social context over what appeared to be more personal. A submerged disagreement existed between the interlocutors.

In the subsequent discussion, some disagreements emerged more openly. Claire made the point that these authors used nontraditional methods, but "at the same time, their arguments wouldn't have been as effective if they didn't have such a firm grasp of the standard conventions." In Bizzell's response, nineteen lines of transcript, she essentially argued for both teaching the traditional academic discourse and "at the same time, giv[ing] the basic writing students models like [Williams, Villanueva, and Rose] for what their target discourse might be." Nancy then raised an objection.

Nancy: There is a contradiction. . . . You have a mixed signal that you are sending your students. You are telling them to do one thing and then you're offering them a chance to do something else. I think that's going to end up being confusing. *I think that academic discourse simply has to change, that the ideals of academic discourse have to be revised.*

Jackie: I kind of agree with Nancy in some ways, but I also think, okay, the students have to learn formal academic discourse. . . . But I don't know. . . . *I have to totally disagree [with Claire] and say that [Villanueva's] argument could have been just as good [had he not used standard conventions], but he wouldn't have been recognized by academia as having his argument be good until they do it, until he does it the way they want him to.* And I think that's exactly what he argues. [Emphasis mine]

I see these students as having mounted a minor insurrection here by calling attention to the fact that academic discourse is necessary for the approval of the system. Or, as Freire puts it, Nancy and Jackie became "critical co-investigators in dialogue with the teacher" (68). I found Bizzell's response to be somewhat evasive. She spoke of Villanueva's self-report on how the book was written, that he had had writer's block until he gave himself permission to use a nontraditional approach, that NCTE published the book and he got tenure. "[I]n some ways he took a gamble that paid off . . . and the canon of academic discourse got enlarged. Maybe that's the answer. There have to be more people like that that take risks." Bizzell's response makes Villanueva appear a bit dehistoricized; it is my feeling that NCTE had been looking for books by academics of color.[2]

Moreover, in responding to her interlocutors, I think Bizzell whitewashed the underlying disagreement. Nancy argued for changing the discourse, not for enlarging it. I am reminded here of Bizzell's more radical comment in "Foundationalism and Anti-Foundationalism" (1986) in which she calls for "political activity that changes the nature of discourse and the institutions whereby the discourse is preserved" (reprinted in *Academic Discourse* 220). Jackie, taking issue with Claire's affirmation of academic discourse, pointed out the need for accommodation in order to get recognition. Nancy and Jackie seemed less loyal to academic discourse than their teacher.[3] [Bizzell noted, "Very interesting analysis."]

Later, when a student commented that nontraditional discourse was not acceptable in most English classes ("I don't consider this an English class, I consider it more of a cross-cultural or sociological perspective on English"), Bizzell became very animated:

> I asked you guys this very question when we were reading Petrosky. You all said (gross generalization), "Oh, Holy Cross professors would love it if we wrote papers that were [inaudible]." Personally I thought that was a lot of baloney. I didn't say that, but personally I was quite struck by . . . your almost universal response.

There was much friendly laughter while she was speaking, as the students seemed to recall that they had, in fact, said these things. ["Whatever I said, it was to the effect that they had claimed earlier that Holy Cross English professors would welcome a lot of personal commentary—'This book made me think about a time in my life when . . .'—*that* was baloney!"] It is my sense that Bizzell herself welcomed personal commentary only when it was explicitly linked to social, "representative" issues.

Caitlin described how she had gotten the "picky" professor of her Judaism class to accept writing he might have ordinarily dismissed. She gave him a draft and sat with him as he read it.

Caitlin: [I]t was so funny to watch him, because I sat there while he read it and he was like [emits a noise]. [Laughter] "That's endearing but I wonder if . . ." We went through the whole thing together and he was like, "I really like the way things are said but I want to make sure you're making your point and it's true." . . . Even if we disagree to the bitter end, he'll give me a good grade having gone to him. . . . I think the key is to, like, get the draft done and, like, not see it as, like, the professor's the enemy but your partner in the education process. [Much affirmative murmuring]

Bizzell: I want to inscribe everything you just said on a scroll and, like, post it on the wall. [Laughter]

Here the community seemed to have reached a consensus: you do what you can to push the boundaries of academic convention without risking getting a poor grade. Bizzell helped facilitate this consensus by not dwelling on the problems raised by Sadiqa, Nancy, and Jackie. Perhaps this process had happened before in the class, but the students were far from silenced by it. [Bizzell noted here: "You seem consistently suspicious of consensus."]

Having noted some unacknowledged disagreements in this part of the class, let me conclude my observations by saying that the other part was characterized by supportive and pragmatic mentoring. The atmosphere felt personal. The class began with Bizzell asking if there were any tutoring problems people wanted to discuss. What ensued was a highly dialogic interchange in which, with a spirit of camaraderie, students eagerly shared their own experiences. The example that follows reflects the level of trust in the classroom, an atmosphere that is absent when confrontational pedagogy predominates. As Bleich puts it, "[C]ollaboration requires more than opening up or expressing ourselves; it demands the patient, gradual buildup of trust and understanding" (*Know* 115).

Jackie: Yesterday was my first time tutoring and I was so nervous. It was only a two-page paper and it took me ten minutes to read, and I couldn't remember what I had read at all [friendly laughter]; and I said, "Oh, no." And I made these little comments, but I had no idea what this paper is about after ten minutes. . . .

Bizzell: What happened when you actually had to open your mouth and say something?

Jackie: I started with something easy. She had like the word order wrong. That was easy. We switched that around and then I sort of went back to the first sentence and we fixed that.

What struck me was the comfort Jackie had in sharing her sense of failure in front of twenty-eight other students, which speaks to the relatively noncompetitive nature of the milieu. Jackie's self-disclosure was especially impressive, as she was one of only a few students of color in the class.

Other tutors, mostly sophomores, raised problems about feeling intimidated by juniors and seniors who sought help with their writing. Bizzell then delivered her longest statement of the class, assuring her students that the feeling of intimidation is part of the vulnerability of teaching.

Remember when we talked about Kaly and Morgan and how self-conscious they were? They were always thinking about, "What are people thinking about me and how am I coming over here?" I think . . . it's a normal part of moving into that role and being a kind of authority. I don't think you ever want to lose that feeling because, if you do, you'd probably become insensitive to the feelings of the people you're working with, but you shouldn't take it as an accurate self-assessment, you know. "I'm feeling inadequate because I am inadequate. I'm feeling inadequate because this is a feeling that people have when they are trying to do this work and I have to just push it over here to the side."

Bizzell's remarks were spoken with warmth, and I experienced them as being both caring and useful to her student tutors.

The State of the Field

I have tremendous respect for what I see as Pat Bizzell's social constructionist pedagogy and for her nearly thirty years of teaching, which undoubtedly raised the critical consciousness of many students and fellow faculty. I was especially struck by the ease with which her students simply embraced the concept of social justice. Her writing and praxis, which are in accord with each other, have contributed enormously to my own professional self-formation.

Bizzell is on call for the "local struggle," which I have come to valorize in a new way after having sat in on her class. As another former sixties radical, Robert Allen Oden Jr. put it,

> "We wanted to change the world. . . . We wanted to stop the war in Vietnam. And we still want to make a difference. . . . *We're fighting now in classrooms and in urban centers for the soul of the country.* That puts it very grandly I know but I like to think that's what we've done." (Flint 16, emphasis mine)

During the antiwar movement, much of the work was devoted to anti-imperialist education. Perhaps we can say that, despite the difficulties I have outlined, the theoretical groundwork for future struggle is being laid now by people like Pat Bizzell, Henry Giroux, Ira Shor, Lil Brannon, and the many unheralded teachers who introduce cultural criticism into the academy. Perhaps some less well known teachers influenced the Ohio State students who, on 18 February 1998, interrupted Secretary of State Madeleine Albright, Defense Secretary William Cohen, and National Security Adviser Samuel Berger as they tried to garner support for bombing Iraq. The students chanted, "One, two, three, four! We don't want your racist war!" Or, as Cy Knoblauch and Lil Brannon argue in regard to gender discrimination, perhaps change is happening through "local, determined interventions in teaching life":

> The reasons for these changes . . . have nothing to do with abrupt, massive, revolutionary change. . . . They have everything to do with small numbers of women, even at first individuals, performing acts of critical intervention amidst political and economic realities organized against their best interests. . . . The historical track of critical pedagogy, leading by small increments toward an increasingly engaged citizenry *unwilling to accept the subordination or mistreatment of any of its members*, will resemble the track of women's rights. (200, emphasis mine)

However, what troubles me about both confrontational pedagogy and the current state of composition studies is that they smack of the same kind of notions of "right" and "wrong" ideas that I saw in the PLP/PWP. Perhaps initiated by the taxonomy of James Berlin and continuing with Lester Faigley's "competing theories of process" ("Competing" 527), the field seems polarized by the social constructionist critique of personal writing in the academy. While the CCCC's evaluation of paper abstracts is conducted through blind review, it feels symbolic that Peter Elbow's proposal "Expressivists Talk Back" was rejected for the 1998 convention in Chicago. As I noted in chapter 1, a composition professor formerly at the University of Texas told me, "The cardinal rule of graduate school is that no one reads Peter Elbow." Theory wars abound, and what I see in our literature and in our graduate classroom discussions seems to be little more than "theory cleansing." As a colleague recently said, "The field *is* dissent."

I see a dangerous trend in the field of composition studies today. Some well-published social constructionists who also sit on several editorial boards, as well as on important professional committees, seem to have an upper hand in a discourse that is either dismissive of the personal narrative or validating only insofar as it is linked to the social. And, as I stated earlier, the social is mysteriously conceived in such a way as to render the family invisible.

I constantly find myself up against this trend, refusing in my own writing and pedagogy to slight narratives about troubling personal experiences. The authoritarian PLP/PWP, as I knew them in the 1960s, paid little or no attention to personal problems not related to overt political struggle. To me, the refusal to respect an aspect of life represents the antithesis of critical consciousness. The personal and the political elements must be seen as interrelated. As Carolyn Kay Steedman puts it her own working-class autobiography, *Land-*

scape for a Good Woman, we need to see the development of class consciousness, not just its expression, a behavior "learned in childhood and often through the exigencies of difficult and lonely lives" (13). Political consciousness emerges from these "difficult and lonely lives," and the awareness of oneself as a sentient being arises from the political. "Class and gender, and their articulations, are the bits and pieces from which psychological selfhood is made" (7). Thus we are back to James Merrill's "tesserae of [the] mosaic" I referred to in the introduction. The political and the personal are grouted together into one whole.

In fact, many times I have found my students' dominant ideology to be fueled by some troubling life experience that they need to reexamine, such as the student who wrote a paper attacking affirmative action because he blamed it for his rejection from Harvard. As I suggested in relation to Faigley's reading of Norma Bennett's essay on her father's alcoholism in *What Makes Writing Good,* I see an antifemale strain in the current hegemonic trivialization of the personal narrative in the academy. Gradin writes, "[T]he fact that expressivism values the autobiographical, the intimate and subjective voice that has been codified as 'feminine' in our culture, may be one reason that expressivism is continually denigrated" (145).

The factional disputes within composition studies especially worry me when I read the social epistemics as essentializing cognitivists and "expressivists." I am reminded of the factionalism on the left in the sixties. Rather than shadow boxing with books and articles that were written over twenty years ago, I think we should be revising and rehabilitating the contact zone in our field so that it incorporates mutual respect and more ethnographic research about what our colleagues are doing today. I see professionals like Elbow, who convened an informal meeting of people from "competing theories of discourse" within the field in the fall of 1994, and Gradin, who calls for a hybrid "social-expressivism," as spearheading a constructive movement in this direction.

In this regard, it is interesting to look at Bizzell's way of responding to criticism. She is fair in her reply to Nancy McKoski in spite of being called "modernist and reactionary" (334). "McKoski does not seem to be aware of . . . developments in my most recent scholarship, and she seriously misrepresents some of my views" ("Are Shared Discourses Desirable?" 273). However, Bizzell does up the ante by equating McKoski's remarks with "what [James] Sosnoski calls 'getting-at-my-truth' criticism, in which the object is to show that the ideas of no one but the present writer have any merit" (275). [Bizzell noted here, "Actually I've thought a lot about how to respond to criticism of my work. I want to avoid the usual agonistic stance and to assume that the point is not defending my work but rather furthering the collective work, the disciplinary project. I was more harsh in my reply to McKoski than I have ever been because I felt she really was unfair and unhelpful."] I too was "harsh" in my commentary on Faigley and Berlin earlier. In fact, one reader had encouraged me to be more "lighthearted" about the misrepresentation of "expressivism." I felt that either no response or a lighthearted one would not be useful in dispelling the perpetuation of an Other in our field that has become serious enough to me to look like a kind of theoretical racism against one's colleagues.

The tendentious and sectarian nature of some of the published writing in composition often seems characterized by careerism and "'getting-at-my-truth' criticism." The dominant view now, which feels like a new foundationalism, involves knee-jerk dismissals of "expressivism" for allegedly encouraging our students to believe in unified selves, of cognitivism for proclaiming universals, and of Marxism for being a "grand narrative." A psychologist recently told me when I tried to describe our differences, "I don't understand this. I thought the idea was to just teach people to write." (I will not go to bat for this remark; after all, mental health professionals have had their own slugfest over how to "cure" us.) [Bizzell noted here: "Debate has to be allowed, even fostered. Funny how easy it is to mock other people's debates (e.g., your psychologist friend)—because the issues don't matter. If they do matter, you have to find a way to develop them productively in dialogue."] It is time to look beyond what each "side" preaches to what it practices.

[Bizzell wrote, "I don't want to write much more here than I've already put in the margins—where my comments belong, I think. It was certainly fascinating and provocative to read such a thoroughgoing study of myself, but enough already. Bizzell's been heard from plenty enough in this essay.

"I'm glad you took the initiative to ask me to visit my class, interview me, and get commentary. I'd be reticent to volunteer such things (and exhausted if many others asked!). Thank you for asking. I really like your paper. Shalom—PB."]

After I made yet another revision to this chapter, Bizzell wrote me a letter (29 August 1999).

> Thank you for sending me the final version of your chapter. I still like it very much. In fact, reading it this time after not seeing it for awhile, I was struck by how careful and insightful your analysis of my work is. Also I was struck by the importance of your point that social-constructionist theorizing tends to neglect the family as a social site. I think this is a neglect that needs to be remedied, even though you and I might disagree about what kinds of writing assignments would properly attend to this site.

Coda

Listening to Bizzell's student tutors express their feelings of inadequacy in their new roles evoked some feelings of inadequacy about my own teaching that year. Had I raised anyone's "critical consciousness" in my FWS? The political feels so personal for me. I conclude this chapter with a teaching story of my own.

Fall of 1993. We are about to discuss Elie Wiesel's *Night*. I just put it on the syllabus. I am not a child or a grandchild of a Holocaust survivor, as my paternal grandfather fled Russia before the Nazi invasion. When they invaded, the Nazis ordered the Jews, including my great grandparents, aunts, and uncles, to dig a pit and line up above it, and then the Nazis shot them from behind so that they fell forward into the pit. Recently I heard a child of a Nazi describe how they used to try to get two starving Jews to stand really close so they wouldn't have to waste more than one bullet.

"All right," I say. "Can someone go to the board and write down what people want to discuss?" Someone goes; I forget whom. The class cranks right up, most unusual for this pulling-teeth crowd. It just hits me, pure abreaction, the kind that you're supposed to have during the ninety-dollar clinical hour. I grew up less than five miles from this school with a mother who hated everybody who was not Jewish (because, I believe, she somehow thought they bore collective guilt for the *Shoah*). Now I'm standing here "teaching" the Holocaust to a room full of Catholics. The urge to cry is astonishing. Somehow I choke it back (you get good practice growing up in an alcoholic family) and manage to get Jen to lead the class discussion. She is not too happy about it but cooperates. After a while, I am able to speak. I only remember saying that the topic was more emotional for me than I anticipated. Is teaching like this for everybody? [Bizzell noted here, "No, only the fortunate. Actually I find it becoming *more* emotional for me as I get older (and my kids get older)—I don't know why—I just seem to cry more easily—my eyes fill, anyway."]

Spring of 1994. Jed, a Jordanian student, transfers into my class because his first instructor chose as the theme for her FWS the Holocaust. "I could not sit in a class for four months and sympathize with her about something that happened so long ago when my people are dying in the West Bank and ethnic cleansing is going on in Bosnia." In conference we talk about the Middle East. With my Star of David glinting in his eye, he listens to me talk about my opposition to the Occupation. I hear his description of Jordanians being strip-searched entering into Israel. Naked groups, their clothes all tangled in a pile on the floor. I feel sick at this reenactment of the Holocaust. Anna Freud might call the Israeli's treatment of the Jordanians "identification with the aggressor."

Black Friday, 25 February 1994. During the prayer of Ramadan, the holiest of Muslim holidays, Baruch Goldstein, doctor–settler–Jewish terrorist enters the Arab side of the Hebron Ibrahimiya Mosque/Cave of the Machpela (Abraham is the father of both our peoples) and shoots and kills thirty-five praying Arabs, wounding many more. At least as many will be killed by the Israeli Army in the ensuing protests. I don't know what to do with myself. I contact the New Jewish Agenda and learn that the Middle East Justice Network is holding a demonstration.

I call Jed and nearly start to cry. I simply say, "I'm sorry." Two other students from the class go to the demonstration. I stay behind to teach and hand out stories from the book *Homeland: Oral Histories of Palestine and Palestinians* (Lynd et al.). Jed agrees to lead the next class on the massacre.

I see the therapist. No "discourse demonstratives" today (Berkenkotter et al. 15). No words at all. "It's good you can cry about this. Jews all over the world feel shame." [Bizzell notes, "Indeed."]

Jed gives a report. Draws a map on the board. Carefully distinguishes between the nation of Israel and Jews, but it's not easy for him. Tells about the history and the massacre. The two students who attended the demonstration give a report. One has written down all the slogans he saw. We talk about the oral history. A fifteen-year-old Palestinian rock thrower loses his leg to a barrage of bullets from Israeli soldiers. Students say this is all new to them; they have never heard the Palestinian side of the story from the media. We talk about this elision as an indication of the U.S. government's support of Israel.

I tell the class how I feel. I believe that the lesson of the Holocaust is that the Occupation is wrong. I have them do a freewrite based on a *Boston Globe* article. I want them to try to simulate and feel the range of reaction at an Israeli high school in Jerusalem and an Arab school in Nazareth. We all write. The period ends. No one leaves.

In conferences I check with the students about how they felt about the class. Was it too intense?

"No. Could we talk about current events more often?"

⇢ CONCLUSION
Responding Responsibly to Personal Narratives

Cura Personalis

In her novel *Oranges Are Not the Only Fruit,* Jeanette Winterson writes,

> And when I look at a history book and think of the imaginative effort
> it has taken to squeeze this oozing world between two boards and type-
> set, I am astonished. Perhaps the event has an unassailable truth. God
> saw it. God knows. But I am not God. And so when someone tells me
> what they heard or saw, I believe them, and I believe their friend who
> also saw, but not in the same way, and I can put these accounts together
> and I will not have a seamless wonder but a sandwich laced with a
> mustard of my own. (95)

I read this statement by Winterson, or rather by Winterson's fictional
persona, as instruction for the ethnographer. She wants us to believe
all sides of the story, even if they contradict each other, and when
we write our version, we acknowledge our subjectivities.

I have told many stories in this book. I have told the story of
how some composition scholars (namely, James Berlin, David Bartholomae, and Lester Faigley) have created a narrative about other
composition scholars, such as Peter Elbow and William Coles and

James Vopat. Their stories are based largely on textual representations, writing on writing about writing. I have told classroom stories: how a young black teacher worked with two dissimilar students,
one coming across as self-confident and judgmental toward the poor,
the other as insecure and judgmental toward people who drink to
excess; and I have told the story of how a middle-aged white teacher
worked with her class's only black student, who tried to write her
way through a racist and humiliating teaching practicum. My final
story was about how Patricia Bizzell worked in one class period with
her students and peer tutors. All of these stories are infused with a
purpose; my intent has been to break up false binaries in the field
of composition. I have represented those teachers identified with
"expressivist" pedagogy or writing programs as inviting such issues
as race and class into their courses (although with varying degrees
of comfort), and I have shown that there was a personal element in
one class meeting of a social constructionist.

However, I also want to argue that autobiography is a viable
genre and that it belongs in the academy along with other more con-
ventional types of writing. While my ethnographic study of the BC
teachers shows that they did not limit their agenda to personal narrative, they did include this genre and saw it as important. Our students loosen up as writers when they are creating texts about matters that are important to them and events that have transpired in
their lives. And I do not think this phenomenon is limited to first-
year college writing. For example, one quarter I taught a course at
Northeastern University called Writing for the Professions for the
"middle-year" student in a five-year undergraduate program. The
writing program at this university was heavily influenced by Bartholomae. In fact, some of the faculty reviewed the additional material in Bartholomae and Petrosky's fifth edition of *Ways of Reading*. However, built into this tight and demanding course was a
narrative assignment in which we asked students to trace their interest in a topic. My student Gillian wrote a fine essay entitled "The
Human Genome Project [HGP]: Scientific Achievement or Ethical
Disaster?" as she moved toward a career in forensic medicine. (The
goal of the HGP is to map all the genes in the human body and keep
records, which may not be confidential.) She located the source of
her interest in DNA and criminal investigation in a family tragedy.
"A little over a year ago my mother's best friend was murdered by
her husband." The man was convicted based on forensic and medi-

cal evidence. As a result, Gillian wanted to be involved in "bringing criminals to justice and bringing peace of mind to families." The etiology of her interest in the subject never directly appeared in her well-written essay; it appeared only in one of the preceding assignments, the narrative. Yet her personal concern and strong voice were infused in the research paper itself. "If we are to consider the HGP as an achievement in the scientific field, then it must not compromise the privacy and security of human beings." What if her instructor had decided to skip the course's narrative assignment? What if Gillian had not had the opportunity to write about something that she thought about frequently, the murder of a close family friend? Would her final paper have been as good? I have no way of knowing because she did write the narrative. However, I would venture to say that she is better able to perform in the difficult courses she takes for having had the space to make public this trying experience, an experience closely linked to her motives as a student. Perhaps her desire to work so hard to achieve her goal of being involved in forensic medicine was reinforced by knowing that the people who assigned such difficult term projects in the middler-year writing course cared about her life experiences.

In the spring of 1999, I accepted the position of director of freshman English at a Jesuit institution in Los Angeles, Loyola Marymount University. One of the reasons that I was drawn to the school is its affirmation of the principle of *cura personalis,* or the care of the whole person. The mission statement of the school reads: "Loyola Marymount understands and declares its purpose to be: the encouragement of learning, the education of the whole person, the service of faith and the promotion of justice." At a time of backlash against autobiographical writing in the academy, it was refreshing to read such a statement. When we invite our students to write about their life experiences, without disqualifying this writing as somehow an unwitting reinscription of a "master narrative" of the family, as does Bartholomae ("Writing" 67), we are explicitly letting them know that the experiences that have shaped them as people and as students matter to us as much as what we have to teach them matters. Whether students want to write about positive or negative life events, describe some sort of awakening, or create profiles of individuals who have impacted their lives, we can find a place for their work in our classrooms. Furthermore, we will not denigrate their efforts by telling the students that they have no agency in producing their texts, that they were always already written by the hegemonic ideology of our culture. And we will not tell them that they can only write their essays using the perspective of an author whose work we have deemed fit to anthologize, thus creating a new "master narrative" for the genre of autobiography. As we learn from the knowledge and experience that our students bring to the university, so they can learn from what we professors have to teach them in an atmosphere of caring and respect.

The Ethics of Required Personal Narratives

Yet I have almost completely ignored one important critique of autobiographical writing in the academy, and it is one that I am not wholly in disagreement with. It has to do with the tension that necessarily arises when people in authority ask those beneath them in an institutional hierarchy to write narratives about their personal lives. As I conclude this volume, I quote variations of this objection, offer a case example of how the projected problems were avoided in one teacher's class, and make some suggestions about how to teach personal narrative responsibly, thus minimizing the potential for abuse of power.

In the following paragraphs, I offer statements from different theorists and my summaries of what their objections are.

Lester Faigley (drawing upon Foucault):

> When a teacher obtains a revealing personal disclosure, a different relation of power is constructed between teacher and student than typically is constructed in transactional forms of writing. (*Fragments* 131)

Faigley thinks that we may be using institutional authority to extract "confessions."

Susan Swartzlander, Diana Pace, and Virginia Lee Stamler (faculty or staff psychologists at Grand Valley State University, Allendale, Michigan):

> Writing about childhood experiences could cause strong feelings of shame to surface; having others read about their experiences could cause additional trauma. . . . Our counseling center has had to aid students who have blocked out unpleasant childhood experiences, only to have an intrusive writing assignment elicit a flood of excruciating memories. (B1)

Writing teachers who require autobiographical writing may be causing their students to relive painful events in their lives.

Judith Summerfield:

> The composition classroom is a curious nexus of the public and the private, particularly in this moment when talk-show culture promotes telling all in lurid detail and we, in composition, promote show-not-tell or, worse, "self-disclosure," or promote personal writing because we believe that it will be healing or transformative or promote personal growth. We need to scrutinize our own complex values, motives, principles, and ideologies for asking students to write in this hybrid form under the description "personal narrative," which is mostly peculiar to the classroom. (170–71)

Have we, as writing teachers, really examined what we are doing and why we are doing it when we assign personal narratives?

Michelle Gibson:

> [S]tudents in the throes of revealing and coping with personal traumas cannot be expected to believe our assertions that we criticize their writing rather than their experiences or their emotions. (26)

Rhetorical assessment by the teacher cannot be extricated from the psychological assessment.

Dan Morgan:

> I have some misgivings about the ethical appropriateness of issuing an unsolicited referral to counseling. So . . . do I work to help this student write a *better* paper about how a person should continue staying in a relationship with an abusive crack addict? . . . What *is* the nature of our "contract" with students, exactly? (320)

Morgan is stunned by some of the papers his students write and is confused about his responsibilities as a teacher of composition.

Catherine (an informant from a class in Smalltown in the United Kingdom in an ethnography conducted by Barnes et al.):

> I prefer to keep my feelings to myself. (91)

Catherine resents it when she feels her teachers are prying into her personal life.

Dorothy Barnes, Douglas Barnes, and Stephen Clarke:

> These researchers wonder how a student is to write on private topics for "a teacher with whom they may not be on easy terms." (109)[1]

The arguments of these critics of personal writing in the academy fall into two areas. The assignment of personal writing either can lend itself to an abuse of power on the part of the teacher that may cause the students pain, or it can lend itself to a crisis of responsibility for a teacher who does not know how to respond to what he or she receives. These are important critical issues. I have no doubt that there is a tremendous potential for abuse when our students are required to write about their lives. However, the potential for abuse lies in another direction as well.

Marilyn Valentino presents a different problem faced by teachers. Despite not requesting personal responses to assignments on literature, she has often been "shocked and certainly ill-prepared" when she gets them (274). She argues that a teacher who does not acknowledge what has been disclosed and solely critiques the assignment is doing that student a disservice. In "Responding When a Life Depends on It: What to Write in the Margins When Students Self-Disclose," an article that won the CCCC Best of 1997 for *Teaching English in the Two-Year College,* Valentino issues her own guidelines for what to do when a student self-discloses. Valentino's essay should be required reading for teachers.[2]

Thomas Newkirk addresses the issue of privacy invasion in *The Performance of Self in Student Writing.* He does not agree with those who problemize the power dynamics surrounding personal writing:

> While it is possible that an insensitive teacher could establish "disclosure" as a tacit criteria, I have been impressed by how rarely this seems to happen. Over the past two decades I have read thousands of anonymous, student written evaluations of teachers in our program [at UNH]. I cannot remember one in which a student made this kind of complaint. The overwhelming and consistent comments we see are those of appreciation for the opportunity to write and reflect on life experiences. (19)

Newkirk finds no empirical evidence in his program that students feel violated when they are asked to write personal essays. In fact, he says, they like it.

A Model for Responding to Personal Narratives

Rather than argue with the critics of "expressivism" here, I simply acknowledge that their concerns are theoretically plausible. Perhaps the personal narrative should not be "required" by teachers. I think that when shocked or disturbed by the narrative content of student essays, teachers can have a wide range of unpredictable responses, including acting as if they are trained psychotherapists. Moreover, those teachers who specifically assign personal narrative can forget the context of the assignment: namely, that they have the power to grade a student's paper, and this authority complicates the "sharing" that transpires in that paper. The task environment is not neutral, and the student who chooses to write about a painful experience is vulnerable. On the other hand, what many of the critics of personal writing assignments do not discuss is how some aspects of postmodern theory may add to the difficulties students experience. Before exploring this possibility, let me offer a case example of what is, in my opinion, an appropriate response to a personal narrative.

I conducted an ethnographic study at the New Hampshire Summer Writing Program in 1996 (see Paley, "Next Week"). My primary informant, teacher Pat McLure, received an essay written in the third person that she correctly intuited was a first-person experience. "Sally's" piece, "The Drive-In," was a masterfully written narrative about a fourteen-year-old girl who took care of the house while her mother worked. One day her friend asked her to go see the movie *The Exorcist,* and they arranged to have her mother call Sally's mother for permission. All worked according to plan except that Sally did not anticipate the fear that the film would trigger in her.

> "If I can just stay calm 'til I get home I'll be alright." . . . While the terror coursed through her veins, she bit back total panic with clamped lips, tight over clenched teeth and her balled-up fists hugged close around her.

The narrator held herself together until she got home and rushed to her mother for the hug and reassurance she so desperately needed.

> As she opened the door she saw her mother standing in the kitchen. Relief washed over her. "Mom, thank God . . ." she burst into tears with her arms held wide stepping toward the older woman, inviting a hug. As she moved forward her mother's right arm shot out, smashing across her right cheek with a jolt. CRACK! "You're not allowed to stay out this late!" Her only explanation.

The slap was actualized in the reader who very much wanted the young girl to be comforted by her mother.

I was able to follow the development of this piece from the pre-writing phase in peer group, to a conference with Pat, to a reading to the whole class. In addition, I interviewed both Sally and Pat individually. The conference provided an example of a composition teacher maintaining the boundaries around her role in the face of an essay that clearly related to an unresolved personal trauma experienced by the author.

Sally read the essay aloud in conference, the first time that either Pat or I heard it. At the end, I jerked my head up from note taking as if struck myself, and I saw the tears streaming down Sally's cheeks. Pat could not seem to prevent herself from emitting, "Oh, my God! That's so strong." The latter was a reference to the ending. Pat's voice was compassionate. That she was emotionally present for the student's pain was evident in her soft, kind voice and pained expression. However, she was completely focused on the text as a piece of writing told by a third-person narrator. She said, "The reaction is so powerful and unexpected." Her reaction was also in the third person. Rather than personalize the character or give direct emotional support to the author, she maintained the student's third-person boundary, yet there was implied empathy. "You develop the main character. You took us through her day. This is really a very capable person. . . . The dinner scene was so quiet and you could feel the tension. You set the stage."

When I interviewed Sally later, she told me that she was satisfied with the response she had received from her teacher.

> [M]y perception of Pat's role in that relationship is someone to be focusing on the writing and she did that. And, as a reader or a listener, the words I wrote would have an emotional impact on her and I would want that from everyone, but her part of the bargain is that she is there to help me see the things that meet my criteria for the piece . . . and to help me problem solve a few ways of taking care of the less effective parts. I wouldn't want more from her. She did that and I don't need the emotional support from her.

Like Helena's student Catherine, who wrote about her father's drinking, Sally did not want "counseling" from the teacher. As Newkirk argues,

> Paradoxically, these writing situations can be therapeutic precisely because we don't act as therapists. . . . [T]he therapeutic power of such

writing may be the experience of having it treated as "normal"—that is, writing that can be responded to, critiqued, even graded. (*Performance* 19)

Subsequently I asked Pat about her experience of hearing the essay.

The ending surprised me. I wasn't expecting that ending to it. . . . I felt for her. You could see the pain that it still carries for her. And even though she was trying to distance herself from the piece by not writing in the first person, you knew she was writing about herself. There's certainly a real emotional connection we make with people when they share stories like that.

Clearly Pat felt the pathos of Sally's essay even though she never expressed it to her; instead she respected the author's decision to write in the third person. Pat understood the self-protective function of the narrative strategy. However, she also commented,

I wonder if I would have responded differently if I was involved in the response earlier in her process with this piece, as she was just starting to talk her way through it. I might have focused more on her experience as opposed to hearing it today as she really had a pretty complete draft done. . . . The other thing I know I was thinking about was the fact that she didn't want to use her name in it, and I kept thinking as she was reading through this, Why wasn't she just calling it herself?

Although Pat was not sure how she would have responded to an earlier draft, it is clear that she was aware of her ethical responsibility to respect the privacy of the author of this essay.

The whole class was the audience for the final reading of "The Drive-In." Sally's peers also respected her privacy. Sally was shaking by the end of the reading, but there was only a hint of tears. Her peers began to discuss the movie itself until Sam, the only male in the class, spoke up, defying my gender expectations. "The essay has a very powerful ending and we're all talking about the movie." That led to other comments like "You don't ever expect the slap across the face," and "You get the insecure child who wants the mother's acceptance." One comment, however, indicated some slippage between the narrator and her classmate. "We become the character; we're as shocked as *you* are" (emphasis mine). Yet, for the most part, both Sally's teacher and her peers allowed the author third-person anonymity.

I tell this story, at least partly, to ask a question. Who *is* the narrator of the personal essay? Postmodern theory has put great distance between the self who writes and the self in the text, between empirical experience and its discursive representation. For example, Summerfield objects to readers who assume that "the writer is the transcriber. That the 'I' writing is naturalized, assumed authentic" (165). Postmodernists see all autobiography as a quasi-literary event, constructed for an audience. I do not disagree that language is representation rather than re-presentation. What I do object to is that this postmodern theory can be used as a tool to remove affective experience from the academy, as a way to distance the student writer from his or her own feelings. When Summerfield invites her students to write about "[their] own life and times," she issues twenty-one guidelines with the assignment. Here are a few of them:

1. The representation is not the event.
2. The memory is not the event.
3. To be "personal," you don't have to "be" personal, that is, to lose control, to spill the beans, to confess, to say what you don't want to say.
4. The "I" of your piece will be an invention, a fiction. . . .
12. Our agreement as readers will be that we will not be allowed to ask: Did this "really" happen? (175–76)

Pat McLure followed the twelfth guideline in her response to Sally's essay; she did not ask. I read Summerfield as attempting to protect her students from an invasion of their privacy and any ensuing ambivalent feelings that might result from such an invasion.

However, when students self-disclose, they do not see their narrational *I* as a fiction. They believe they are describing events as they experienced them. In fact, labeling as fiction the personal narrative could cause a student to feel that he or she is not being believed; such disbelief could retraumatize the writer. The postmodern separation between writer and textual self ignores a point made by Irena Klepfisz. In her feminist history of Yiddish women writers, she tells us that "many of these stories . . . use narrators closely identified with the women protagonists" (53). The writer may not be the same as the narrator, but he or she is closely identified with that narrator.

Additionally, I would argue that authors of Holocaust testimonials would be greatly offended by the notion that the narrational *I* is a fiction. Many of them state as their purpose wanting the feelings described to be actualized in the reader; the author wants the audience to know exactly how the Nazis treated people. Furthermore, as Earl Miner describes the responses of Eastern readers,

> [I]n the absence of countervailing evidence, it is presumed that poets speak *in propria persona*. . . . [T]he east Asian idea holds that the author is speaking out to the reader, commonly as if there were no lyric speaker, no narrator of a story. (30)

Summerfield's application of postmodern theory can be too dismissive of students' efforts to transmit experience, a dismissal that can border on inappropriate distancing or disengaged response.

I am, therefore, suggesting that there may be times when we do want to ask if the student is describing a life experience; and, when we learn that he or she is relating an actual event, we should respond to that personal narrative with great sensitivity, a sensitivity that is informed by a belief that the student is trying hard to describe the past or present self and relationships as that student currently sees them. In other words, there are times when we may want initially to respond as if we were East Asian readers. Responding sensitively might mean following Valentino's suggestions. Ask if the student is describing something that actually happened and then respond with "reflective statements": "'This must have been horrible for you.' 'That must have been upsetting.' 'You seem upset. Is there someone you can talk to about this? Would you like to speak to a counselor?'" (278–81).

Earlier I tried to convey the caution that Helena used in conferences when discussing Catherine's personal essay. After reading the paper, Helena immediately acknowledged to Catherine that she understood the weight of the material. This acknowledgment allowed Catherine to consider her essay as a piece of writing that would be subject to revision. I also showed Debby's empathy toward Tanya as they discussed several versions of the hybrid paper on her METCO experience. By using the metaphor "sea of white teachers," and by disclosing the marginalization that Jews like her feel at a Jesuit college, Debby positioned herself as someone who had some understanding of what Tanya went through in her practicum. If either Helena or Debby had refused to acknowledge the reality of the experiences their students were trying to share, I think it would have been distancing and potentially hurtful to these students.

So far I have suggested alternative responses to personal narratives about difficult life experiences: ask if the student is writing about an actual event and express compassion, or act as if the essay is not about the student but about the narrator. Deciding which course of action to take is somewhat a matter of intuition based either on one's experience working with the student or on the awareness of a deliberately distancing narrative strategy, such as Sally used in her paper on *The Exorcist*. However, once the paper comes under discussion as a piece of rhetoric, it is my opinion that writing teachers ought *always* to refer to the *I* of the essay as *the narrator*. The purpose here is to separate out our critique of the essay from what could be seen as an attempt to revise either the student's life or the student's perception of a life experience. I am distinguishing here between the textual moment of the essay and the psychological moment of the event itself and its aftermath. In the model I am suggesting, the student who has disclosed that the essay is about an event has already experienced some brief empathetic statement from the teacher. For the student who has not disclosed the reality of the event, it is my hope that the teacher will find a way both to protect the wish for privacy and to demonstrate concern. Pat McLure's sensitive and boundaried approach was in evidence both through her tone of voice and her positive remarks about the character of the protagonist.

I want to acknowledge that my proposal for a responsible pedagogy may not be as simple as I try to make it sound. The most salient difficulty is that making a decision regarding whether to ask the student if the story is "really" about him or her is based on what I call *intuition*. This word may be unfashionable in its attempt to psychologize the situation rather than contextualize it using any number of cultural factors. As I see it, the teacher's response does constitute a psychological moment as opposed to a political moment.[3] I am using *psychological* here not in its usual sense, namely, as something intrapsychic within each participant, but as perhaps interpsychic, referring to the dynamics in the student-teacher dyad.

As teachers, we bring our subjectivities to student texts and student conferences. Some of us may not feel equipped to self-reflect on these subjectivities and thus may avoid teaching the personal essay. Doing so requires what bell hooks refers to as an "engaged pedagogy," which calls for "a union of mind, body, and spirit." She draws upon the work of Buddhist philosopher Thich Nhat Hanh. Like Freire, Hanh wants students to be "active participants." Unfortunately, according to hooks, Freire "was primarily concerned with the mind." Hanh emphasizes the unity of the mind with the body and the spirit.

> [Engaged pedagogy] means that teachers must be actively committed to a process of self-actualization that promotes their own well-being if they are to teach in a manner that empowers students. Thich Nhat Hanh emphasized that "the practice of a healer, therapist or teacher or any helping professional should be directed toward his or herself first, because if the helper is unhappy, he or she cannot help many people." (hooks 15)

Hooks is not promoting that we practice therapy on our students. She wants us instead to be mindful that students want more than decontextualized knowledge. They want "spaces in the academy where the will to be self-actualized can be affirmed" (18). Yet she thinks students who only want to dwell on personal experience in classrooms that connect "ideas learned in university settings and those learned in life practices" abuse the freedom in such classrooms.

Some teachers may opt to exclude the personal narrative from their repertoire of rhetorical teachings. Such teachers know that they are not comfortable reading essays about harrowing experiences and that their discomfort may play out in responses that are either too distant from or too overly involved in their students' emotional lives. Instead they could assign writing on positive significant moments or profiles of individuals who have impacted the students' lives in important ways. Or they could use the Bartholomae–Petrosky approach of having the essays shaped by others' perspectives. (Frankly, I have no problem with this approach, as long as the teacher simply acknowledges to the student that he or she is not a good audience for intensely personal essays about family or childhood experiences, and as long as the teacher does not project the blame for his or her discomfort onto the student by telling that student "it is not wise" to write such essays.) In reality, I think students self-censor and would most likely not write about traumatic personal experiences for teachers they sense would be too shocked to evaluate the essay.

By the same token, some teachers do not feel equipped to introduce into their courses politically provocative material pertaining to issues of race or gender or class. I recall an instructor at BC who had leaders of rival political groups on campus in the same class and felt some obligation to allow them to air the debate in her class, yet she was quite anxious about the possibility of them doing so. Her colleagues told her that, since the students had many other arenas for their debate, her classroom did not have to be one of them. If there is the luxury of choice, some teachers specifically avoid hot topics. They are extremely uncomfortable in the face of conflict and thus do not feel capable of managing a discussion in which there is a strong possibility of losing control of the class. (I describe such a moment when a group of Italian males nearly got into a fistfight in my class over the use of the racial slur *guinea* [see "Writing" 295].) Similarly, Maureen Fitzsimmons describes a class she taught on Martin Luther King Jr.'s "Letter from Birmingham Jail."

> Suddenly Jake, a white male student, jumped up and began yelling. I can't remember what he said, but my sense was he wanted to shut down the discussion on Martin Luther King, Jr.'s letter. In one of those moments when everything stops, the students and I sat stunned as Jake raged. (23)

These moments are difficult; even the experienced teacher asks, "What should I do? How should I respond? What can I do to make students feel safe? What can I do to calm Jake?" (23). If we want to raise politically provocative issues in our classrooms, we must develop the pedagogy necessary to handle strong student outbursts, whether they emerge from the political right or from the political left.

Because each of us brings more than pedagogical training into the classroom, because each of us has a self, in fact, as William Coles puts it, "plural 'I's,'" we have instructional areas in which we feel competent and others in which we feel incompetent. I am proposing that, while constantly seeking to expand our areas of expertise in the classroom and to keep up with the pedagogical developments in our field, we teach to our strengths. If we want our students to be active participants in the classroom, we cannot ask them to take risks that we would not ourselves take. As hooks puts it, "It is often productive if professors take the first risk, linking confessional narratives to academic discussion so as to show how experience can illuminate and enhance our understanding of academic material" (21).

Let us expend less energy in disparaging pedagogy that is different from ours and more energy in introducing each other, in a collegial manner, to different approaches to teaching writing. Perhaps the way to develop our pedagogical community in composition is to form local, noncompetitive faculty groups to share teaching stories, so that we can collectively figure out how to more successfully motivate our students to improve their writing. Newkirk suggests that we "create forums for telling failure stories" ("Silences" 27). Competitiveness is somewhat kept in check when these groups work to build trust. Walvoord and McCarthy, in their long-term ethnography of writing across the disciplines, write, "We moved to create a climate of trust in which team members could—and did—say that their feelings had been hurt or that another team member's interpretation was inadequate or mistaken" (45). Of course, there are major obstacles to building trust when some group members have authority to influence the tenure and promotion of other group members. In many cases, working toward the ideal of sharing pedagogies may require building groups across departments or across institutions.

I know of two examples of attempts to build pedagogical community. At BC, a group of faculty met for three years with counseling staff. We read and discussed student papers that we felt to be disturbing and discussed how to respond to them as writing teachers. Another example of a relatively noncompetitive faculty group is the one described by Margaret Himley, Kelly Le Fave, Allen Larson, Susan Yadlon, and the Political Moments Study Group that met at Syracuse University for two years: teachers shared difficult moments in the classroom (Himley et al.). Just as we ask our students to work in peer groups, let us create more of our own and publish our experiences. In this way, composition professionals can demonstrate a model of the cooperative discourse community that does not work toward consensus but rather respects the variety of approaches to teaching writing that might best fit the mixture of personal and political dispositions of the individual teacher and the many different students that we are hired to teach.

→ NOTES

1. The Social Construction of "Expressivist" Pedagogy

1. According to Karen R. Melton, the director of marketing for Bedford–St. Martins, more than a quarter of a million copies of *Ways of Reading* had sold as of 2 December 1999. This total "makes it one of the most successful readers on our list (an impressive feat) and in the industry as a whole."

2. W. Ross Winterowd traces a similar genealogy:

Plato represents and is the father of a tradition that sees the goal of composition as helping the writer develop his or her own "voice" or expressivity, just as Aristotle is the ultimate source of composition as entering a discourse community. (xii)

3. Susan Wall also notes that Berlin's critique of expressionism emerges from his responses to scholarly texts and not from "qualitative research that might contextualize expressivism in specific teaching situations." She sees a certain irony in a social epistemic critique that fails to examine context because of "its own theoretical claim that discourses . . . are socially constructed and politically interested, shaped by specific and historically contingent material circumstances" (252).

4. Again, I am not alone in my objections to Berlin's work. Cassity notes that, writing in 1987 *(Rhetoric and Reality),* Berlin comments only on

Elbow's first book, *Writing Without Teachers* (1973) and ignores *Writing with Power* (1981). Wall argues that "in the expressivist works [that Berlin] critiques (publications of the sixties and seventies), the authors do not generally define the self as isolated or knowable apart from language" (241).

4. Confronting Bias in Student Texts

1. Again, Helena commented that what Janet did is common for those who have a "missionary complex." The complex is

> typical for middle class (even working class) people, and typical, in particular, for kids in Catholic school—having attended Catholic school all my life, I know. Trinh T. Minh-ha talks about this complex a little in *Woman, Native, and Other*, I think. The problem is that when we are in a position of some privilege and when we help others, we think we can know them and speak for them. After her volunteer experience, Janet had a certain sense of what you might call entitlement. She felt entitled to insider status after she helped the homeless women; I think that's why she speaks in her paper without hesitation and with such authority. Missionaries work this way, too. They go in with clothes and food, sure—and they also, often, impose their value system on the people they help without giving consideration to facts like: the people they are working with already have a value system; the people they are interacting with might know complex realities that the helper can never know, etc. (E-mail 4 June 1998)

2. An example of psychoneuroimmunology would be oncologist Bernie Siegel's descriptions of "exceptional patients" whose will to live and emotional resources combine to put their cancer into remission.

3. Of course, we can never simply re-present reality. As Kirsch and Ritchie put it, all researchers need "to recognize the impossibility of ever fully understanding another's experiences and to question their motives in gathering, selecting, and presenting those stories" (13). Patricia Sullivan points out that even when Denny Taylor invites her informants—substance abusers and homeless persons—to share the stage with her at academic conference presentations, it is a performance. The informants become actors who

> are visibly uncomfortable as they address their stories to the rapt academic audience that sits before them. They are uprooted from the streets and shelters and families they call home. The stories they tell are rendered in their own terms, but not on their own terms or turf. ("Ethnography" 105)

4. I do not have access to the source as Janet's paper was missing a works cited list.

5. In her essay "The Cultural Translator: Toward an Ethnic Womanist Pedagogy," Bonnie TuSmith discusses teaching multicultural literature in "a monocultural environment." She "had to get white students to understand that they, too, had specific cultural roots" (21). In this way, TuSmith participates in their culture; the students feel somewhat safe in this exploration, and then she moves with them to the unfamiliar territory of ethnic women's writing. I wonder how having the students explore their own class and cultural backgrounds might have impacted the subsequent discussions of poverty in Helena's FWS.

5. "I'm Just Really Struggling in This Class": Facing Student Self-Doubt

1. The phrase *scorched earth* is from Philip Morse's study of writing conferences. He concluded that, for the most part, teachers do not use the communication skills that are defined as effective in helping relationships. "About fifty percent of the time they used directives and closed-ended questions. . . . In a few cases one had the impression that the writer could have walked away from the conference without the teacher even noticing" (19). "Frequently, a sort of 'scorched earth approach' emerged with the teacher trying to deal with all the problems as he or she marched through the piece of writing" (17).

2. I did not receive a works cited page from Catherine.

6. Developing Voice, Developing Agency

1. The director of Prose Writing at BC was Paul Lewis, who received his doctorate at UNH in 1977. While there, he took a graduate seminar with Donald Murray, and Murray invited Lewis to teach English 501, the precursor to BC's Prose Writing. Lewis was the first Ph.D. candidate to teach that course.

2. Drawing on an essay by Frances Mascia-Lees and her colleagues, David Bleich encourages ethnographers to engage in "socially generous research" that "'contributes to the welfare of the community or society being studied'" (qtd. in Bleich, "Ethnography" 178). In my classroom ethnography, it was the researcher who was the recipient of some social generosity. After observing Debby's class for the semester, I was given the opportunity to teach the course myself. Thus my observation time also served as an apprenticeship.

3. In an interview later in the semester, Rachel presented a different view. She was disturbed that the FWS had not prepared her for the kinds

of papers she would have to write as a sophomore English major in a required course called Narrative and Interpretation, a course she had to repeat because she initially failed it.

4. Because of a scheduling conflict, I was not able to sit in on Mark's conferences with Debby, so my perspective on his work may be a bit more distant than it was with Janet, Catherine, and Tanya.

7. "African Americans Have This Slang": Grammar, Dialect, and Racism

1. On the other hand, Maryann Semons, in her ethnographic study of multiethnic schools, points out that when the balance begins to tip and both students of color and students from working-class families begin to represent a majority, the community regards the school as having what has been called a "spoiled identity." "Whether or not there is any objective evidence, the community starts to believe that the quality of their schooling is declining" (4).

2. Tanya grew up in a black working-class family, and the persona she created in her personal narrative in the hurricane paper provided a counterexample to a long-term study done by Dorothy Barnes, Douglas Barnes, and Stephen Clarke in England. The purpose of their study was to research the effect of James Britton's methods on English studies. They write,

> Among the young people whom we talked to it was those from professional homes who moved most easily into a persona that allowed them to deal with personal experience without feeling at risk. . . . [They] are often able to engage in successful personal writing without making public any vulnerable areas. (153)

While not from a "professional" home, Tanya produced a successful piece of personal writing while protecting her vulnerable areas.

3. Debby had brought this incident up at a faculty meeting earlier in the year, and clearly she still felt remiss. Faculty had suggested that we all preface such readings to the class with a comment about the difference between a black writer using the word *nigger* in a novel and a white person using it as an epithet. In *Know and Tell,* David Bleich writes about another type of pedagogical discomfort that white teachers might feel in a class with a black majority. The high school students "read [Zora Neale Hurston] with and through a sense of membership in ways that urged us as teachers to recognize our status as students in this class" (117).

8. The Personal in Social Constructionist Pedagogy: A Visit to the Classroom of Patricia Bizzell

1. While not itself a top-down confrontational pedagogy, in Mary

Louise Pratt's model of the contact zone, the emotional atmosphere is complex and "no one is safe":

> All the students in the class had the experience, for example, of hearing their culture discussed and objectified in ways that horrified them; . . . all the students experienced face-to-face ignorance and incomprehension, and occasionally the hostility, of others. . . . Along with rage, incomprehension and pain, there were exhilarating moments of wonder and revelation, mutual understanding, and new wisdom—the joys of the contact zone. (39)

2. In addition, NCTE's CCCC instituted Scholars of the Dream awards to provide travel assistance to scholars of color attending the conference for the first time.

3. Bizzell's ongoing loyalty to academic discourse is a bit puzzling in the light of some of her recent written remarks. In the introduction to *Academic Discourse and Critical Consciousness,* Bizzell writes, "I reject the idea that any form of literacy in and of itself can provide critical distance on the world or, one may as well say, critical consciousness" (26). In "Are Shared Discourses Desirable?" she explains,

> I justified teaching [academic discourse] primarily on grounds that it would enable previously disenfranchised students to succeed in college and gain access to more power in the wider culture. I did not claim that it would teach them to *think.* . . . I no longer advocate teaching traditional academic discourse to all students. (272, emphasis mine)

Since academic discourse is the product of the elitist institution, its class content is not neutral; neither is "thinking" neutral. Bizzell falls short of critiquing the class implications of the discourse she once embraced.

Conclusion: Responding Responsibly to Personal Narratives

1. However, they do *not* recommend the exclusion of personal writing. They conclude, "In our view, personal reflective writing should continue to have a place in the curriculum for those who can make use of it, but [it] should not provide the dominant model for language use" (Barnes et al. 251–52).

2. Valentino's guidelines include: "Assume nothing. Ask questions before rescuing. . . . Don't keep it a secret. . . . Keep a professional distance and set limits. . . . Make a contract for schoolwork; outline responsibilities. . . . On paper use reflective statements" (278–81).

3. Margaret Himley and her collaborators report on a "political moments" study group at Syracuse University in which, over a two-year pe-

riod, teachers met to share stories about such moments in their writing classes and how to handle them. Himley writes of these discussions, "[T]he risk has been either to over-psychologize (and erase the cultural and institutional context) or to over-politicize (and erase the autobiographical and particular context)" (58). It is this tension that I have in mind.

➤ WORKS CITED

Agueros, Jack. "Halfway to Dick and Jane: A Puerto Rican Pilgrimage." *English*. McGraw-Hill Primis. Boston: McGraw, 1997. 27–72.

Anderson, Paul V. "Simple Gifts: Ethical Issues in the Conduct of Person-Based Composition Research." *College Composition and Communication* 49 (1998): 63–89.

Annas, Pamela J., and Deborah Tenney. "Positioning Oneself: A Feminist Approach to Argument." *Argument Revisited, Argument Redefined: Negotiating Meaning in the Composition Classroom*. Ed. Barbara Emmel, Paula Resch, and Deborah Tenney. Thousand Oaks, CA: Sage, 1996. 127–52.

Aristotle. *Rhetorica. The Basic Works of Aristotle*. Ed. Richard McKeon. New York: Random, 1941. 1325–1451.

Barnes, Dorothy, Douglas Barnes, and Stephen Clarke. *Versions of English*. London: Heinemann, 1984.

Bartholomae, David. "Response." *College Composition and Communication* 46 (1995): 84–87.

———. "Writing with Teachers: A Conversation with Peter Elbow." *College Composition and Communication* 46 (1995): 62–71.

Bartholomae, David, and Anthony Petrosky, eds. *Ways of Reading: An Anthology for Writers*. 5th ed. Boston: Bedford–St. Martin's, 1999.

Berent, Jonathan, and Amy Lemley. *Beyond Shyness*. New York: Simon, 1993.

Berkenkotter, Carol, Thomas N. Huckin, and John Ackerman. "Conventions, Conversations, and the Writer: Case Study of a Student in a Rhetoric Ph.D. Program." *Research in the Teaching of English* 22 (1988): 9–44.

Berlin, James. "Contemporary Composition: The Major Pedagogical Theories." *College English* 44 (1982): 765–77.

———. "Rhetoric and Ideology in the Writing Class." *College English* 50 (1988): 476–94.

———. *Rhetoric and Reality: Writing Instruction in American Colleges, 1900–1985.* Carbondale: Southern Illinois UP, 1987.

———. *Rhetorics, Poetics, and Cultures.* Urbana: NCTE, 1996.

Berthoff, Ann. *The Making of Meaning: Metaphors, Models, and Maxims for Writing Teachers.* Upper Montclair, NJ: Boynton/Cook, 1981.

Bishop, Wendy. "The Perils, Pleasures, and Process of Ethnographic Writing Research." *Taking Stock: The Writing Process Movement in the '90s.* Ed. Lad Tobin and Thomas Newkirk. Portsmouth: Boynton/Cook, 1994. 261–79.

Bissex, Glenda L., and Richard H. Bullock. *Seeing for Ourselves: Case-Study Research by Teachers of Writing.* Portsmouth: Heinemann, 1987.

Bizzell, Patricia. *Academic Discourse and Critical Consciousness.* Pittsburgh: U of Pittsburgh P, 1992.

———. "Are Shared Discourses Desirable? A Response to Nancy McKoski." *Journal of Advanced Composition* 14 (1994): 271–77.

———. "Cognition, Convention, and Certainty: What We Need to Know about Writing." *Academic Discourse and Critical Consciousness.* Pittsburgh: U of Pittsburgh P, 1992. 75–104.

———. Letters to the author. 2 June 1994; 23 June 1994; 29 Aug. 1999.

———. "The Politics of Teaching Virtue." *ADE Bulletin* No. 103 (Winter 1992): 3–7.

———. "Power, Authority, and Critical Pedagogy." *Journal of Basic Writing* 10.2 (Fall 1991): 54–70.

———. "Theories of Content." CCCC Convention. Nashville. 19 Mar. 1994. *ERIC* 372 403.

Bizzell, Patricia, and Bruce Herzberg. *Negotiating Difference: Cultural Case Studies for Composition.* Boston: Bedford–St. Martin's, 1996.

Bleich, David. "Collaboration and the Pedagogy of Disclosure." *College English* 57 (1995): 43–61.

———. "Ethnography and the Study of Literacy: Prospects for Socially Generous Research." *Into the Field: Sites of Composition Studies.* Ed. Anne Ruggles Gere. New York: MLA, 1993. 176–92.

———. *Know and Tell: A Writing Pedagogy of Disclosure, Genre, and Membership.* Portsmouth: Boynton/Cook, 1998.

Bloom, Lynn Z. "Why I (Used to) Hate to Give Grades." *College Composition and Communication* 48 (1997): 360–71.

Britton, James. *Prospect and Retrospect: Selected Essays of James Britton.* Ed. Gordon Pradl. Upper Montclair, NJ: Boynton/Cook, 1982.

Brodber, Erna. *Louisiana.* London: New Beacon, 1994.

Brodkey, Linda. "Writing Ethnographic Narratives." *Written Communication* 4 (1987): 25–50.

Brooke, Robert, and John Hendricks. *Audience Expectations and Teacher Demands.* Carbondale: Southern Illinois UP, 1989.

Cain, Mary Ann. *Revisioning Writers' Talk: Gender and Culture in Acts of Composing.* Albany: State U of New York P, 1995.

Cassity, Kathleen J. E-mail to the author. 27 Jan. 1998.

———. "Embracing Student Voices: A Journey into Peter Elbow's Composition Classroom." Master's thesis. U of Hawaii, 1997.

"Catherine." E-mail to the author. 24 Apr. 1997.

"Cause-and-Effect Analysis." *English.* McGraw-Hill Primis. Boston: McGraw, 1997. 51–56.

Chiseri-Strater, Elizabeth. *Academic Literacies: The Public and Private Discourse of University Students.* Portsmouth: Boynton/Cook, 1991.

Chiseri-Strater, Elizabeth, and Bonnie Stone Sunstein. *FieldWorking: Reading and Writing Research.* Upper Saddle River, NJ: Prentice, 1997.

Coles, William E., Jr. *The Plural I—and After.* Portsmouth: Boynton/Cook, 1988.

Coles, William E., Jr., and James Vopat. *What Makes Writing Good: A Multiperspective.* Lexington: Heath, 1985.

Connors, Robert. "Personal Writing Assignments." *College Composition and Communication* 38 (1987): 166–83.

Corbett, Edward P. J. *Classical Rhetoric for the Modern Student.* 3rd ed. New York: Oxford, 1990.

Dautermann, Jennie. "Social and Institutional Power Relationships in Studies of Workplace Writing." *Ethics and Representation in Qualitative Studies of Literacy.* Ed. Peter Mortensen and Gesa E. Kirsch. Urbana: NCTE, 1996. 241–59.

"Debby." E-mails to the author. 30 Sept. 1997–4 Aug. 1998.

———. Interviews with the author. 24 Dec. 1997; 10 Feb. 1999.

Deletiner, Carole. "Crossing Lines." *College English* 54 (1992): 809–17.

———. E-mail to the author. 26 Nov. 1997.

Delpit, Lisa. "The Silenced Dialogue: Power and Pedagogy in Educating Other People's Children." *Harvard Educational Review* 58 (1988): 280–98.

Dewey, John. *Experience and Nature.* 1925. New York: Dover, 1958.

DiPardo, Anne. "Narrative Knowers, Expository Knowledge: Discourse as Dialectic." Berkeley: Center for the Study of Writing. Jan. 1989. *ERIC* 304 688.

Eagleton, Terry. "The Subject of Literature." *Cultural Critique* 2 (1985–1986): 95–104.

Eastburg, Mark, and W. Brad Johnson. "Shyness and Perceptions of Parental Behavior." *Psychological Reports* 66 (1990): 915–921.

Elbow, Peter. "Being a Writer vs. Being an Academic: A Conflict in Goals." *College Composition and Communication* 46 (1995): 72–83.

———. E-mail to the author. 4 Dec. 1997.

———. "Freewriting." *English*. McGraw-Hill Primis. Boston: McGraw, 1997. 16–18.

———. "Introduction to the New Edition of *Writing without Teachers*." Unpublished essay, 1997.

———. "Response." *College Composition and Communication* 46 (1995): 87–92.

———. "Revisioning the Personal." CCCC Convention. San Francisco. Dec. 1999.

———. *Writing Without Teachers*. New York: Oxford, 1973.

———. *Writing with Power: Techniques for Mastering the Writing Process*. New York: Oxford, 1981.

Emerson, Robert, Rachel Fretz, and Linda Shaw. *Writing Ethnographic Fieldnotes*. Chicago: U of Chicago P, 1995.

Emig, Janet. *The Composing Process of Twelfth Graders*. Urbana: NCTE, 1971.

English. McGraw-Hill Primis. Boston: McGraw, 1997.

Faigley, Lester. "Competing Theories of Process: A Critique and a Proposal." *College English* 48 (1986): 527–40.

———. *Fragments of Rationality: Postmodernity and the Subject of Composition*. Pittsburgh: U of Pittsburgh P, 1992.

Fitzsimmons, Maureen. "Learning to Tell Stories: The Maureen Story." *Political Moments in the Classroom*. Margaret Himley, Kelly Le Fave, Allen Larson, and Susan Yadlon, and the Political Moments Study Group. Portsmouth: Boynton/Cook, 1997. 23–31.

Flint, Anthony. "Days of Protest; Days of Age." *Boston Globe* 9 June 1994: 1, 16.

Flower, Linda. "Writer-Based Prose: A Cognitive Basis for Problems in Writing." *To Compose: Teaching Writing in High School and College*. Ed. Thomas Newkirk. 2nd ed. Portsmouth: Heinemann, 1990. 125–52.

Ford, Marjorie, and Jon Ford. *Dreams and Inward Journeys: A Rhetoric and Reader for Writers*. 3rd ed. New York: Longman, 1998.

Foucault, Michel. *Power/Knowledge*. Ed. Colin Gordon. Trans. Colin Gordon, Leo Marshall, John Mepham, and Kate Soper. New York: Pantheon, 1980.

———. "What Is an Author?" *Contemporary Literary Criticism*. Ed. Robert Con Davis and Ronald Schleifer. 2nd ed. New York: Longman, 1989. 263–75.

Freire, Paulo. *Pedagogy of the Oppressed*. New York: Continuum, 1973.

Geertz, Clifford. "Thick Description: Toward an Interpretive Theory of Culture." *The Interpretation of Cultures: Selected Essays by Clifford Geertz*. New York: Basic, 1973. 3–30.

———. *Works and Lives: The Anthropologist as Author*. Stanford: Stanford UP, 1988.

Gibson, Michelle. "An All-Too-Familiar Paradox: Familial Diversity and the Composition Classroom." *Writing on the Edge* 7.2 (Spring–Summer 1996): 19–30.

Giroux, Henry. "Who Writes in a Cultural Studies Class? Or, Where Is Pedagogy?" *Left Margins: Cultural Studies and Composition Pedagogy*. Ed. Karen Fitts and Alan W. France. Albany: State U of New York P, 1995. 3–16.

Goldmann, Lucien. "Introduction to the Problems of Sociology in the Novel." *Telos* 18 (1973–1974): 122–35.

Gradin, Sherrie L. *Romancing Rhetorics: Social Expressivist Perspectives on the Teaching of Writing*. Portsmouth: Boynton/Cook, 1995.

Graham, Robert J. *Reading and Writing the Self: Autobiography in Education and in the Curriculum*. New York: Teacher's College P, 1991.

Gusdorf, Georges. "Conditions and Limits of Autobiography." *Autobiography: Essays Theoretical and Critical*. Ed. James Olney. Princeton: Princeton UP, 1980. 28–48.

Harris, Jeanette. *Expressive Discourse*. Dallas: Southern Methodist UP, 1990.

Heath, Shirley Brice. *Ways with Words: Language, Life, and Work in Communities and Classrooms*. Cambridge: Cambridge UP, 1983.

"Helena." E-mails to the author. 7 Jan. 1997–4 June 1998.

———. Interviews with the author. Oct. 1997–Jan. 1999.

———. Speech. Donald J. White Teaching Excellence Award Ceremony. Boston College. 28 Apr. 1997.

———. Syllabus. EN010-19. Freshman Writing Seminar. Spring 1997.

Herzberg, Bruce. "Community Service and Critical Teaching." *College Composition and Communication* 45 (1994): 307–19.

Hesford, Wendy S. "Women Reading the Self, the Word, the World: A Descriptive Study of the Metaphorical Constructs of Self and

Composing in the Autobiographical Writings of Eight College Women." Diss. New York U, 1992.

Himley, Margaret, Kelly Le Fave, Allen Larson, and Susan Yadlon, and the Political Moments Study Group. *Political Moments in the Classroom.* Portsmouth: Boynton/Cook, 1997.

hooks, bell. *Teaching to Transgress: Education as the Practice of Freedom.* New York: Routledge, 1994.

Jackie. Interview with the author. 6 May 1997.

"Jane." E-mail to the author. 30 Sept. 1996.

Kaye/Kantrowitz, Melanie. *The Issue Is Power: Essays on Women, Jews, Violence, and Resistance.* San Francisco: Aunt Lute, 1992.

Kinneavy, James L. *A Theory of Discourse.* New York: Norton, 1971.

Kirsch, Gesa E., and Joy Ritchie. "Beyond the Personal: Theorizing a Politics of Location in Composition Research." *College Composition and Communication* 46 (1995): 7–29.

Klepfisz, Irena. "Queens of Contradiction: A Feminist Introduction to Yiddish Women Writers." *Found Treasures: Stories by Yiddish Women Writers.* Ed. Frieda Forman, Ethel Raicus, Sarah Silberstein Swartz, and Margie Wolfe. Toronto: Second Story, 1997. 21–62.

Knoblauch, Cy H., and Lil Brannon. *Critical Teaching and the Idea of Literacy.* Portsmouth: Boynton/Cook, 1993.

Kutz, Eleanor. "Authority and Voice in Student Ethnographic Writing." *Anthropology and Education Quarterly* 21.4 (Dec. 1990): 340–57.

Langer, Lawrence. *Versions of Survival: The Holocaust and the Human Spirit.* Albany: State U of New York P, 1982.

Lopate, Phillip. Introduction. *The Art of the Personal Essay: An Anthology from the Classical Era to the Present.* Ed. Phillip Lopate. New York: Anchor, 1995. xiii–liv.

Loyola Marymount University. *Mission, Goals, and Objectives.* Los Angeles, 1992.

Lynd, Staughton, Sam Bahour, and Alice Lynd. *Homeland: Oral Histories of Palestine and Palestinians.* New York: Olive Branch, 1994.

Mahala, Daniel, and Jody Swilky. "Telling Stories, Speaking Personally: Reconsidering the Place of Lived Experience in Composition." *Journal of Advanced Composition* 16 (1996): 363–88.

"Mark." Interview with the author. 27 April 1997.

McKoski, Nancy. "A Postmodern Critique of the Modern Projects of Frederic Jameson and Patricia Bizzell." *Journal of Advanced Composition* 13 (1993): 329–44.

Melton, Karen. E-mail to the author. 2 Dec. 1999.

Merrill, James. *A Different Person: A Memoir.* New York: Knopf, 1993.

——. *Selected Poems: 1946–1985.* New York: Knopf, 1992.

Miller, Susan. *Textual Carnivals: The Politics of Composition*. Carbondale: Southern Illinois UP, 1991.

Miner, Earl. *Comparative Poetics: An Intercultural Essay on Theories of Literature*. Princeton: Princeton UP, 1990.

Minuchin, Salvador, Bernice Rosman, and Lester Baker. *Psychosomatic Families: Anorexia Nervosa in Context*. Cambridge: Harvard UP, 1978.

Moffett, James. Foreword. *Through Teachers' Eyes: Portraits of Writing Teachers at Work*. By Sondra Perl and Nancy Wilson. Portsmouth: Heinemann, 1986. ix–xi.

Morgan, Dan. "Opinion: Ethical Issues Raised by Student Writing." *College English* 60 (1998): 318–25.

Morse, Philip. "The Writing Teacher as Helping Agent: Communicating Effectively in the Conferencing Process." NCTE Convention, Seattle. 22–27 Nov. 1991. *ERIC* 342 012.

Newkirk, Thomas. "Locating Freshman English." *Nuts and Bolts: A Practical Guide to Teaching College Composition*. Ed. Thomas Newkirk. Portsmouth: Boynton/Cook, 1993. 1–15.

———. *The Performance of Self in Student Writing*. Portsmouth: Boynton/Cook, 1997.

———. "The Politics of Composition Research: The Conspiracy Against Experience." *The Politics of Writing Instruction: Postsecondary*. Ed. Richard Bullock and John Trimbur. Portsmouth: Boynton/Cook, 1991. 119–35.

———. "Seduction and Betrayal in Qualitative Research." *Ethics and Representation in Qualitative Studies of Literacy*. Ed. Peter Mortensen and Gesa E. Kirsch. Urbana: NCTE, 1996. 3–16.

———. "Silences in Our Teaching Stories: What Do We Leave out and Why?" *Workshop 4: The Teacher as Researcher*. Ed. Thomas Newkirk. Portsmouth: Heinemann, 1992. 21–30.

Newkirk, Thomas, with Pat McLure. *Listening In: Children Talk about Books (and Other Things)*. Portsmouth: Heinemann, 1992.

O'Donnell, Thomas. "Politics and Ordinary Language: A Defense of Expressivist Rhetorics." *College English* 58 (1996): 423–39.

Ohmann, Richard. *English in America*. New York: Oxford, 1976.

Oliver, Eileen. *Crossing the Mainstream: Multicultural Perspectives in Teaching Literature*. Urbana: NCTE, 1994.

Paley, Karen Surman. E-mail to "Debby." 25 Dec. 1999.

———. "I Remember, Nana." *Na'amat Woman* 9.4 (Sept.–Oct. 1994): 24–25.

———. "My Mother and the Man who Called the Ambulance." *Kerem* 5 (Spring 1997): 60–72.

———. "'Next Week I'll Do a Tear Jerker': A Look at Personal Disclosure and Response in the New Hampshire Writing Program." Unpublished paper, 1998.

———. "Writing and Rewriting Racism: From the Dorm to the Classroom to the Dustbowl." *Journal of Advanced Composition* 16 (1996): 285–96.

Perl, Sondra, and Nancy Wilson. *Through Teachers' Eyes: Portraits of Writing Teachers at Work.* Portsmouth: Heinemann, 1986.

Pratt, Mary Louise. "Arts of the Contact Zone." *Profession 91* (1991): 33–40.

Rich, Adrienne. "Split at the Root." *The Art of the Personal Narrative: An Anthology from the Classical Era to the Present.* Ed. Phillip Lopate. New York: Anchor, 1995. 640–55.

Roberts, Patricia. *The Harcourt Brace Sourcebook for Teachers of Writing.* Fort Worth: Harcourt, 1998.

Rosie's Place: A Solution Not a Shelter. Boston.

Roskelly, Hephzibah, and Kate Ronald. *Reason to Believe: Romanticism, Pragmatism, and the Teaching of Writing.* Albany: State U of New York P, 1998.

Rossi, Peter H., and James D. Wright. "The Urban Homeless: A Portrait of Urban Dislocation." *English.* McGraw-Hill Primis. Boston: McGraw, 1997. 161–71.

Said, Edward W. *Orientalism.* New York: Random, 1978.

Salvatori, Mariolina. "The Personal as Recitation." *College Composition and Communication* 48 (1997): 566–83.

Schaub, Lorianne. "On Having Your Cake and Eating It, Too: The Strategic Employment of the Personal in Academic Texts by Women." Unpublished paper, 1995.

Schilb, John. "The Ideology of 'Epistemological Ecumenicalism': A Response to Carol Berkenkotter." *Journal of Advanced Composition* 10 (1991): 153–56.

Scholes, Robert E. *Textual Power: Literary Theory and the Teaching of English.* New Haven: Yale UP, 1985.

Schultz, Lucille M. *The Young Composers: Composition's Beginnings in Nineteenth-Century Schools.* Carbondale: Southern Illinois UP, 1999.

Schweickart, Patrocinio P. "Reading Ourselves: Toward a Feminist Theory of Reading." *Gender and Reading: Essays on Readers, Texts, and Contexts.* Ed. Elizabeth A. Flynn and Patrocinio P. Schweickart. Baltimore: Johns Hopkins UP, 1986. 31–62.

Semons, Maryann. "Ethnographic Depiction of a Multiethnic School: A Comparison to Desegregated Settings." American Educational Association Annual Meeting. San Francisco. 31 Mar. 1989. *ERIC* 309 214.

Shor, Ira. *Empowering Education: Critical Teaching for Social Change.* Chicago: U of Chicago P, 1992.

———. Foreword. *Sharing Pedagogies: Students and Teachers Write about Dialogic Practices.* Ed. Gail Tayko and John Paul Tassoni. Portsmouth: Boynton/Cook, 1997. ix–xiii.

Siegel, Bernie. *Love, Medicine, and Miracles: Lessons Learned about Self-Healing from a Surgeon's Experience with Exceptional Patients.* New York: Harper, 1986.

Smith, Summer. "The Genre of the End Comment: Conventions in Teacher Responses to Student Writing." *College Composition and Communication* 48 (1997): 249–68.

Sommers, Nancy. "Between the Drafts." *College Composition and Communication* 43 (1992): 23–31.

———. "Responding to Student Writing." *College Composition and Communication* 33 (1982): 148–56.

Spellmeyer, Kurt. "After Theory: From Textuality to Attunement with the World." *College English* 58 (1996): 893–913.

Spiegelman, Art. *Maus II: A Survivor's Tale and Here My Troubles Began.* New York: Pantheon, 1991.

Steedman, Carolyn Kay. *Landscape for a Good Woman: A Story of Two Lives.* New Brunswick, NJ: Rutgers, 1987.

Sullivan, Patricia. "Ethnography and the Problem of the 'Other.'" *Ethics and Representation in Qualitative Studies of Literacy.* Ed. Peter Mortensen and Gesa E. Kirsch. Urbana: NCTE, 1996. 97–114.

———. "Social Constructionism and Literary Studies." *College English* 57 (1995): 950–59.

Summerfield, Judith. "Principles for Propagation: On Narrative and Argument." *Argument Revisited, Argument Redefined: Negotiating Meaning in the Composition Classroom.* Ed. Barbara Emmel, Paula Resch, and Deborah Tenney. Thousand Oaks, CA: Sage, 1996. 153–80.

Swartzlander, Susan, Diana Pace, and Virginia Lee Stamler. "The Ethics of Requiring Students to Write about Their Personal Lives." *Chronicle of Higher Education* 17 Feb. 1993: B1+.

Tayko, Gail, and John Paul Tassoni. *Sharing Pedagogies: Students and Teachers Write about Dialogic Practices.* Portsmouth: Boynton/Cook, 1997.

Tobin, Lad. Interview with the author. 29 Jan. 1998.

———. *Writing Relationships: What Really Happens in the Composition Class.* Portsmouth: Boynton/Cook, 1993.

Trimbur, John. "Reviews: *English in America: A Radical View of the Profession* and *The Politics of Letters,* Richard Ohmann." *College Composition and Communication* 44 (1993): 389–92.

TuSmith, Bonnie. "The Cultural Translator: Toward an Ethnic Woman-ist Pedagogy." *MELUS* 16.2 (Summer 1989–1990): 17–29.

———. "The Englishes of Ethnic Folk: From Home Talkin' to Testifyin' Art." *College English* 58 (1996): 43–57.

———. "Teaching Evaluations and the Color Line: An Ethnic Womanist Perspective." MLA Convention. San Francisco. Dec. 1998.

Valentino, Marilyn J. "Responding When a Life Depends on It: What to Write in the Margins When Students Self-Disclose." *Teaching English in the Two Year College* 23.4 (Dec. 1996): 274–83.

Villanueva, Victor. *Bootstraps: From an American Academic of Color.* Urbana: NCTE, 1993.

Wall, Susan. "'Where Your Treasure Is': Accounting for Differences in Our Talk about Teaching." *Taking Stock: The Writing Process Movement in the '90s.* Ed. Lad Tobin and Thomas Newkirk. Portsmouth: Boynton/Cook, 1994. 239–60.

Wall, Susan, and Glenda Hull. "The Semantics of Error: What Do Teachers Know?" *Writing and Response: Theory, Practice, and Research.* Ed. Christopher Anson. Urbana: NCTE. 261–92.

Walvoord, Barbara E., and Lucille Parkinson McCarthy. *Thinking and Writing in College: A Naturalistic Study of Students in Four Disci-plines.* Urbana: NCTE, 1990.

Winterowd, W. Ross, with Jack Blum. *A Teacher's Introduction to Composition in the Rhetorical Tradition.* Urbana: NCTE, 1994.

Winterson, Jeanette. *Oranges Are Not the Only Fruit.* New York: Atlantic, 1987.

Wolf, Thia. "Conflict as Opportunity in Collaborative Praxis." *Writing With: New Directions in Collaborative Teaching, Learning, and Research.* Ed. Sally Barr Reagan, Thomas Fox, and David Bleich. Albany: State U of New York P, 1994. 91–110.

Woolf, Virginia. "A Sketch of the Past." *Virginia Woolf's Moments of Being: Unpublished Autobiographical Writings.* Ed. Jeanne Schul-kind. London: Sussex UP, 1976. 61–138.

⇝ INDEX

KAREN SURMAN PALEY is an assistant professor and the director of freshman English at Loyola Marymount University in Los Angeles, where she is also developing writing across the curriculum. Her essays have appeared in the *Journal of Advanced Composition, Reader, Assessing Writing, Diversity,* and *Women and Language.*